DC Jazz

DC
Jazz

Stories of Jazz Music in Washington, DC

Maurice Jackson and Blair A. Ruble, Editors

HISTORICAL SOCIETY *of*
WASHINGTON, D.C.

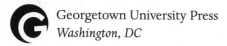

Georgetown University Press
Washington, DC

The publisher is not responsible for third-party websites or their content. URL links were active at time of publication.

Chapters 1–6 and 10 were previously published in Washington History 26, Special Issue: Jazz in Washington (Spring 2014), www.jstor.org/stable/i23728033. These chapters have been edited and, in some cases, updated.

Poems on page xvi used by permission of the author. © 2010 E. Ethelbert Miller.

Library of Congress Cataloging-in-Publication Data
Names: Jackson, Maurice, 1950- editor. | Ruble, Blair A., 1949- editor.
Title: DC Jazz : Stories of Jazz Music in Washington, DC / Maurice Jackson and Blair A. Ruble, editors.
Description: Washington, DC : Georgetown University Press, 2018. | Includes bibliographical references and index.
Identifiers: LCCN 2017047948 | ISBN 9781626165892 (hardcover : alk. paper) | ISBN 9781626165908 (pbk. : alk paper) | ISBN 9781626165915 (ebook)
Subjects: LCSH: Jazz—Washington (D.C.)—History and criticism. | Jazz musicians—Washington (D.C.)
Classification: LCC ML3508.8.W27 D3 2018 | DDC 781.6509753—dc23
LC record available at https://lccn.loc.gov/2017047948

♾ This book is printed on acid-free paper meeting the requirements of the American National Standard for Permanence in Paper for Printed Library Materials.

20 19 18   9 8 7 6 5 4 3 2   First printing

Printed in the United States of America

Editorial, permissions, and production assistant: Regina Andreoni
Composition: Graphic Composition, Inc.
Cover design: Spencer Fuller, Faceout Studio
Cover image: John Malachi courtesy of the William P. Gottlieb/Ira and Leonore S. Gershwin Fund Collection, Music Division, Library of Congress

Furthermore:
a program of the J.M. Kaplan Fund

Support for this publication was provided by Furthermore: a program of the J.M. Kaplan Fund

To

Roger "Buck" Hill
1927–2017

Geri Allen
1957–2017

and

Reuben Brown
1939–2018

Contents

Illustrations

Photographs

Tables

Foreword

Part of what I have always loved about coming to DC to perform is what can happen after the set. For a few years, my routine was that, after a concert at the Kennedy Center, I'd hop in a taxi and head over to Bohemian Caverns to catch the tail end of someone else's set. My friend Omrao Brown was running the club, and there was so much sympathetic energy there, I knew it would be a place I could learn more about the diversity of the DC jazz scene. I could go there and hear Christian Scott. A saxophonist who has toured with Scott, and played with him there, Braxton Cook, is from the area and attended Georgetown University before going on to Julliard. Or I could hear the big band, the Bohemian Cavern All-Stars, or Craig Taborn. The club had it all. It literally had it all. On the ground level was a restaurant, and above that was a multigenre room that booked hip-hop and rock acts. This was amazing to me. There were so many layers to understanding why this felt like the right series of events. And I think it stemmed from the feeling that we were in a space where people had been gathering since the early 1920s. The Crystal Caverns, the Bohemian Caverns' predecessor, is one of America's oldest jazz clubs; up until a year ago, it still supported the scene musicians in DC and nationwide. Designed with an underground faux cavern with plaster stalactites hanging from the ceiling, this space was special because we, as patrons, continued to descend the stairs to look for the heavens. The music was uplifting. In the nation's capital, it would seem that DC needs the abstract improvisations of jazz musicians to make sense of a country built on so many contradictions.

The history of how the space gets started begins to tell the story of how jazz in DC is also related to community. Jazz has always been about community because of a revolutionary idea: the song is shared by every member of the band. In most jazz bands, every musician feels they are making a valuable contribution to the song. And in small groups, everyone gets a solo that often gives agency to audiences who recognize themselves in the musicians. And for the African American who visited that club, there was the feeling of being with some of the first groups of emerging middle-class folks. This is big. How and where do we relax? Where do we gather to drink and celebrate? The places are important. And the city's complex urban design by Pierre Charles L'Enfant and Benjamin Banneker lets you know that it is a cyclical space—round and round the circle, choruses and choruses of music changing hands from one player to another. It is a city and capitol building that enslaved people helped build.

Duke Ellington may be the most important musician to emerge from the city of Washington, DC. He had a strong sense of himself. As a young man, he shared his visions of his fame with his family. All of it came true, as he became one of America's greatest ambassadors. Elegant, musical, and charming, he had the opportunity and the access. Following behind him came Dr. Billy Taylor, a man who continued to be an ambassador as he shared his world of jazz on *CBS Sunday Morning* and who implemented the Kennedy Center jazz program. Dr. Taylor's sense of history is unique because he was the pianist that the elders loved. And by elders, I mean Art Tatum, Willie "the Lion" Smith, and James P. Johnson. He witnessed Duke's rise to fame and followed those same footsteps in teaching America—and the world—to understand that jazz was a rich music, and the people who create it are rich in character as well. There is something about these two figures, Duke Ellington and Dr. Taylor, that if I pause at their impact on the greater understanding of jazz, I can't help but equate their work to the DC environment they were raised in.

There is something twofold that happens with this kind of power. By Ellington's and Taylor's movements, they both left DC for New York City but kept close ties. Of course, Duke Ellington School of the Arts is named after Ellington. Scores of new musicians like mezzo-soprano Denyce Graves and pianist Marc Cary came from the school and have gone on to have touring careers.

DC is a city where the relationship to historical narratives in music is strong, from Ellington's "A Tone Parallel to Harlem" to Taylor's "I Wish I Knew How It Would Feel to Be Free." Musicians like DC-born James Reese Europe have attached the story to the land and the music. DC has produced some great pianists, like Ellington and Taylor but also Shirley Horn, John Malachi, Reuben Brown, and Marc Cary. And here at Howard University it produced my late friend Geri Allen. That thread continues to be pulled along by artists today such as Akua Allrich, Kris Funn, and Herb Scott, local musicians carrying the nature of songs.

Because the city is home to great jazz clubs like Blues Alley and Twins and to institutions hosting musicians in concert and conversation like the Kennedy Center, the Library of Congress, and the Washington Performing Arts Society and to universities like Howard University, Georgetown University, and the University of the District of Columbia, there is always something happening. The DC Jazz Festival is also becoming an institution. Maybe jazz is behind closed doors or is simply incidental music in a restaurant, but jazz has always been the backdrop of DC. It lives in the speakers and on the stages. But it also lives in the shadows of its northeastern neighbors, Philadelphia and New York—so much so that many musicians drive I-95 frequently between New York and DC to perform. The corridor has been tread for generations, and scores of choruses have been played on those roads. The exchange not only with the jazz scenes in the northeast but also by virtue of DC being the nation's capital keeps the relationship to jazz open to the global perspective. Turkish ambassador Mehmet Munir Ertegun hosted jazz concerts in the 1940s because his sons Nesuhi and Ahmet, founders of Atlantic Records, loved jazz. More recently the embassy hosted jazz concerts featuring musicians like Cecile McLorin Salvant, Orrin Evans, and Helen Sung. Recently I performed at the Swiss Embassy for the DC Jazz Festival. Audiences in DC know the music well and continue to support it to make sure the fabric of the city is still felt in the sounds that occupy it.

What will the future hold for this great city? The music will always continue to mature, but now, as the city changes and U Street begins another shift, where will the venues and musicians go? Recently a new condominium development was built named The Coltrane. The real estate developers framed the location with terms used to define the sound that John Coltrane created on his groundbreaking recordings. All the while, the developers are deleting the very art that brought the neighborhood its acclaim. This I might say is also DC jazz: a country that defines itself by its erasure of history, not only locally but globally. And as jazz is the art form that is American born and documented with sound recordings, it is our best textbook for how the city and how the country has changed. The future of jazz in the District is still a tough one. Fortunately, there is no shortage of citizens who are highly aware that this city thrives off the sounds of change and the sounds of freedom.

This book brings together stories of jazz in Washington, DC. And it shows us how the music we call jazz has been so important in documenting the history of people, places, and events and in itself has made history.

Jason Moran
Artistic Director for Jazz, John F. Kennedy Center for the Performing Arts
Distinguished Artist in Residence at Georgetown University

Acknowledgments

A volume such as this depends on the support, good cheer, and wisdom of far too many people to thank. This particular effort began as a special issue of *Washington History*, the journal of the Historical Society of Washington, DC. We would like to thank all those who made that special issue possible, including John Suau, executive director; Anne W. Rollins and Jane Freundel Levey, managing editors; Mary Beth Corrigan, editorial consultant; Laura Barry, editorial assistant; and Karen Harris, events and publications coordinator. We also would like to thank the generous contribution from Mica Ertegun, who supported the journal issue to honor the legacy of her late husband Ahmet Ertegun, cofounder of Atlantic Records.

We are indebted to Richard Brown, then director of Georgetown University Press, for his generosity and encouragement of expanding the original special issue into the published volume you see here. We also would like to thank the members of the Georgetown University Press team, including Glenn Saltzman and especially Regina Andreoni, without whose assistance and hard work this volume could not have been produced.

Without question, this book is a product of the enthusiasm and hard work of all of the contributors, for whom we have the deepest affection and appreciation. Our wives, Laura Ginsburg and Sally Ruble, have remained steadfast supporters throughout.

Finally, we would like to thank all the talented Washington musicians who have added their own special beauty to our lives and to our city. Accordingly, we dedicate this work to three outstanding Washington jazz legends, Geri Allen (1957–2017), Reuben Brown (1939–2018), and Roger "Buck" Hill (1927–2017).

Ask Me Now

like Thelonious Monk

I record my love for you
and no one understands it

the complexity of my
declarations

the strange way
it makes you feel

Do Nothin' Till You Hear From Me

what did Ellington mean
when he said

"I love you madly"

his hands touching a
piano not made of flesh

The Ear Is an Organ Made for Love

It was the language that left us first.
The Great Migration of words. When people
spoke they punched each other in the mouth.
There was no vocabulary for love. Women
became masculine and could no longer give
birth to warmth or a simple caress with their
lips. Tongues were overweight from profanity
and the taste of nastiness. It settled over cities
like fog smothering everything in sight. My
ears begged for camouflage and the chance
to go to war. Everywhere was the decay of
how we sound. Someone said it reminded
them of the time Sonny Rollins disappeared.
People spread stories of how the air would
never be the same or forgive. It was the end
of civilization and nowhere could one hear
the first notes of *A Love Supreme*. It was as
if John Coltrane had never been born.

Poems by E. Ethelbert Miller

Introduction

The history of jazz has developed a durable, conventional story line that takes the music from Congo Square in New Orleans up the Mississippi to Chicago and then by rail to New York before exploding across the globe. As is so often the case with accepted wisdom, there is considerable truth behind this way of telling the tale. Yet it glosses over a multitude of other places where players, venues, and communities have meaningfully advanced the music. Washington is one such corner of the jazz world that has not received the attention that it deserves.

As the contributors to this book demonstrate, the nation's capital has been a fertile city for jazz for a century. Some of the most important clubs in the jazz world have opened and closed their doors here, some of its greatest players and promoters were born and grew to maturity in this town and still play here, and some of the institutions so critical to supporting the music remain active.

The verbal portraits that follow cannot pretend to offer a comprehensive picture of the vibrant and still-vital DC jazz scene. Instead, they represent important, idiosyncratic, even syncopated, stories about Washington jazz. They tell as much about the city as they do about the music. We hope to provoke interest: for researchers, to delve even more deeply into the world of DC music, and for readers, to go out and hear what is being played all around you.

Collectively, these stories underscore the deep connection between creativity and place. Sitting astride the cultural borders between North and South, DC has long been a place that has promoted exciting new directions in jazz and other musical forms, nurturing players who often set out for New York, Nashville, Chicago, and Los Angeles to leave their marks. The city is home to some of the most important institutional sponsors for jazz, including the U.S. Armed Forces, the Smithsonian Institution, the Library of Congress, and the Kennedy Center. Closer to the ground, a close network of universities—especially Howard University and the University of the District of Columbia—and schools like the Duke Ellington School of the Arts as well as churches, informal associations, media, and clubs keep the music more than alive to this day.

Musical invention needs places in which creativity can take flight. As Maurice Jackson's examination of the emergence of Great Black Music in Washington and the United States demonstrates, the jazz scene in DC was always about more than music; it played an integral role in reshaping the city through desegregation. Blair Ruble argues that Seventh Street was just such a place, a pulsating, cultural wetlands where music transcended the boundaries of race, class, ethnicity, and income.

Photo I.1 *Tommy Myles Orchestra*
A young Billy Eckstine, ca. 1933, fronts the Tommy Myles Orchestra,
a popular dance band in Washington in the 1930s and 1940s.

Such varied musical inclinations and backgrounds require musicians of considerable creativity to give them new life. The DC jazz scene is noteworthy because it has been home to some of the most protean inventors in the music and its presentation to the world at large. John Hasse amplifies the role of individual musicians in creating the Washington jazz scene by demonstrating the connections between Washington native son Edward "Duke" Ellington and the community that gave him life before he moved on to New York and the world.

Music promoter Bill Brower tells the story of a later explosive period in the history of Washington jazz—the 1970s and 1980s—in an interview with jazz journalist Willard Jenkins. That scene was interwoven with particularly noteworthy jazz radio personalities, as becomes evident in Rusty Hassan's personal reflections on his long career as a local jazz radio host.

Institutions provided important anchors for all of these achievements. As Lauren Sinclair reveals, Howard University emerged as a leading center for studying and promoting jazz during the late twentieth century. The University of the District of Columbia—at first under the inspired direction of Calvin Jones and later the mastery of Allyn Johnson—has long provided an essential foundation for Washington jazz. As Judith Korey recounts, the university's music program, concert and outreach series, radio station, and Felix Grant Jazz Archives have played essential roles in the development of the music in the city.

Washington is, of course, not just a great city; it is also home to myriad national institutions that have played a role in supporting local music as they have sought to promote national and international music. Anna Celenza amplifies these connections by exploring how jazz—and the local jazz scene—became intertwined with national legislative and foreign policy goals.

There are many more stories to tell about Washington jazz than can be contained between the covers of any one volume. Michael Fitzgerald's guide to resources for researching Washington jazz reveals many places for readers to explore on their own. And as Ethelbert Miller's poems reveal, jazz has influenced every American cultural form, including the written word.

1 Jazz, "Great Black Music," and the Struggle for Racial and Social Equality in Washington, DC

Maurice Jackson

After years of abolitionist activities, by black and white, President Abraham Lincoln on April 16, 1862, eight and one-half months before the Emancipation Proclamation, signed the DC Emancipation Act, freeing more than three thousand enslaved African Americans in the District of Columbia.[1] Yet Washington remained a town with Southern sensibilities, customs, and traditions. Over the years a system of de facto and de jure segregation emerged in the city. For more than a hundred years after slavery ended, African Americans in the nation's capital continued to seek equality under the law. While they fought for justice through the legal system and in Congress, they gave full expression to their pride and determination through music in all its forms, from folk, gospel, and spirituals to the blues, classical, and jazz. The result is today called Great Black Music, and it continues in constantly reinvented forms.[2] Washington, as one of the most vibrant centers of African American culture in the country, has been both enriched by the music created and performed here and changed, however slowly, by its presence. During the long struggle for desegregation, jazz in particular provided a common ground for blacks and whites to find a space and a place to mingle and celebrate great music together.

Progenitors: From Will Marion Cook to James Reese Europe

Washington was home to two of the founders of Great Black Music, Will Marion Cook and James Reese Europe. A concert violinist, Cook received excellent classical training in both this country and Europe but as an adult found inspiration in traditional African American folk tunes and spirituals, incorporating them in his compositions. Bandleader and composer Europe was outspoken in his belief that "we colored people have our own music that is part of us. It's the product of our souls; it's been created by the sufferings and miseries of our race."[3] Both men lived in Washington when they were young, and their outlooks on life were inevitably shaped by DC's social landscape.

Between 1890 and 1918, the African American population in Washington grew dramatically. Blacks moved to the city in large numbers to flee the lynch mobs, political and economic oppression, and poverty of the South. The prospect of steady employment in the federal government provided unique opportunities for African Americans and accounted in part for this migration. These federal jobs also contributed to the emergence

Photo 1.1 *Leadbelly and Martha*
Folklorist Alan Lomax photographed newlyweds Huddie "Leadbelly" Ledbetter and his wife,
Martha, in 1935, while Lomax was recording Leadbelly for the Library of Congress. Leadbelly's
country blues were part of an African American idiom that black musicians had turned to
for inspiration, drawing from traditional songs and melodies to create their own music. The
resulting works together have been called Great Black Music, of which jazz is a vital part.

of a black middle class, who generally lived near Howard University. Paul Laurence Dunbar wrote in 1901: "Here comes together the flower of colored citizenship from all over the country. . . . The breeziness of the West here meets the refinement of the East, the warmth and grace of the South, the culture and fine reserve of the North."[4]

The election of Woodrow Wilson marked a turning point for this population. In 1912, before Wilson's inauguration, the founder of Tuskegee Institute, Booker T. Washington, believed that "the eyes of the entire country are upon the 100,000 Negroes in the District of Columbia."[5] But the next year, after Wilson became president, Washington was less optimistic about the prospect of black advancement, telling a colleague: "I have recently spent several days in Washington and I have never seen the colored people so discouraged and bitter as they are at the present time."[6] Wilson had begun to implement policies that segregated black employees within the federal government. Between 1910 and 1918 the proportion of black employees within the federal service declined from nearly 6 percent to 4.9 percent.[7]

During these years, racial lines hardened in other ways. Despite the presence of a black middle class, the overwhelming majority of Washington's black population was poor. Most lived in crowded neighborhoods and slum-like alley dwellings because of racially restrictive housing and economic segregation. The Alley Dwelling Act of 1918 (and, later, 1934) condemned the small hovels, primarily inhabited by blacks, and ultimately forced entire neighborhoods to relocate to the southeast quadrant of the District, across the Anacostia River. Labor unions resisted black membership, so there were few ways to escape poverty. Most blacks continued to work as domestic and low-skilled laborers with little hope of advancement.[8]

Within this milieu, Washington native Will Marion Cook emerged as one of the founders of Great Black Music. Born in 1869, Cook was the son of John Harwell Cook, the dean of the Howard University Law School. At age fifteen he began violin studies and composition at the Oberlin Conservatory.[9] Then, with the support of Frederick Douglass and members of the First Congregational Church, where Douglass had organized a recital, money was raised for Cook to attend the Hochschule für Musik in Berlin, Germany, from 1887 to 1889.[10] In September 1890, the *Indianapolis Freeman*, an early African American newspaper, noted "the formation of a new Washington, D.C. orchestra with Frederick Douglass as President and Willie Cook as director."[11] But, according to Europe biographer Reid Badger, it "failed to last a year—despite the backing of Frederick Douglass and the leaders of Washington's black society—in part because it followed too closely the European 'high culture' model."[12]

Cook then attended the National Conservatory in New York, where he studied in 1894 and 1895 with the Czech-born composer and conductor Antonín Dvořák. Dvořák had been recruited to the conservatory in 1892, and in 1893, not many months after his arrival, composed the symphony *From the New World* (No. 9 in E minor), which incorporates American folk tunes. Dvořák's association at the conservatory with African American composer Harry Burleigh inspired him to write "Goin' Home."[13] In an interview in the *New York Herald Tribune* on May 21, 1893, he said, "I am now satisfied that the future of this music must be founded upon what are called Negro melodies. This must be the real foundation of any serious and original school of composition to be developed in the United States. . . . These are the folk songs of America, and your composers must turn to them. All of the great musicians have borrowed from the songs of the common people." Dvořák also said, "In the Negro melodies of America I discover all that is needed for a great and noble school of music."[14] A few days later the *Tribune* editorialized that "Dr. Dvořák's explicit announcement that his newly completed symphony reflects the Negro melodies, upon which . . . the coming American school must be based . . . will be a surprise to the world."[15] The same week the *Paris Herald* carried articles on and interviews with Dvořák, May 26–28, and ran the commentary of Joseph Joachim, "a distinguished violinist and pedagogue who may have already been exposed to American Negro music through his student, Will Marion Cook."[16]

A few years later W. E. B. Du Bois, in his classic essay "The Sorrow Song" in *The Souls of Black Folk*, wrote, "The Negro folk song—the rhythm cry of slavery—stands today not simply as the sole American music, but as the most beautiful expression of human experience born this side of the seas. It has been neglected, it has been persistently mistaken and misunderstood; but notwithstanding, it still remains as the singular spiritual heritage of the nation and the greatest gifts of the Negro people."[17]

In 1898 Will Marion Cook, in collaboration with poet Paul Laurence Dunbar, composed the musical *Clorindy; or, The Origin of the Cakewalk*. Cook wrote that he borrowed

Photo 1.2 *Will Marion Cook*
Native Washingtonian Will Marion Cook was trained as a concert violinist, studying abroad and at the National Conservatory in New York, but came to believe that African Americans needed to look to their own musical folk traditions in composing and performing. Through his own works and personal connections with rising musicians like Duke Ellington, he had a profound effect on the emergence of Great Black Music and, ultimately, of jazz.

ten dollars and went to Washington to find Dunbar. They "got together in the basement of my brother John's rented house on Sixth Street, just below Howard University, one night and about eight o'clock . . . where without a piano or anything but the kitchen table, we finished all the songs and all the libretto and all but a few bars of the ensemble by four o'clock the next morning."[18] Drawing on African American language and melody, the one-act musical opened that year in July, the first all-black cast to appear on Broadway. After the success of *Clorindy*, according to musicologist Eileen Southern, Cook "became a conductor of syncopated orchestras and a composer of art music . . . [and] 'composer in chief' for a steady stream of musicals, most of which featured the celebrated vaudeville team of George Walker and Bert Williams."[19] Like Dvořák, Cook also began to incorporate folk music into his compositions and in 1912 published *A Collection of Negro Songs*.

Cook was extremely important to the early development of another Washington native, Duke Ellington, both in Washington and after he moved to New York. In his autobiography, *Music Is My Mistress*, Ellington wrote:

Will Marion Cook, His Majesty the King of Consonance . . . I can see him now with that beautiful mane of white hair flowing in the breeze as he and I rode uptown through Central Park. . . . It was always when I was browsing around Broadway, trying to make contacts with my music, that I would run into Dad Cook. . . . Several times, after I had played some tune I had written but not really completed, I would say, "Now, Dad, what is the logical way to develop this theme? What direction should I take?". . . . He would answer, . . . "First you find the logical way, and when you find it, avoid, it, and let your inner self break through and guide you. Don't try to be anybody but yourself." That time with him was one of the best semesters I ever had in music.[20]

The National Theatre, which had opened in 1835, for the first time in 1838 refused to seat African Americans in the main gallery and forced them to sit in the balcony. Then, in 1873, they were refused entry in the theater altogether. Blacks found their own performance spaces, and from the 1870s on African Americans saw classical, folk, church, and choral music concerts at the Lincoln Temple Congregational Church, the Asbury United Methodist Church, the Nineteenth Street Baptist Church, and the Fifteenth Street Presbyterian Church. John Esputa founded the short-lived Colored American Opera Company in Washington, and on February 3 and 4, 1873, its first performance of *The Doctors of Alcantara* was presented.

Henry Lewis organized the Amphion Glee Club in 1892. It found success performing all over the city and was active well into the 1930s. In 1902 the Samuel "Coleridge-Taylor Society was formed with John Turner Layton as the musical director."[21] The next year, 1903, Harriet Gibbs Marshall founded the Washington Conservatory of Music to provide young African Americans with classical musical training. She had been the first black woman to receive a diploma in music from Oberlin and later studied in Boston, Chicago, and eventually France before coming back to DC and teaching in its public schools.[22]

The Coleridge-Taylor Society was named after Samuel Coleridge-Taylor (1875–1912), the Afro-British composer who became known for his trilogy of cantatas, *Hiawatha's Wedding Feast* (1998), *The Death of Minnehaha* (1899), and *Hiawatha's Departure* (1900). The society brought Coleridge-Taylor to Washington in 1904 and 1906 as part of his United States tour, performing at the Metropolitan African Methodist Episcopal Church.[23] In addition to the *Washington Bee*, *The Music Master*, and *The Negro Musician*, the official organ of the Washington Conservatory of Music, *The Negro Journal of Music*, also covered local productions of Great Black Music.

Coleridge-Taylor again came to the United States in 1910, the guest of the Litchfield (Connecticut) Choral Union Festival. He had seen the Fisk Jubilee Singers perform in England in 1899, and this sparked his interest in the "Negro spirituals" and folk songs. Influenced by Paul Laurence Dunbar, whom he had met in London, he made an arrangement of many of these songs in his *Twenty-Four Negro Melodies Transcribed for the Piano* in 1905. The composer also set some of Dunbar's poems to music. An early Pan-Africanist, he composed *African Suite* in 1898. Among its movements are "A Negro Love Song." The *Suites* finale is titled "Danse Negre," based on Dunbar's poem of the same title.[24]

Du Bois first met Coleridge-Taylor, who also attended the first Pan African Conference in the summer of 1900. Of their first meeting Du Bois wrote, "I remember the Englishman, like the Colensos, who sat and counseled with us; but above all I remember Coleridge-Taylor."[25] So taken by the music of Coleridge-Taylor was W. E. B. Du Bois that it inspired him to write a pageant, *The Star of Ethiopia*. First drafted in 1911, it became what Du Bois biographer David Levering Lewis called "a three-hour extravaganza in six episodes, featuring a thousand creamy complexioned young women and tawny, well-built men and flocks of school children marching through history."[26] The work was intended as a history of the struggles and achievements of the African American people. With the exception of two compositions from Verdi's *Aida*, all the music was composed by blacks, including Coleridge-Taylor and J. Rosamond Johnson, brother of James Weldon Johnson. It was first performed in 1913 at the Twelfth Regiment Amory in New York as part of the celebrations surrounding the fiftieth anniversary of the Emancipation Proclamation, where Du Bois wrote that at least thirty thousand attended the premier.

Of its Washington October 1915 premier, Du Bois wrote that "we used the great ball field of the American League," officially called the American League Ball Park, where "a committee of the most distinguished colored citizens of Washington co-operated with me . . . and fourteen thousand saw the pageant."[27] Eloquently, he described his own feelings: "Wonderfully, irresistibly, the dream comes true. You feel no exaltation, you feel no personal merit. It is not yours. It is its own. You have simply called it and it comes."[28] The guide program for the pageant said, "The Story of the Pageant covers 10,000 years of the history of the Negro race and its work and suffering and triumphs in the world. The pageant combines historic accuracy and symbolic truth. All the costumes of the thousand actors, the temples, the weapons, etc., have been copied from accurate models."[29] The *Washington Bee* called the event "electrical, spiritual."[30]

James Reese Europe, noted his biographer, Reid Badger, "was born on February 22, 1880, in Mobile, Alabama. Fifteen years after the end of the Civil War, seven years after the birth of W. C. Handy, and one year before Booker T. Washington began his work at Tuskegee."[31] He was almost ten when he and his family arrived in Washington. They settled at 308 B Street, SE, not far from where his father worked at the post office, first as a clerk and later as a supervisor. By coincidence, John Philip Sousa, the famed musician and director of the U.S. Marine Corps band, and his family moved in a few doors down the street, at 318 B Street. Badger notes that "the Marine Band itself had a long standing relationship with African American community in Washington" and "regularly took part in such important events in the black community as Howard University's commencement ceremonies, and band members often provided musical instruction to promising Black children. One of these young men was Jim Europe," who took lessons in piano and violin from the assistant bandmaster of the U.S. Marine Corps.[32] March music, performed with precision by military bands and in parades, had long played a role in New Orleans, where it combined with African and Creole rhythms. Marches were also a big part of the annual DC Emancipation Day parades, so it was not unusual for youngsters to hear and enjoy them. Years later W. E. B. Du Bois would write appreciatively in the *Crisis*, the voice of the National Association for the Advancement of Colored People (NAACP), that Europe had a "genius for organization" and that his marches "all in all . . . are worthy of the pen of Sousa."[33]

For two years, Europe attended the M Street High School, founded in 1870 as the Preparatory High School for Colored Youth, the first public high school for blacks in the country. Europe was soon recruited to the school's new cadet corps, started by Sgt. Maj. Christian A. Fleetwood, a recipient of the Medal of Honor for his Civil War services. Over the years the Cadet Corps attracted many other outstanding students, including "historian Rayford W. Logan, poet Sterling Brown, scholar and diplomat Mercer Cook (son of Will Marion Cook), Army Lieutenant Colonel West Hamilton, federal judge William H. Hastie, and blood-plasma researcher Dr. Charles H. Drew."[34] Europe also joined "Captain Joseph Montgomery's prized drill company and served as Color Sergeant for the corps." Both of these experiences served him well, as Badger notes: "His cadet training would later prove useful when he sought to organize black musicians of New York; it was undoubtedly helpful to him as an officer in the 15th New York Infantry Regiment in World War I."[35] M Street School was renamed the Paul Laurence Dunbar High School in

1916 and, as Mary Gibson Hundley wrote, had "a remarkable history which chronicles the achievements of an underprivileged people."[36]

After his father died in 1899, Europe dropped out of M Street School and in 1904 headed to New York City. Europe set his sights on New York both to escape the city's crippling discrimination and to make his name in music. At the time, many artists preferred Harlem, where, as Langston Hughes wrote, "people are not so ostentatiously proud of themselves, and where one's family background is not much of a concern," as he believed was the case with the black elite of Washington.[37]

Europe quickly became part of the New York black theater and musical scene, writing songs, composing, and directing stage shows, always employing the African American idiom. In 1910 he founded the Clef Club, "a combination musicians' hangout, labor exchange, fraternity club, and concert hall," while also serving as a contracting agency for black musicians.[38] At the time, W. E. B. Du Bois noted the significance of the Clef Club: "Before [black musicians] were prey to scheming head waiters and booking agents, now they are performers whose salaries and hours are fixed by contracts."[39] Europe then formed the Clef Club Symphony Orchestra, and on May 2, 1912, the 125 musicians performed at Carnegie Hall a concert of early jazz music, all by black composers, titled "A Concert of Negro Music," "the first performance ever given by a black orchestra at the famous bastion of white musical establishment."[40] The *New York Evening Post* called the collection of musicians "one of the most remarkable orchestras in the world."[41]

On November 21, 1913, at the Metropolitan AME Church, James Reese Europe's Afro-American Folk Singers and his National Negro Symphony Orchestra presented the works of Samuel Coleridge-Taylor as well as works by Will Marion Cook, Harry Burleigh, and J. Rosamond Johnson. They performed folk songs, arrangements by Dvořák, Pyotr Tchaikovsky, and Felix Mendelssohn. The vocal soloists were Burleigh, J. Rosamond Johnson, and Abbie Mitchell.[42]

In 1913 Europe began performing with the famed white dancers Irene and Vernon Castle, serving as their bandleader, with Ford Dabney as the arranger. The Castles developed the fox-trot "from steps Europe had learned from W. C. Handy, and a score thrown off from Europe." Although some saw such collaboration of white and black music and dancing as "the devil's work," eventually even the *Ladies Home Journal* wrote approvingly of the Castles and their dancing.[43]

Ford Dabney was a lesser-known early Washington musician who, with Will Marion Cook and James Reese Europe, made up "three composers and bandleaders who moved to New York City from Washington, D.C. to make their fortune."[44] Born in Washington in 1883, he showed such talent that in 1903 he added an international element to Washington jazz circles when he became the "court pianist to Haitian President Noro Alexis, remaining in that post until 1907."[45] He moved to New York in 1913, where he worked with Europe's orchestra and wrote songs for the Castles and for Florenz Ziegfeld at Ziegfeld's New Amsterdam Theatre and its roof garden.[46]

When the United States entered World War I, brave men like James Reese Europe served among the 325,000 black soldiers in the segregated U.S. military. He saw action with Harlem's famed 369th Regiment and put together an outstanding regimental band, which he led. The 369th was originally the Fifteenth Infantry Regiment of the New

York National Guard, which was formed after many African Americans had presented petitions for it in early 1912. New York governor John Dix agreed to form the unit, but nothing was actually done until 1916, when then-governor Charles S. Whitman said that "either the regiment ought to be built and given a fair chance of proving itself, or the law ought to be repealed."[47]

Europe did not join the Fifteenth Infantry Regiment simply out of patriotism. When first approached by one of the few black officers in the National Guard, he resisted. But over time he came to believe that such a unit would enhance the status of his race. He told his good friend Noble Sissle, the composer and bandleader who also joined the Fifteenth, that in his sixteen years in New York, "there has never been such an organization of Negro men that will bring together all classes of men for a common good." He added, "Our race will never amount to anything, politically or economically, in New York or anywhere else unless there are strong organizations of men who stand for something in the community."[48] Europe was commissioned as an officer and the leader of the regimental band, and Sissle enlisted as a private, played violin, and became the drum major.

Of the four black regiments under the American Expeditionary Force, led by Gen. John J. "Black Jack" Pershing, three, including Europe's regiment, were positioned under French command. As Gail Buckley wrote, "They weren't really *American*, anyway, so giving them to the French seemed to satisfy both Wilson's expressed desire to serve humanity and his racism. They would be adopted with fulsome gratitude by the French Fourth Army."[49]

Although the members of the Fifteenth Infantry Regiment preferred to call themselves "Men of Bronze," they were nicknamed the "Enfant Perdus" (the lost or abandoned children) by the French and the "Hellfighters" by the Germans. The band's performances helped introduce European audiences to African American musicians and to ragtime, the blues, and jazz. When they played a snazzy rendition of "Marseillaise," the French crowd did not at first recognize their national anthem, but then, according to Sissle, "there came over their faces an astonished look, quickly alert, snap-into-attention and salute by every French soldier and sailor present."[50] At performances at an opera house in Nantes to honor Abraham Lincoln's birthday, the band played the "Stars and Stripes Forever" and W. C. Handy's "Memphis Blues." Sissle described first "the fireworks," then a "soul rousing" crash of the drum cymbals, when "the audience could stand it no longer the 'jazz germ' hit them and it seemed to find the vital spot." He added, "We played to 50,000 people at least, and had we wished it we might be playing yet."[51]

The unit fought with black soldiers from Morocco and Senegal who had distinguished themselves at the Battle of Marne in 1914. According to Emmet J. Scott, France declared that "it is because these soldiers are brave and just as devoted as white soldiers that they receive exactly the same treatment, every man being equal before death which all soldiers face."[52] Europe became the first African American officer to experience combat, on April 20, 1918. Injured during a German poison attack, he wrote "On Patrol in No Man's Land" from his hospital bed.

Before the war was over, the regiment had amassed 191 combat days. For their fighting, without loss of life or an inch of ground, the French government awarded the unit the Croix-de-Guerre, the French Army's highest honor. They also won 171 decorations for bravery, the most of any U.S. regiment.

On its return on February 17, 1919, the regiment marched up Fifth Avenue in New York City to thunderous applause. W. E. B. Du Bois wrote of their bravery in war and of the racism they came home to in his article "Returning Soldiers." There he declared:

> We return.
> We return from fighting.
> We return fighting.
> Make way for Democracy! We saved it in France, and by the Great Jehovah, we will
>   save it in the United States of America, or know the reason why.[53]

Postwar Washington

With the coming of peace, the few advances made by blacks during the war became grounds for increasing resentment among some white Americans. Returning white soldiers found themselves competing with blacks for the jobs they had left to go to war. Black soldiers seldom found the respect and benefits they had been promised but instead encountered disdain for taking pride in their wartime heroism.[54] During their time in the service, many African Americans like Europe had experienced a bit of equality and opportunity they were reluctant to relinquish. Others were influenced by the Pan-Africanist ideas of W. E. B. Du Bois or by socialism. By the "Red Summer" of 1919, postwar ethnic and economic tensions following demobilization, combined with fear of the Bolshevism that had taken hold in Russia, flared into violence in some Northern cities, including Washington.

On Friday, July 18, 1919, Elsie Stephnick, the wife of a Naval Aviation Department employee, was allegedly assaulted by a black man on D Street, SW. Several hundred angry white soldiers, sailors, and marines, recently returned from World War I, gathered in Southwest Washington armed with clubs, pipes, and pistols and began attacking African Americans they saw on the streets.[55] Both the *Washington Post* and the *New York Times* reported with incendiary headlines about the reported sex crime by a "negro fiend."[56] Similar headlines read "Armed and Defiant Negroes Roam about Shooting at Whites," "Negro Runs Amuck, Wounding Many in Flight," and "Race War in Washington."[57] Armed whites rampaged through Sunday morning, despite the efforts of reserves from the nearby military outpost and officers from three police stations on the scene.[58]

On Sunday, July 20, 1919, more than a thousand civilians and several hundred soldiers and marines resumed the riots, attacking black pedestrians and dragging others from their cars.[59] Then on Monday afternoon, the superintendent of police, Maj. Raymond W. Pulliam, and the District commissioner, Louis Brownlow, called up all police officers, reserve soldiers, and four hundred regular army troops recruited from Fort Myer cavalry, and order was gradually restored. Although President Wilson was "greatly concerned," he never made any public comment on the matter, nor did he declare martial law (as some congressmen desired). Of the nearly one hundred people arrested, only eight or nine were white. In the end, at least four blacks and three whites died.[60]

African Americans, however, did not perceive the violence in the same manner as the *New York Times* and the *Washington Post*. Former diplomat and NAACP president James Weldon Johnson warned America that blacks would not sit silent in the face of white violence.[61] "The Negroes saved themselves and saved Washington by their determination not to run, but to fight, fight in defense of their lives and their homes," he noted.[62] This riot marked a milestone for black citizens as they banded together and fought the white oppression that had come to define DC's social dynamic. Shocked when African Americans began to fight back in defense of their communities, white mobs retreated. Unwilling to see racism as the cause of violence, they blamed outside agitators and socialist and Bolshevik propaganda.

Over the next decade, Howard University philosopher and scholar Alain Locke advocated the development of the "New Negro" and a new self-awareness and confidence in racial identity. Locke noted "a renewed race-spirit that consciously and proudly sets itself apart," a result of the "ripening forces as culled from the first fruits of the Negro Renaissance." Coming amid what he saw as a new intellectual and cultural self-awareness, he believed that the "New Negro is keenly responsive as an augury of a new democracy in American culture," who is "contributing his share to the new social understanding."[63] This concept ignited a Washington renaissance for blacks, creating new cultural opportunities and in many ways preceding the better-known Harlem Renaissance.[64] Blacks in the nation's capital adopted the words of the poet Claude McKay, who captured their spirit and determination in his "If We Must Die":

> Like men we'll face the murderous pack,
> Pressed to the wall, dying, but fighting back![65]

A New Era of Racial Solidarity Through Cultural Protests

This new racial solidarity promoted by Locke was tested in June 1922. Robert Russa Moton, the successor to Booker T. Washington at Tuskegee, was a featured speaker at the dedication of the Lincoln Memorial. Although his name was listed on the official invitation and program, Moton and other blacks were cordoned off in a segregated section far from the dais. In response to this indignity, the *Baltimore African American* reported, "twenty-one distinguished guests of the nation at the dedication of the Lincoln Memorial yesterday got up from their seats and left the exercises when they found they had been jimcrowed." The newspaper speculated that "Dr. Moton may have been referring to this incident when he said in his address that he hoped that 'black and white, North and South are going to strive to finish the work Lincoln so nobly began—to make America an example for the world of equal justice, and equal opportunity for all who strive and are willing to serve under the flag that makes men free.'"[66]

Marian Anderson

A concert by internationally celebrated contralto Marion Anderson in 1939 exposed Washington's segregated society to the rest of the country. For several years the Howard University Music Department had presented an annual concert featuring Anderson, using space at Dunbar High or local auditoriums. In 1939 Anderson was fresh from a successful European tour, and her promoters, along with Howard officials, decided to move the event to Constitution Hall, owned by the Daughters of the American Revolution (DAR), not realizing that the DAR had in its leasing agreements a "white artist only" clause. Unlike the National Theatre, which denied black audience admittance but allowed black performers, Constitution Hall allowed black patrons to sit in roped off areas but did not allow African American performers.[67]

When denied the use of Constitution Hall, the newly formed Marian Anderson Citizens Committee (MACC) then tried to reserve Central High School (which was for whites), but the school board denied the auditorium to any events with either African American performers or audience members.[68] Finally, with the support of First Lady Eleanor Roosevelt, who resigned her DAR membership over the issue, Secretary of the Interior Harold Ickes arranged for Anderson to perform on the steps of the Lincoln Memorial.

On Easter Sunday, April 9, 1939, the concert was held at the Lincoln Memorial with more than seventy-five thousand in attendance. Anderson sang Negro spirituals such as "Nobody Knows the Trouble I've Seen" and "My Soul Is Anchored in the Lord" and "Gospel Train," arranged by her old friend Harry Burleigh, as well as Franz Schubert's "Ave Maria" and a moving rendition of "America." The program was broadcast over NBC Radio, so millions in America and the world heard it live or in rebroadcasts in newsreels at movie houses. Others read about it in newspapers, broadsheets, and magazines.

Mary McLeod Bethune, head of the National Council of Negro Women, an appointee to the National Youth Administration, and a member of President Franklin Roosevelt's Kitchen Cabinet, wrote to Charles Hamilton Houston, special litigation counsel of the

Photo 1.3 *Marian Anderson at the Lincoln Memorial*
Marian Anderson performs before thousands at the Lincoln Memorial in April 1939, after being denied the use of the DAR Constitution Hall. The concert brought national attention to Washington's pervasive segregation and was hailed by Mary McLeod Bethune as "our triumphant entry into the democratic spirit of American life."

NAACP and dean of the Howard Law School, that Anderson's performance "cannot be described in words. There is no way. History may well record it, but it will never be able to tell what happened in the hearts of the thousands who stood and listened yesterday. . . . Through the Marion Anderson Protest Concert we made our triumphant entry into the democratic spirit of American life."[69] Historian Constance McLaughlin Green later wrote that "no one who was present at that moving performance ever forgot it. . . . It was a turning point, one man averred, in Washington Negroes' seventy-year old fight against discrimination. And it was no longer a local affair only. Race relations in the nation's capital thenceforward were a matter of interest to Americans everywhere."[70]

The MACC saw the concert as just part of its mission. They also decided to challenge the school board's decision to deny Anderson the right to sing at Central High. At a mass meeting on March 26, a few days before the scheduled concert, Herbert Marshall, head of the DC branch of the NAACP, declared that "the denial of the use of the Central High School auditorium is the very antithesis of democracy."[71] Their appeal was denied. Historian Raymond Arsenault notes that, while the DAR battle had been won, "the battle over racial justice in the nation's capital was just beginning," and "it would be years before black Washingtonians achieved anything approaching fundamental reform in the District's schools."[72]

A few weeks later, Anderson performed at the White House for a private audience of President Roosevelt, Mrs. Roosevelt, King George VI, and Queen Elizabeth of Great Britain. Mrs. Roosevelt's education in civil rights did not end with the DAR event. She later read Countee Cullen's poem "Black Majesty" from his book *The Black Christ* and other poems that were dedicated to Toussaint L'Ouverture, Jean-Jacques Dessalines, and Henri Christophe. One line reads "Lo, I am dark, but comely, Sheba sings, and we were black, three shades reply, but kings." Mrs. Roosevelt was so moved that she wrote years later in her newspaper column that everyone should be required to read *The Black Christ*.[73] During the 1963 March on Washington, Anderson again performed at the Lincoln Memorial. Scheduled to sing the national anthem, she was, like many, caught up in a massive traffic jam, but she did arrive in time to sing "He's Got the Whole World in His Hands."

The DAR's bigotry did not stop with African American performers. Michael Terrace (Michael Gutierrez) wrote of being part of Mambo USA, a mixed-race Latino touring company in the summer of 1952. The review was set for its Washington premier. As Terrace describes it,

> Constitution Hall was a munificent auditorium, the highest ceiling and plush seats. It made one feel proud to be an American but it didn't last long. The following day we went to Constitution Hall in Washington, DC and this time at our rehearsal we met again with a similar confrontation that was belittling coming from three ladies that claimed to belong to the Daughters of the American Revolution, in their own Southern lady like fashion, that n - - - - rs were not allowed to perform on the stage of Constitution Hall with whites. . . . We were told that we were mix breeds and could not perform on the Constitution Hall stage.[74]

The DAR finally relented after the show was sold out, although at the show all blacks were searched and the whites were not. At the performance, one of its stars, Myrta Silvia, said, "Why should we continue on a stage that only belongs to the supreme whites?"[75]

To this the audience stood and cheered "love refrains" until she sang her next song. Feeling victorious, the mixed-race review and many from the audience went to the local Arthur Murray Dance Studio for a celebration. This was during the time of the early picket lines and protests against segregation, just a few years before the court rulings that desegregated the city.

Billie Holiday

The same April of 1939, when Marion Anderson performed at the Lincoln Memorial, Billie Holiday first performed "Strange Fruit" at New York's Café Society, a midtown club that attracted a varied audience, from Nelson Rockefeller to Lillian Hellman and Langston Hughes. Other performers there included such stars as Lena Horne, Sarah Vaughan, and Imogene Coca. According to David Margolick, "It was probably the only place in America where 'Strange Fruit' could have been sung and savored."[76] The song was written by Abel Meeropol under the pen name Lewis Allan, who explained, "I wrote 'Strange Fruit' because I hate lynching and I hate injustice and I hate the people who perpetuate it."[77] Holiday told how a hush enveloped the room as she sang the song, then one by one audience members began to applaud as they understood the meaning and the sadness of the song about lynchings in the South. The song was then studio recorded on April 20 and released a few months later. "Strange Fruit" had a riveting effect on jazz and on the struggle against lynching.

Holiday had signed on as vocalist with Artie Shaw, a Jewish clarinetist and bandleader, in 1938. Shaw was the first to hire and the first to tour the segregated South with a black female singer. The singer endured Southern bigotry for months, but by the time of her April 1939 club date at Café Society, she "had just quit Artie Shaw's band in part because she had been forced to take the freight elevator during a gig at a New York hotel. And not just any hotel, but one named after Abraham Lincoln."[78] But Holiday respected Shaw: "There aren't many people who fought harder than Artie against the vicious people in the music business or the crummy side of second-class citizenship which eats at the guts of so many musicians. He didn't win. But he didn't lose either."[79] In later years Shaw came to DC with integrated bands and to lobby President Roosevelt for federal support for the arts.

The *Baltimore Afro-American* newspaper reported in March 1940 that "Miss Holiday recently sang ['Strange Fruit'] at the Howard Theatre in Washington," and "speculation became rife as to whether it actually will incite or condemn mob action," but the paper said the song "immediately won praise from both the hot and classical schools." The paper also speculated "that Holiday might have even won the NAACP's prestigious Spingarn Medal, given annually to blacks for special achievements, had the black church not disapproved of entertainers at the time."[80]

Even the more conservative National Urban League's Lester Granger praised the song. Holiday continued to sing "Strange Fruit" at progressive and antiracist events, including a benefit in 1943 "for Ben Davis Jr., a black man elected as a Communist to the New York City Council (Paul Robeson, Teddy Wilson, Josh White, Ella Fitzgerald and Hazel Scott participated in the same event)."[81]

Holiday performed regularly in Washington and was especially fond of playing at Club Bali, staying at the Dunbar Hotel. In 1949 she had a three-week engagement there, breaking the club record and ending on April 7, her birthday. Around this time pianist Carl Drinkard, a twenty-year-old Howard University senior, caught her attention while he was playing at a small club called Little Harlem. After hearing him play, Holiday "marched over to the piano and said 'You! You're coming with me!'"[82] He soon joined her at the Club Bali, and on his first night one of the greatest piano players, Art Tatum, was in the audience and gave young Drinkard his approval.

Georgianne Williamson of the *Washington Post* wrote in 1949, "There's a singular kind of repose about [her features]: Billie is earthy, but with complete good grace. More factual than suggestive, still she's got a gallop that has the bar sitters, around her in a semi circle at her feet, supplying a chorus of adulation."[83]

Duke Ellington

Washington-born Duke Ellington also made his contribution to the desegregation of his native city. He knew well the works of the prolific African American historian Rayford Logan, his old family friend, who in 1941 published *The Diplomatic Relations of the United States with Haiti*. According to Ellington biographer John Edward Hasse, Duke Ellington "owned 800 books on black history, and had underlined passages about Denmark Vesey and Nat Turner." Ellington was also familiar with the art of Jacob Lawrence, the poetry of Langston Hughes, and the prose of W. E. B. Du Bois related to the Haitian Revolution and Toussaint L'Ouverture.[84] Although some writers have noted Ellington's social conservatism, especially in his later years, Terry Teachout offers another view of Duke: "Ellington, like many other blacks, appreciated the Communist Party's stance against racism, and his sentiments were widely shared in Harlem." While noting that the maestro, like many of his generation, was a Republican, Teachout points out that Ellington "himself would actively support the candidacy of Benjamin J. Davis Jr., when he ran for New York's city council on the Communist ticket in 1943," siding with a black man he admired for openly fighting racism.[85]

Ellington also made a statement with his symphony *Black, Brown and Beige.* Duke said that he composed the suite as "a tone parallel to the history of the Negro in America."[86] He told columnist Belle Ayer that "five of the 10 years which have gone into writing the piece were put into research, and the other five years were required to write the book and the music" to his suite.[87] The suite was influenced by the blacks that fought at the Battle of Savannah and by his appreciation of the Haitian Revolution. "I have gone back to the history of my race and tried to express it in rhythm," Ellington wrote. "We used to have a little something in Africa, a 'something' we have lost. One day we shall get it again."[88]

In 1943 *Black, Brown and Beige* was ready for its opening in New York. Ellington knew that when the film *Emperor Jones*, starring Paul Robeson, premiered in September 1933, it opened simultaneously to segregated audiences. Whites viewed it at the Rivoli Theater in the downtown theater district, and blacks viewed it at the Roosevelt Theater uptown in Harlem. Duke wanted better.[89] On January 23, 1943, Duke Ellington's *Black, Brown and Beige* premiered at New York's Carnegie Hall. Count Basie, Jimmie Lunceford, and Benny Goodman attended the performance as well as First Lady Eleanor Roosevelt and Leopold Stokowski. According to the *Washington Afro-American*, "Frank Sinatra left his engagement at the Paramount to visit backstage." Among the African American celebrities in attendance were Marian Anderson, Langston Hughes, and Alain Locke. Tickets to the concert sold out two weeks before the premiere and "an overflow crowd of about 2,000 persons milled about the sidewalks and lobby of [3,000-person capacity] Carnegie Hall . . . in the hopes of securing tickets."[90] The concert, which was done in support of Russian War Relief, grossed $7,000 and netted $5,000. The concerts were repeated in Boston on January 28, 1943, and in Cleveland on February 20, 1943, all for integrated audiences.[91] Ellington, who said that he was not a street protester, used his *Jump for Joy* (1941), *Symphony in Black* (1934), and *Creole Rhapsody* (1931) in addition to *Black, Brown and Beige* to express himself through his music. He wrote that "jazz is based on our native heritage. It is an American idiom with African roots—a trunk of soul with limbs, reaching in every direction, to the frigid North, the exotic East, the miserable, swampy South, and the wild swinging West."[92]

Ahmet Ertegun

Ahmet and Nesuhi Ertegun, sons of the Turkish ambassador to the United States, had a profound impact upon the Washington jazz scene. Arriving in Washington in 1935, the young men and their sister, Selma, quickly developed a love and appreciation of African American music of all kinds: blues, spirituals, gospels, jazz, and, later, rhythm and blues. They learned about the city and about African Americans from the embassy's custodian, Cleo Payne, an ex-prizefighter who taught Ahmet Ertegun to box and took him to boxing matches, "introduced him to beer joints, and . . . gave him an appetite for soul food."[93] Often they traveled the streets of black Washington driven by the embassy's African American chauffeur and spent long hours going to record stores and visiting the homes of blacks to listen to and purchase jazz recordings.

Despite segregation, the Erteguns socialized with the African American community. "In the forties, Washington was like a Southern town," Ahmet later wrote. "There was total segregation. Black people had their own movie theatres in their own section of town and were not allowed in the white movie theatres." Except, that is, for the burlesque shows where whites sat downstairs and blacks in the balcony. "Black and white musicians did play together, but it was not easy. It was more possible in New York, particularly Harlem, but in Washington at that time it was virtually impossible."[94] They began to meet "the black professors at Howard University, especially the Dean of the School of English Literature, Sterling Brown" and others in

> the black intelligentsia and members of the Washington black society. Our common interest in jazz brought all of us together. . . . We had a lot of friends in Washington, and we could never go to a restaurant together, never go to a movie, or to the theater with them. . . . It was impossible to go out. I couldn't even take Duke Ellington, who is one of the geniuses of our country, to a restaurant. Or Count Basie. That's how it was and we could not accept it.[95]

Beginning in 1940 the brothers began to invite musicians they had seen play on Saturday nights at the Howard Theatre and elsewhere to the embassy for Sunday lunches, where jazz-loving friends and whichever band was in town would play, including Duke Ellington, Louis Armstrong, Johnny Hodges, Benny Carter, Rex Stewart, Joe Marsala, Lester Young, and Meade Lux Lewis.[96]

Photo 1.4 *The Erteguns and Gottlieb*
Nesuhi (left) and Ahmet Ertegun (center),
with their friend, photographer Bill Gottlieb
(right), were the Turkish ambassador's
sons who arrived in Washington in 1935
and soon fell in love with jazz. They
haunted the clubs and theaters downtown
and befriended jazz musicians.

Some Washington residents with strong Southern sensibilities were disturbed to see blacks entering the embassy through the front door. Ertegun often told the story of a Southern senator who lived nearby complaining to his father, Mehmet, about African Americans entering the embassy through the front door. Ahmet said, "My father would respond with a terse one-sentence reply such as: 'In my home, friends enter by the front door—however, we can arrange for you to enter from the back.'"[97]

Ahmet Ertegun called himself "leftish intellectually" while living "in an embassy with sixteen servants with a limousine," yet he detested segregation. Frustrated, the Ertegun brothers decided to hold jazz concerts open to integrated audiences in 1942. While whites had long gone to U Street and the Howard Theatre to hear Great Black Music, there had not been events that promoted blacks and whites listening to music together. According to Ahmet:

As Nesuhi and I had become friends with Duke Ellington, Lena Horne and Jelly Roll Morton, we decided to put on the first integrated concert in Washington. We had black and white musicians onstage, people like Sidney Bechet, Joe Turner, Pete Johnson, Pee Wee Russell, and others—and also we had an integrated audience. We had a lot of trouble finding a place in Washington where we could stage this event. The first concert we held was at the Jewish community centre, which was the only place that would allow a mixed audience and a mixed band. After that the National Press Club broke down and let us to use their auditorium. Leadbelly used to come to some of our open jam sessions at the embassy and he sang at the first concert we gave at the National Press Club. When he peeked out from the wings backstage and saw the size of the crowd, he said 'Man, you gotta give me double the price, otherwise I'm not going on.' So of course we did—we gave him everything we could, and you know, we certainly weren't pretending to be experienced promoters, we were just doing it for the love of the music.[98]

The Erteguns smashed boundaries posed by culture and race when they organized this first interracial concert in Washington, located on Sixteenth Street about a mile north of the White House. As Nesuhi remembered in a 1979 interview with the *Washington Post*, "Blacks and whites couldn't sit together in most places. So we put on concerts. . . . jazz was our weapon for social action."[99] Ahmet recalled later that many who came to the Jewish Community Center "did not know it would be integrated" and that the Press Club relented and allowed their next concert because he promised "to make a big scene out of it if they didn't let us rent it."[100] The music was played by a racially mixed jazz orchestra for a mixed audience. Interracial audiences began to be more common in the DC jazz clubs.[101] The Erteguns also saw this as an effort to bring African Americans, Jewish people, and Muslims together. Perhaps they had read the evil words of Adolf Hitler that "the large mass of Jews is a race culturally unproductive. That is why they are more drawn to the Negro than to the culturally higher world of the truly creative races."[102] The Erteguns wanted to denounce anti-Semitism and racial hatred of any kind. And they did so using the music of the truly creative African American and Jewish peoples.

Soon the Erteguns were known throughout the city for their activities in the jazz scene. In a *Washington Post* article on May 16, 1943, titled "Two Turks, Hot for U.S. Swing," William Gottlieb wrote that "from the beginning, the young Erteguns treated the music of Morton, Armstrong, Oliver, Ellington and the rest with sincere enthusiasm and scholarly discrimination, an attitude that, strangely enough is more typical of Europeans than Americans."

When Leadbelly performed in the Erteguns' second concert, he was familiar with the realities of segregation in Washington, having visited the city years before, in the 1930s. Born Huddie Ledbetter, Leadbelly was initially brought to the city to record music at the Library of Congress by folklorist Alan Lomax. According to Lomax biographer John Szwed, "the Ledbetters were to have stayed with the Lomaxes in their apartment, but when the landlord got word that they had Negroes as guests he threatened to call the police and, under Washington's segregated housing laws, have them all put out of the building." The next day Lomax and Leadbelly searched the town looking for a black hotel or rooming house, and when, with their wives, they sought a place to eat together, they were denied entrance to the restaurants. Leadbelly wrote "Bourgeois Blues" to reflect his views of race and class in the capital city, first recorded in 1938.

> Me and my wife went all over town,
> And everywhere we went people turned us down
> Lord in a bourgeois town

And the last stanza:

> I tell all the colored folks to listen to me
> Don't try to find no home in Washington, D.C.
> Cause it's a bourgeois town.

Over the years this song has been used to describe unflatteringly the city's "black bourgeoisie." When Lomax sang the song, he emphasized this and called it a "Bush-wa Town."[103]

Ahmet Ertegun also got to know Jelly Roll Morton, born in 1890 as Ferdinand Joseph Lamothe, a Creole with both French and African ancestry. Renaming himself Jelly Roll Morton, he was one of the founders of what we now call jazz, mixing opera, French quadrilles, and Latin American and European marching band traditions. Popular in the 1920s when jazz centered in New Orleans, he moved between California, Chicago, and New York. But as ragtime declined and he was down on his luck, he moved to DC, where Ertegun said "he had hit rock bottom . . . didn't have a place to stay, didn't have anything."[104] Still, in 1935 his music was influential, "as Benny Goodman's rendition of Morton's 'King Porter's Stomp,' arranged by Fletcher Henderson, ushered in the Swing Era."[105] In 1938, as with Leadbelly, Lomax conducted interviews with Morton for the Library of Congress, and the next year he made eight new recordings as a result of the interviews. Although Leadbelly recorded "Bourgeois Blues" in 1938, some of his words reflect those of Jelly Roll, who wrote to his wife in January 1937, "Darling Wife, I don't want you to worry. Things are tough everywhere and we are not the only ones that's catching hell." Lomax sums up Morton's condition: "another month of striving up and down U St.—another month of acting up to the part of top composer in jazz on coffee and cakes in the most class-ridden small town in the U.S.—the colored bourgeois ghetto of Washington, D.C."[106] Ertegun recalled, "For me Jelly Roll is still, to this day, one of the greatest musicians of all time."[107]

Another musician who indirectly influenced the integration of the city was Elizabeth Cotten, the author of the monumental folk song "Freight Train." According to Mike Seeger, a folksinger and cousin to the legendary Pete Seeger, "beginning in the early 1940s she lived with her daughter and five grandchildren in Washington, D.C." While working at the Lansburgh's department store she "returned a lost Peggy Seeger to her mother. They quickly became friends and soon Elizabeth Cotten was working for the Seegers. After a few years she remembered that she, too, used to play, took the family guitar down and started playing again, recalling one by one many of the songs and tunes of her childhood and youth."[108] On the streets near Lansburgh's department store, along Seventh and E Streets in downtown DC, all races heard her and the message about the dignity of African Americans. With the help of the Seeger family, she joined the folk festival circuit, playing at the Newport Folk Festival and the Smithsonian Festival of American Folklife on the National Mall.

Ahmet and Nesuhi Ertegun moved to New York and in September 1947 founded Atlantic Records, where they worked with the greats of American and world music of all colors, races, and religions. The noted pianist, composer, jazz educator, and Dunbar graduate Dr. Billy Taylor later wrote in appreciation, "In their own way, the Erteguns defied segregation to frequent our neighborhood and patronize our music. They also produced jazz concerts that featured racially mixed groups, shocking the Washington, D.C. establishment and delighting their friends."[109] In a 2007 PBS documentary about Atlantic Records, Ahmet comments, "All popular music stems from black music, be it jazz or rock and roll." Reflecting on his career, he adds, "I'd be happy if people said that

Photo 1.5 Jazz at the Turkish Embassy

In 1940 the Ertegun brothers started to invite visiting bands to come to the embassy on Sunday for lunch and a casual jam session. This ensemble includes members of the Ellington and Marsala bands: *left to right*, Johnny Hodges (partly hidden in back), Rex Stewart, unidentified saxophonist, Harry Carney, Adele Girard, Barney Bigard, unidentified person (partly hidden in the back), and Joe Marsala.

I did a little bit to raise the dignity and recognition of the greatness of African American music."[110]

A Changed City

The Erteguns left Washington a different city. Through their insistence on breaking racial barriers, they had cracked open a door to greater integration in entertainment venues and, ultimately, much more. In 1946 David Rosenberg, the owner of Club Bali, where legendary artists such as Lester Young, Billie Holiday, Louis Armstrong, and Sarah Vaughan had appeared, made news with plans to build a space where there would be a nondiscriminatory policy for both musicians and audience. On January 12, 1947, Rosenberg opened the Music Hall—one of the first professional venues in Washington that allowed mixed-race bands and audiences—with great fanfare at Ninth and V Streets, NW, featuring a one-week engagement by Louis Armstrong. By late April the Music Hall had hosted Billy Eckstine, Ella Fitzgerald, Cootie Williams, Lionel Hampton, Tony Pastor, Cab Calloway, Rex Stewart, Jimmie Lunceford, Illinois Jacquet, Erskine Hawkins, Andy Kirk, Dizzy Gillespie, Art Tatum, and Sam Donahue. Charlie "Yardbird" Parker also performed there, while he and Dizzy Gillespie were leading the new bebop revolution in jazz.[111]

The next year jazz continued to weaken the hold of segregation through concerts promoted by Willis Conover, a popular disc jockey on radio station WWDC. Conover held the first of many integrated jazz concerts on Saturday, April 24, 1948, at the All Souls Unitarian Church on Sixteenth Street, NW, a fitting place to hold a socially pioneering performance. Long a bastion of social liberalism, the church's bell rang on Emancipation Day, January 1, 1863, and would again during the March on Washington on August 28, 1963. Among its founders in 1821 was John Quincy Adams, called by some "the Abolitionist" for his role arguing the *Amistad* case before the U.S. Supreme Court.[112] The church has continued its activism for freedom and racial equality to this day.

With the success of the first "jam session" at All Souls Church, "Willis Conover Presents Jam Session No. 2" was held at the National Press Club on May 9, 1948, which by then had adopted a policy of nondiscrimination, in part because of the efforts of the Ertegun brothers, journalist and photographer William Gottlieb, and Conover. The third and last of that first series of concerts was held two weeks later, on Sunday afternoon, May 23, at the Music Hall, advertised in the *Washington Daily News* as "Dixieland vs. Bebop and featuring Charlie Parker."[113] Ron Frits writes that the Music Hall was a good choice: "Venues in the Washington area that would accommodate patrons regardless of race and charge reasonable rent, while offering amenities far and above the standard in 1948, [were] few and far between."[114]

Conover later became famous internationally as a jazz broadcaster for the Voice of America. Although he made thousands of fans for American jazz around the world, he was little known outside the jazz community in this country. He described himself as a "lower case voice identified with the music that symbolized freedom," perhaps equating black freedom with the Voice of America's broadcasting from "the free world" to behind the Iron Curtain. "A program should play music, not talk about it," he wrote, and he did not think that he should discuss US racial issues on air.[115] However, as noted author Gene Lees has written, "During [Conover's] military service, he acted to desegregate Washington. His part in this effort was to present musicians in nightclubs, insisting that blacks be admitted. He also produced a series of Saturday midnight concerts at the Howard Theater. His opposition to racism was lifelong, and deeply felt."[116]

Pianist and jazz authority Bill Potts, who toured with the likes of Ella Fitzgerald and Stan Getz and who often led the house band at Olivia's Patio Lounge, wrote that, "in the fifties, Washington was a mecca for jazz in the country. There was an abundance of young, experienced musicians from all around the country living in the D.C. area."[117] These included Shirley Horn, June Norton, Bill Potts, Buck Hill, John Malachi, and many others. Willis Conover was producing shows under the name "Willis Conover Presents the Orchestra, Joe Timer, Musical Director," with guest musicians like Dizzy Gillespie, Stan Getz, Lee Konitz, Zoot Sims, and Charlie Parker when they came to Washington. On February 22, 1953, Charlie Parker appeared and may have played the plastic saxophone "Bird" was known to use when he had pawned his horn.

A New Push

The 1940s brought the emergence of the modern civil rights movement, as African Americans worked more aggressively for equality through the courts, the federal government, unions, and civic organizations. Many regard a planned march on Washington in June 1941 as its beginning. Labor leader A. Philip Randolph threatened to bring a hundred thousand people to Washington to protest discrimination in federal agencies but agreed to call off the march when President Roosevelt issued Executive Order 8802, which prohibited such discrimination. Roosevelt also established the Fair Employment Practices Committee in 1942 to address some of the same issues. When African Americans began returning home from the war, they brought expectations that the idea of "Double V"— Victory against fascism abroad and Victory against racism and injustice at home—meant they would return to a more equitable Washington.

Newly emboldened African Americans sought the integration of cultural venues beyond jazz clubs. The Actors' Equity, representing thousands of actors and stage managers, took a stand against segregation at theaters such as the National in 1947. The actors' union issued a statement that read, "We state now to the National Theatre—and to a public which is looking to us to do what is just and humanitarian—that unless the situation is remedied, we will be forced to forbid our members to play there."[118] Rather than integrate, the National Theatre closed in 1948 and stayed shut until 1952, when new owners agreed to allow interracial audiences.

Late in 1947 the President's Committee on Civil Rights, appointed by President Harry S. Truman, issued a report titled "To Secure These Rights," which "shocked the nation with its revelations of how deeply racial segregation and discrimination were rooted" in the city and the nation.[119] Within a year, President Truman issued Executive Order 9981, which desegregated the military and other areas of federal employment.[120] This was particularly significant for Washington, with its thousands of federal employees and military personnel, many of them black.

Another landmark of 1948 was the Supreme Court's ruling in *Shelly v. Kraemer*, which stated that racially restrictive housing covenants were not enforceable. As a result, some middle-class blacks moved into neighborhoods where they had been barred before, such as Shepherd Park, Brightwood, and Brookland near Catholic University. One of the four cases joined to *Brown v. Board of Education*, *Bolling v. Sharpe*, originated in Washington. That same year a report titled "Segregation in Washington" was published with the endorsement of some ninety prominent Americans, including Eleanor Roosevelt, Hubert Humphrey, and Walter Reuther.

The Lost Laws

In 1949 the Coordinating Committee for the Enforcement of DC Anti-Discrimination Laws began a campaign against segregation in restaurants and public facilities. Longtime resident and activist Marvin Caplan described the city at midcentury: "By 1950, segregation by law and by custom was firmly entrenched in Washington. Segregated restaurants were only one reflection of a racially divided city. Black Washingtonians encountered segregation in the most fundamental aspects of their daily lives. . . . Blacks who ventured downtown found most hotels and movie houses closed to them."[121] The Coordinating Committee focused on certain antidiscriminatory "lost laws" passed in 1872 and 1873. Although never repealed, as were many such laws after Reconstruction, even when the city codes were revised in 1901, the laws were not enforced. On January 27, 1950, eighty-six-year-old Mary Church Terrell and three others entered Thompson's Cafeteria on

Fourteenth Street downtown and tried to purchase food. The restaurant's refusal to serve them formed the basis of the suit in the *District of Columbia v. Thompson Co.* First the municipal court (1950) and then the appellate courts (1951) ruled against their complaint, and the case went on to the Supreme Court. Picket lines and marches continued in downtown DC as the boycott spread to other restaurants and to People's Drug Store, Hecht department store on Seventh Street, and G.C. Murphy's on F Street. On one occasion "Josephine Baker, the celebrated singer and dancer and friend of Mrs. Terrell (who seemed to know everyone), spared a moment during a visit to the capital to come down to Hecht's, and when she was refused service, took a turn on the picket line."[122]

Entertainers and public citizens also played another role. The Coordinating Committee began publishing a list of eating establishments "which are reported to serve meals to well behaved persons irrespective of race." The headline of the January 24, 1951, *Afro-American Newspaper* read "List Published of the 36 White-Owned Restaurants in D.C. Serving All Comers," as well as "All Federal Building Cafeterias." The *Afro-American* also wrote that foreign embassies and the U.S. State Department kept updated lists of places that served all races.[123] This policy no doubt was reflective of the larger number of diplomats of color coming to the city. In fact, some years later during the height of the civil rights struggles, African Americans were known to wear African dresses, headdresses, and other attire, seeking to "pass" as diplomats in DC or in their travels south to visit relatives, hoping to escape discrimination. Some who believed that blacks from the Caribbean or Latin America were treated better also claimed to speak Spanish or another language.

Finally, in 1953 Justice William O. Douglas wrote in the majority opinion in the Thompson case "that we find no other intervening act which would effect repeal of the [lost laws]." As the Coordinating Committee successfully tested the laws, movie theaters, hotels, public facilities, and restaurants were integrated.

As the civil rights movement grew stronger in the 1950s, the federal government responded. President Dwight D. Eisenhower, in his first State of the Union Address in 1953, said that Washington must be an "honored example for all communities of our nation" and declared that "not one single penny of federal money should be spent in a way that would discriminate against anyone."[124] Over the next several years he ordered the integration of all U.S. military academies and the end of segregated schools at military bases as well as the elimination of the few all-black military units that had not been integrated under President Truman. In his 1956 State of the Union message Eisenhower described the low black voter turnout as "disturbing," speculating that it was because of intimidation at the polls.[125]

Satchmo Speaks His Mind

Then, in September 1957, nine African American students were blocked from entering the all-white Central High School in Little Rock, Arkansas. Defying federal law, Gov. Orval Faubus stationed National Guard troops around the school to prevent their entry.[126]

Louis Armstrong, who had been approached by the State Department to visit the Soviet Union as part of the Jazz Ambassadors program, was angered.[127] After seeing pictures of white mobs throwing objects at young black girls, Armstrong told a reporter, "My people—the Negroes—are not looking for anything—we just want a square shake. But when I see on television and read about a crowd in Arkansas spitting and cursing at a little colored girl—I think I have a right to get sore—and say something about it."[128] Referring to his trips abroad representing the United States, he told another reporter on September 19, "The way they are treating my people in the South the Government can go to hell. The people over there ask me what's wrong with my country. What am I supposed to say?" Accusing the president of being "two faced" and having "no guts," he added, "It's getting so bad a colored man hasn't got any country."[129] Because of his outspokenness, some concerts and TV appearances were canceled, but Armstrong found a new appreciation among black Americans and throughout the world. On September 24, perhaps affected by the man known throughout the world as Satchmo, Eisenhower sent 1,200 paratroopers from the 101st Airborne to Little Rock to escort the Little Rock Nine into Central High. Satchmo then sent a message to Ike: "If you decide to walk into the schools with the little colored kids, take me along, daddy. God Bless You."[130]

This had a tremendous impact in Washington in the same year that African Americans became the majority population. In his own way "ole Satch" had reached the president, not just with his trumpet or his singing but with his spoken word. And his actions directly contributed to democracy in the nation's capital.

New Avenues

Washington's sports teams were also slow to integrate. Although Jackie Robinson had integrated Major League Baseball in 1947, the Washington Senators owner, Clark Griffith, refused to sign black ballplayers. At last, "in September 1954, four months after the *Brown* and *Bolling* decisions Griffith finally integrated his team but in his own perverse way."[131] He used Carlos Paula, a twenty-six-year-old black Cuban player. The *Pittsburgh Courier* editorialized, "Mr. Griffith would give Washington fans dark players from other lands but never an American Negro."[132] The team relocated to Minnesota in 1960 without ever having signed one African American.

Football was little different. On November 31, 1961, *Washington Post* sportswriter Dave Brady noted "83 Negroes on Pro Teams, including seven at Dallas, but none" on the Washington football team. He added that they "have no Negroes and no victories." By 1962 the National Football League had over fifty black players but none in DC until the team obtained the all-star wide receiver Bobby Mitchell from the Cleveland Browns in 1962.[133]

Jazz at Lorton

Perhaps events in the Washington area also influenced Armstrong. On July 2, 1957, Louis Armstrong & His All-Stars with Jack Teagarden appeared at the 2nd Lorton Jazz Festival. The festival first began in 1956 at the Lorton prison complex, where offenders from Washington, DC, were sent. Conceived by the prison's Catholic chaplain, Father Carl J. Breitfeller, the first annual concert featured Sarah Vaughan. Performing before a large audience of black and white inmates, Satchmo told the large audience that it was at the Waif's Home in New Orleans, when he was sentenced for eighteen months for shooting a pistol when he was twelve years old, that he learned to play the trumpet. Armstrong told them "they made me the bugler—I didn't know one end of the horn from the other—and later I picked up the cornet." He added, "if it had not been for Professor Jones, the man who headed the Waifs' home, who got me interested in music—Well, thank God for the good men, he put on this earth."[134] He appeared at the Lorton festival again in 1960, this time with the great singer Velma Middleton.[135] In 1965 at the 10th Annual Lorton Jazz Festival, Frank Sinatra appeared with the Count Basie Orchestra and Ella Fitzgerald with the Tommy Flanagan Trio. The crowd of 1,500 inmates witnessed history, as this was the first time that Mr. Sinatra and Ms. Fitzgerald had ever performed on the same program. In a documentary on Sinatra, narrated by the legendary Walter Cronkite, the broadcaster tells of the chaplain inviting him and notes the obvious fun that "Ole Blue Eyes is having" and "that he not only came but brought the whole Count Basie Band with him." Cronkite added, "at this affluent point in his career he responds more quickly to the request for a benefit performance than to the opportunity to make money."[136]

Also appearing were Eddie Harris, Ramsey Lewis, Bobby Timmons, and Quincy Jones.[137] This was Fitzgerald's fourth appearance, Basie's second, and Sinatra's first. At the 1965 concert, inmates from the District of Columbia Jail and the Women's Reformatory at Occoquan were bused in.[138]

The New Thing

It was at this moment when The New Thing Art and Architecture Center began to play a major role in bringing black, white, and brown people of different ages and classes together to listen to jazz, to socialize, and to help educate young people of color. The New Thing was founded in 1967 by Colin "Topper" Carew, a one-time member of the Student Nonviolent Coordinating Committee.[139] The twenty-eight-year-old former Howard University architecture student had dropped out; he recalled: "I wanted to be a people's architect. So I opened a storefront in the Adams-Morgan community." Soon the kids would "come by and stare in the window at me, . . . wondering 'Who is this guy? . . .' So one day I just opened the door, let the kids come in, and started explaining what I did. They began coming by every day after school."[140] He added, "We were taking kids past drugs and stimulating the whole cultural community of Washington."[141] He estimated that, between 1967 and 1970, the center held many performances bringing different groups of people together which "usually involve thirty, but in workshops there are many more," that employed the "collective energies of 100 to 125 people." Up to "250 kids are involved on a continuing basis, seventy-five young adults" and "fifty older adults." The New Thing gave performances with as many as "2,500 people in attendance," and had "600 monetary contributors."[142] Its most noteworthy events were weekly jazz concerts held at the St. Margaret's Episcopal Church on Connecticut Avenue between Adams Morgan and DuPont Circle. DC-born jazz greats Shirley Horn and Andrew White were among the performers.

A special role was played by Eric Gravatt, a student at Howard University. Carew observed that "the little boys have a cat named Eric, who's their idol, teaches them percussion, but its more than just teaching percussion, it's a whole relationship. . . . When he comes in, he just has a whole line of kids walking behind him. It's partly because they can go see him at the jazz workshop." Carew added, "Eric's twenty-one. He's played with Pharaoh Sanders, he's recorded about three albums, Miles Davis wants him to play."[143] Gravatt later become best known for his long association, as the drummer and percussionist, with pianist McCoy Tyner, who himself came to prominence playing with John Coltrane. Carew later said, "I wanted jazz recognized as the only true American art form.

This was really important. But you know, what I was trying to say was that black artists deserved their due. I wanted cultural institutions in Washington to acknowledge and accept the reality of Washington's black population."[144] A magnificent outgrowth of the concerts was the launching, on July 1969, of a legendary jazz program on WAMU, later hosted by Rusty Hassan and aptly named *The New Thing Root Music Show*.[145]

At its storefront spaces, Carew noted that The New Thing offered classes to young people in "photography, film making, African American design, Afro-American sculpture, karate, black history, and a workshop on practical life experiences." The center, located in the area of the city populated by African Americans and Latinos, offered classes in "Afro-Cuban percussion, Latin percussion, blues guitar, blues harmonica, and blues theory."[146] The New Thing operated out of five buildings and gained national recognition.[147] One location sat near the headquarters of the local branches of the Students for a Democratic Society and the Black Panther Party.

Melvin Deal was also a member of The New Thing. As founding director of the African Heritage Dancers and Drummers, he became known worldwide for his pioneering instruction of African dance and drumming to young people most notably in wards 7 and 8. As reported in the *Washington Post*, "the troupe was started in 1967 with 15 children. Demands now are heavy on the 38 positions in the troupe. There are nearly 100 youngsters in the dance workshops."[148] Among those who came to work with the kids was the legendary percussionist Babatunde Olatunji. In late 1968 and early 1969 alone, the troupe had played concerts at schools such as Yale University, Bennington College, Columbia University, and Williams College. The youth drummers also visited the nation of Colombia.

Deal's vision along with Carew's, and especially the guidance and leadership of Peggy Cooper Cafritz, dancer Michael Malone, and others helped lay the foundation for the Duke Ellington School of the Arts. Deal, in summarizing the need for groups like The New Thing, believes that "so many advances are being undone. I see a tremendous need for another New Thing in about 10 years. Because it was a conscience for the power establishment. It received great impetus after the riots of '68. The way things are going, there might be more trouble. And then it will be needed again."[149]

The New Thing also sponsored the Washington Blues Festival at Howard University in November 1970. It was the first such effort in the city and the first ever major blues festival organized by blacks. "'We wanted to bring the blues back home and make people more conscious of their cultural heritage,' said The New Thing's Carew, its principal organizer."[150] Performing at the festival were B. B. King, Howlin' Wolf, the Junior Wells and Buddy Guy Blues Band, and Richie Havens, the famed folksinger who performed for free. On three successive nights, blacks and whites attended en masse, with 1,500 on Thursday, 1,200 on Friday, and 1,000 on Saturday. At one point, Howard University students protested, as did some other blacks who wanted to attend, because tickets were sold out and they noted large numbers of whites in the audience. "Why do those whites from Georgetown get all the privileges? This is black music," said some of the protesters.[151] Carew explained that the tickets had been sold by mail, so sales were colorblind. Carew received funding aid from organizations like the Friends of the John F. Kennedy Center. Said Carew, the festival was an assault of cultural racism. "Washington is 70 percent black, but the city's cultural style is neo-European," he told the *Washington Post*.[152] In the end, though plagued by disorganization and faulty audio equipment, the event was a success. Never before had so many whites gone to a musical event at Howard University, and never had the school seen such an integrated audience for such a venue.

Conclusion

Lawrence Levine has observed that "culture is not a fixed condition but a process, the product of interaction between the past and the present. Its toughness and resiliency are determined not by a culture's ability to withstand change, which indeed may be a sign of stagnation not life, but by its ability to reach creatively and responsively to the realties of the new situation."[153] The many forms of Great Black Music changed, developed, and played a major role in the struggle for equality in the nation's capital. It started with Will Marion Cook, who wrote that "we must strike out for ourselves, we must develop our own ideas and conceive an orchestration adopted to our own abilities and instincts."[154]

The Great Black Music created in Washington and by Washingtonians highlights how this music advanced both music and society. It helped to bring the races together in the fight for equality. By the 1960s Washington was moving slowly, if not to a city of "equals," then at least to a place where "equal rights" were the law. By this time Washington had become the first major city in the country with a majority black population. The Twenty-Third Amendment was ratified in 1961, allowing Washington residents, black and white, to vote in presidential elections. The following year at Pierce Hall in All Souls Church on February 13, 1962, guitarist Charlie Byrd, tenor sax giant Stan Getz, and bassist Keter Betts recorded their groundbreaking session *Jazz Samba*, bringing the multiethnic Brazilian sounds to the nation.

Washingtonians voted for president in 1964 for the first time since 1800, and the Civil Rights Act of 1964 was passed. That same year the Ramsey Lewis Trio recorded *The Ramsey Lewis Trio at the Bohemian Caverns* and repeated their success with the Grammy-winning *The "In" Crowd with the Ramsey Lewis Trio* in 1965. Al Clarke of WOOK Radio wrote in the album's liner notes, "Nowhere in the country has the trio been more enthusiastically received than in the nation's capital, where they enjoy the praise of fans of all nations. It is a small wonder that hundreds of global neighbors waited in line to enter the beautiful, sculptured, world renowned Bohemian Caverns, the home of the 'In' crowd."[155]

Shortly after the Voting Rights Act of 1965 was passed, James Reeb, the white assistant minister of All Souls Unitarian Church, where John Quincy Adams had worshiped and blacks and whites like Keter Betts and Charlie Byrd had performed, was murdered by a gang of white men in Selma, Alabama, because of his efforts to win equality for African Americans. Great Black Music and the men and women, black and white, who performed, promoted, and went to hear it, played their parts in integrating the city and the nation. As Washington, DC, jazz historian Thomas J. Porter has pointed out, "National consciousness has always been inherent in Black music, but the music has always embodied both the class and national characteristics in its criticism of the society."[156] Nowhere has this been more evident than in Washington, DC, the nation's capital, where Great Black Music played its part in securing the rights that Reverend Reeb died for.

Washington-born musicians continued to express their desire for equality. Billy Taylor, who graduated from Dunbar High in 1939, reflected on his years in Washington, DC. "I had much reinforcement in terms of who I was, what I was about and the tremendous contributions that black people have made to science, music, art, government. Black accomplishment was very visible in Washington what with judges, lawyers and other over achievers."[157]

Dr. Taylor, as he was universally known, wrote of the racial situation in America when he recorded "I Wish That I Knew How It Would Feel to Be Free," in 1963, two weeks before the assassination of President John Kennedy.[158] Taylor said, "The lyrics were about freedom, which for African Americans was the clarion cry of that era." He believed that the song "captured the essence of the Civil Rights Movement" and that Martin Luther King Jr. was especially fond of Nina Simone's popular recording of it in 1967. Taylor noted that King "was a lover of Jazz," but because he could never remember the title always asked him to play "that Baptists sounding song."[159]

In May of 1971, one of the largest demonstrations in US history, the May Day Peace protest against the war in Vietnam, was held in the capital city. That year Washington-born Marvin Gaye released one of biggest-selling albums in history. *What's Going On* also ranks among the top as music of social protest. Gaye was deeply moved by the letters his brother had sent from Vietnam and the conditions of black people in America. One of the songs on the album, "Inner City Blues (Make Me Wanna Holler)" is a song reflecting the chaos of the times and, with it, violence, poverty, and the plight of ghetto youth who took the song as their own. The beginnings words, "Rockets moon shots / Spend it on the have not's," took "the government to task for probing outer space while leaving the poor to fend for themselves."[160] The song is about inequality and the denial of democratic rights. Gaye said, "What mattered was the message. For the first time I felt like I had something to say."[161]

Gil Scott-Heron, who had lived in DC and once taught at Federal City College, also wrote songs about life in Washington, his most famous being "H20Gate Blues." He said that many of his "songs began taking shape in DC" as he observed the black condition. "Instead of just glossing over the problem," he "generally used an individual or an individual circumstance as an example of a larger thing"—the plight of impoverished black Washingtonians.[162]

Washingtonians still do not have a voting representative in the US Congress, so the struggle for democracy and equal rights continues. Scott-Heron said it best in a song on his 1982 album *Moving Target*. Titled "Washington D.C.," a key verse reflects the city in 2018. "It's a mass of irony for all the world to see, It's the nation's capital, It's Washington, DC."[163]

Notes

1. See Maurice Jackson, "Washington, D.C.: From the Founding of a Slaveholding Capital to a Center of Abolitionism," *Journal of African Diaspora Archeology and Heritage* 2, no. 1, special issue, "Atlantic Approaches on Slave Resistance in the Americas" (May 2013): 38–64.

2. The term "Great Black Music" was coined in the 1960s by members of the Association for the Advancement of Creative Musicians, founded by band members of Art Ensemble of Chicago

and others. Musicologist George E. Lewis writes that Great Black Music "could easily encompass nonblack musicians and non jazz music within its purview." George E. Lewis, *A Power Stronger Than Itself: The AACM and American Experimental Music* (Chicago: University of Chicago Press, 2008), 449.

3. James Reese Europe, interview with the *New York Evening Post*, March 15, 1914.

4. Paul Laurence Dunbar, "Negro Society in Washington," *Saturday Evening Post*, December 1901, 9.

5. R. W. Washington, "Dr. Booker T. Washington Speaks," *Washington Bee*, May 15, 1909, 1.

6. Booker T. Washington to Oswald Garrison Villard, August 10, 1913, Washington Papers 28: 186–87, Library of Congress; and Louis R. Harlan and Raymond Smocks, eds., *The Booker T. Washington Papers*, vol. 12, *1912–1914* (Urbana: University of Illinois Press, 1982), 248.

7. Samuel S. Krislov, *The Negro in Federal Employment: The Quest for Equal Opportunity* (Minneapolis: University of Minnesota Press, 1967). Although the percentage fell, the government's overall expansion during the war meant that more blacks could obtain federal jobs.

8. S. E. Tolney and E. M. Beck, "Racial Violence and Black Migration in the American South," *American Sociological Review* 57, no. 1 (1992): 103–16; James Borchert, *Alley Life in Washington: Family, Community, Religion, and Folk Life in the City, 1850–1970* (Urbana: University of Illinois Press, 1982); and S. E. Tolnay, R. M. Adelman, and Kyle D. Crowder, "Race, Regional Origin, and Residence in Northern Cities at the Beginning of the Great Migration," *American Sociological Review* 67, no. 3 (2002): 456–75.

9. Cook named his son William Mercer Cook. So indebted was Duke Ellington to Cook that he named his own son Mercer.

10. Marva Griffin Carter, *Swing Along: The Musical Life of Will Marion Cook* (New York: Oxford, 2008), 17.

11. Ibid., 17.

12. Reid Badger, *A Life in Ragtime: A Biography of James Reese Europe* (New York: Oxford, 1995), 56. Badger adds: "It may have been a competent (or even superb) orchestra, but it was not—in instrumentation, performance, or material—an African-American one."

13. Harry Burleigh was accepted to the National Conservatory for vocal training, but he also played the double bass and timpani. He played in one of the orchestras conducted by Antonín Dvořák and eventually worked with him as a copyist. Most important, the two musicians spent hours together as Burleigh sang Negro spirituals and folk songs.

14. *New York Herald Tribune*, May 21, 1893. See also Maurice Jackson, liner notes to *Come Sunday*, by Charlie Haden (bassist, producer) and Hank Jones (piano), Emarcy 0602527503684, CD, 33⅓, 2011; and Maurice Jackson, liner notes to *Steal Away: Spirituals, Folksongs and Hymns*, by Charlie Haden (bassist) and Hank Jones (pianist), Verve Records 527 249-2, CD, 33⅓, 1995.

15. *New York Herald Tribune*, May 28, 1893.

16. Maurice Peress, *Dvořák to Duke Ellington: A Conductor Explores America's Music and Its African American Roots* (New York: Oxford, 2004), 24.

17. W. E. B. Du Bois, *The Souls of Black Folk* (New York: Fawcett, 1961), 182.

18. Will Marion Cook, "Will Marion Cook," in *Readings in Black American Music*, ed. Eileen Southern (New York: Norton, 1971), 228.

19. Ibid., 226.

20. Duke Ellington, *Music Is My Mistress* (New York: Da Capo Paperbacks, 1973), 95, 97.

21. Eileen Southern, *The Music of Black Americans: A History*, 3rd ed. (New York: Norton, 1997), 295.

22. Ibid., 288.

23. See Doris E. McGinty, "The Washington Conservatory of Music and School of Expression," *Black Perspective in Music* 7, no. 1 (1979): 59–74; Doris Evans McGinty, "'That You Came

So Far to See Us': Coleridge-Taylor in America," *Black Music Research Journal* 21 (2001): 197–234; Doris E. McGinty, "The Black Presence in the Music of Washington, D.C.: 1843–1904," in *More than Dancing: Essays on Afro-American Music and Musicians*, ed. Irene V. Jackson, 81–106 (Westport, CT: Greenwood, 1985); and Sarah Schmalenberger, "The Washington Conservatory of Music and African-American Musical Experience, 1903–1941," PhD diss., University of Minnesota 2004, UMI: 3124757.

24. Liner notes to CBS Records, *Black Composers Series*, The College Music Society, New York, 1986, series insert, ed. Samuel A. Floyd, Jr., p. 7.

25. W. E. B. Du Bois, *Darkwater: Voices from within the Veil* (1920; repr., New York: Schocken Books, 1969), 193.

26. David Levering Lewis, *W. E. B. Du Bois: Biography of a Race, 1868–1919* (New York: Henry Holt, 1993), 460.

27. W. E. B. Du Bois, *Dusk of Dawn: An Essay Toward an Autobiography of a Race Concept* (New York: Harcourt, Brace, 1940; New York: Schocken Books, 1968), 272.

28. Ibid., 273.

29. Quoted in Mack Tucker, "The Renaissance Education of Duke Ellington," in *Black Music in the Harlem Renaissance: A Collection of Essays*, ed. Samuel A. Floyd Jr. (Knoxville: University of Tennessee Press, 1990), 117–18.

30. "The Great Pageant," *Washington Bee*, October 23, 1915, p. 1.

31. Badger, *A Life in Ragtime*, 10.

32. Ibid., 20.

33. W. E. B. Du Bois, "Men of the Month: James Reese Europe," *The Crisis* 4, no. 2 (June 1912): 66–67.

34. Mark Tucker, *Ellington: The Early Years* (Urbana: University of Illinois Press, 1995), 7.

35. Badger, *A Life in Ragtime*, 22.

36. Mary G. Hundley, *The Dunbar Story, 1870–1955* (New York: Vantage Press, 1965), 20; see also Alison Stewart, *First Class: The Legacy of Dunbar, America's First Black Public High School* (New York: Lawrence Hill, 2013); and Mary Church Terrell, "History of High School for Negroes in Washington," *Journal of Negro History*, 2, no. 3 (1917): 255.

37. Langston Hughes, "Our Wonderful Society: Washington," *Opportunity* 5 (August 1927): 226–27.

38. David Levering Lewis, *When Harlem Was in Vogue* (New York: Penguin, 1979), 31; and Gail Buckley, *American Patriots: The Story of Blacks in the Military from the Revolution to Desert Storm* (New York: Random House, 2001), 192.

39. Du Bois, "Men of the Month."

40. Henry Louis Gates and Evelyn Brooks Higginbotham, eds., *African American Lives* (Oxford: Oxford University Press, 2004), 350.

41. Quoted in Robert Kimball and William Bolcom, *Reminiscing with Sissle and Black* (New York: Viking Press, 1973), 59–61. The orchestra had "forty-seven mandolins, twenty seven harp guitars, eleven banjos, eight violins, eight trombones, thirteen cellos, seven cornets, five trap drums, two double basses, two clarinets, one tuba, one timpani, and ten pianos crowded onto the Carnegie Hall stage and stunning the audience"; they were also accompanied by two church choirs. Lewis, *When Harlem Was in Vogue*, 31.

42. Tucker, "Renaissance Education of Duke Ellington," 122, 125; Badger, *A Life in Ragtime*, 93; and Carter, *Swing Along*, 96.

43. Lewis, *When Harlem Was in Vogue*, 33.

44. James Weldon Johnson, quoted in Peress, *Dvořák to Duke Ellington*, 199.

45. "Ford Dabney," in *Harlem Renaissance Lives from the African National Biography*, ed. Henry Louis Gates and Evelyn Higginbotham (New York: Oxford University Press, 2009), 141.

46. Peress, *Dvořák to Duke Ellington*, 24.

47. Stephen L. Harris, *Harlem's Hell Fighters: The African-American 369th Infantry in World War I* (Washington, DC: Brassey's, 2003), 31.

48. Quoted in Badger, *A Life in Ragtime*, 142.

49. Buckley, *American Patriots*, 165.

50. Quoted in Badger, *A Life in Ragtime*, 163.

51. Quoted in Geoffrey C. Ward and Ken Burns, *Jazz: A History of America's Music* (New York: Alfred A. Knopf, 2000), 68. Sissle said they played alongside "the greatest concert bands in the world—the British Grenadier's Band, the band of the *Garde Républicain*, and the Royal Italian Band. My band, of course could not compare with any of these, yet the crowd deserted them for us."

52. Emmett J. Scott, *Official History of the American Negro in the World War* (1919; repr., New York: Arno Press, 1969), 118. Scott was the principal deputy to Booker T. Washington and the highest-ranking African American in the U.S. military during the war, serving as special advisor for black affairs to Secretary of War Newton Baker.

53. W. E. B. Du Bois, "Returning Soldiers," *Crisis* 18 (May 1919): 13–14. James Reese Europe was killed after returning to the United States on May 19, 1919, by a deranged band member.

54. "The Rights of the Black Man," *Washington Bee*, August 2, 1919.

55. "Race Riots Renewed," *Washington Post*, July 21, 1919; "Race Riot at Capital," *New York Times*, July 20, 1919; and "Servicemen Beat Negroes in Race Riot at Capital," *New York Times*, July 21, 1919.

56. Peter Perl, "Race Riots of 1919 Gave Glimpse of Future Struggles," *Washington Post*, October 29, 2007, www.washingtonpost.com/wp-srv/local/2000/raceriot0301.htm.

57. "Capital Clashes Increase," *New York Times*, July 22, 1919; "Detective Sergeant Wilson Victim; Other Officers Hurt; Negro Runs Amuck, Wounding Many in Flight," *Washington Post*, July 22, 1919; and "Race War in Washington," *Washington Post*, July 23, 1919.

58. Michael Schaffer, "Lost Riot," *Washington City Paper*, April 3, 1998.

59. "Detective Sergeant Wilson Victim."

60. Constance M. Green, *The Secret City: A History of Race Relations in the Nation's Capital* (Princeton, NJ: Princeton University Press, 1967), 192.

61. "Riots Elsewhere, Forecast by Negro," *Washington Post*, July 25, 1919.

62. James Weldon Johnson, *The Washington Riots: An N.A.A.C.P. Investigation* (Washington, DC: National Association for the Advancement of Colored People, 1919).

63. Alain Locke, ed., *The New Negro: An Interpretation* (New York: Albert & Charles Bonni, 1925), xvii, 9.

64. Edward Christopher Williams, *When Washington Was in Vogue* (New York: Amistad, 2004); Tucker, *Ellington*; and Blair A. Ruble, *Washington's U Street: A Biography* (Washington, DC: Woodrow Wilson Centre Press; and Baltimore: Johns Hopkins University Press, 2010).

65. Claude McKay, "If We Must Die," *Liberator* 2 (July 1919), 21.

66. "Colored Folk Defy Jim Crow: Near Riots Marks Enforcement of Segregation by Soldiers with Guns and Bayonets," *Baltimore Afro-American*, June 2, 1922.

67. Langston Hughes, "Trouble with Angels: National Theater (1935)," in *D.C. Noir 2: The Classics*, ed. George Pelecanos, 45–52 (Washington, DC: Akahashic Classics, 2008).

68. Central High School, at Thirteenth and Clifton Streets, NW, was later renamed Cardozo. Washington writer Edward P. Jones is a 1968 graduate.

69. Quoted in Raymond Arsenault, *The Sound of Freedom: Marian Anderson, The Lincoln Memorial and the Concert that Awakened America* (New York: Bloomsbury Press, 2009), 163; for more about Houston, see Kenneth Mack, *Representing the Race: The Creation of the Civil Rights Lawyer* (Cambridge, MA: Harvard University Press, 2013).

70. Green, *Secret City*, 249.

71. Quoted in Arsenault, *Sound of Freedom*, 174.

72. Ibid.

73. Blanche E. Ferguson, *Countee Cullen and the Negro Renaissance* (New York: Apollo, 1966), 115.

74. Michael Terrace, aka Michael Gutierrez, "A Mambo Musical Dance Show in the Summer of 1952 that Made History," http://michaelterrace.blogspot.com/2013/04/mambo-usa.html. My thanks to WPFW "Latin Flavor" host Jim Byers and the Jim Byers Archive. According to Terrace, this was the same week that several Puerto Rican Nationalists were arrested in a shoot-out on Capitol Hill.

75. Ibid.

76. David Margolick, *Strange Fruit: Café Society and the Early Cry for Civil Rights* (Philadelphia: Running Press, 2000), 42.

77. Ibid., 29. Meeropol, a Jewish American, and his wife, Anne, later adopted the children of Ethel and Julius Rosenberg, who were executed in 1953 for providing secrets to the Soviets at the height of the Cold War.

78. Ibid., 37.

79. Quoted in Tom Nolan, *Artie Shaw, King of the Clarinet: His Life and Times* (New York: Norton, 2011), 104.

80. Quoted in Margolick, *Strange Fruit*, 96, 98.

81. Margolick, *Strange Fruit*, 98.

82. Julia Blackburn, *With Billie: A New Look at the Unforgettable Lady Day* (New York: Vintage, 2005), 228; and W. Royal Stokes, *Growing Up with Jazz: Twenty-Four Musicians Talk about Their Lives and Careers* (New York: Oxford, 2005).

83. Quoted in John De Ferrari, *Historic Restaurants of Washington, D.C.: Capital Eats* (Charleston, SC: American Palate, 2013), 100.

84. Rayford Whittingham Logan, *The Diplomatic Relations of the United States with Haiti, 1778–1841* (Chapel Hill: University of North Carolina Press, 1941); John Edward Hasse, *Beyond Category: The Life and Genius of Duke Ellington* (New York: Simon & Schuster, 1993), 254; and Maurice Jackson, "No Man Could Hinder Him: Remembering Toussaint L'Ouverture and the Haitian, Revolution," in *African Americans and the Haitian Revolution*, ed. Maurice Jackson and Jacqueline Bacon, 141–64 (New York: Routledge, 2010).

85. Terry Teachout, *Duke: The Life of Duke Ellington* (New York: Gotham, 2013), 226.

86. *The Duke Ellington Carnegie Hall Concerts: January 1943*, Prestige P-34004, 1977, 33⅓ rpm; see Jackson, "No Man Could Hinder Him," 141–64.

87. Quoted in Harvey G. Cohen, "Duke Ellington and *Black, Brown and Beige:* The Composer as Historian at Carnegie Hall," *American Quarterly* (Winter 2004): 1006–7.

88. James Lincoln Collier, *Duke Ellington* (New York: Oxford University Press, 1987), 216.

89. Ken Vail, *Duke's Diary*, part 1: *The Life of Duke Ellington, 1927–1950* (Lanham, MD: Scarecrow Press, 2002).

90. Cohen, "Duke Ellington and *Black, Brown and Beige*, 1010–11.

91. Jackson, "No Man Could Hinder Him," 154–56.

92. Ellington, *Music Is My Mistress*, 436.

93. Dorothy Wade and Justine Picardie, *Music Man: Ahmet Ertegun, Atlantic Records and the Triumph of Rock 'n Roll* (New York: Norton, 1990), 29.

94. Ahmet Ertegun, *"What'd I Say": The Atlantic Story, 50 Years of Music* (New York: Welcome Rain, 2001), 12.

95. Quoted in Wade and Picardie, *Music Man*, 30–31.

96. In the past two years a series of jazz events were held at the Turkish Embassy to commemorate the 1940s events, sponsored by the embassy and by Jazz at Lincoln Center.

97. Ertegun, *What'd I Say*, 7. In 1944 Ambassador Mehmet Ertegun died, and his widow and some of the family returned to Turkey. Ahmet and Nesuhi elected to stay in the United States to finish their studies.

98. Ibid., 12.

99. Quoted in J. Freedom du Lac, "A Chord of Jazz History to Echo at Turkish Embassy," *Washington Post*, February 3, 2011.

100. Robert Greenfield, *The Last Sultan: The Life and Times of Ahmet Ertegun* (New York: Simon & Schuster, 2011), 32.

101. Maurice Jackson, "Remembering the Turkish Brothers Who Helped Change Race Relations in America," *Hill*, November 1, 2013.

102. Quoted in Peter Adam, *Art of the Third Reich* (New York: H. N. Abrams, 1995), 62.

103. John Szwed, *Alan Lomax: The Man Who Recorded the World* (New York: Penguin, 2010), 105.

104. Ertegun, *What'd I Say*, 8.

105. Julia Rolf, ed. *The Definitive Illustrated Encyclopedia of Jazz and Blues* (London: Star Fire Books, 2007), 61.

106. Alan Lomax, *Mister Jelly Roll: The Fortunes of Jelly Roll Morton, New Orleans Creole and "Inventor of Jazz"* (New York: Pantheon, 1950), 276.

107. Ertegun, *What'd I Say*, 8; see also William Barlow, *Looking Up at Down: The Emergence of Blues Culture* (Philadelphia: Temple University Press, 1989), 72–75.

108. Mike Seeger, liner notes to *Elizabeth Cotten: Freight Train and other North Carolina Folksongs and Tunes*, Smithsonian Folkways Records SF CD 40009, 1989, CD.

109. Billy Taylor with Teresa L. Reed, *The Jazz Life of Dr. Billy Taylor* (Bloomington: Indiana University Press, 2013), 29.

110. Ahmet Ertegun, quoted in *American Masters*, season 21, episode 2, "Atlantic Records: The House that Ahmet Built," written and directed by Susan Steinberg, aired on May 2, 2007, on PBS.

111. Ron Frits, liner notes to *Charlie Parker: Washington, D.C., 1948*, by Charlie Parker (saxophonist), Uptown Records UPCD 27.55, recorded at the Bebop Concert-Music Hall, Washington D.C., May 23, 1948, released 2008, CD.

112. Marcus Rediker, *The Amistad Rebellion: An Atlantic Odyssey of Slavery and Freedom* (New York: Viking, 2012).

113. *Washington Daily News* advertisement, May 23, 1948.

114. Ron Frits, liner notes to *Charlie Parker: Washington, D.C., 1948*.

115. Willis Conover, *Music USA Newsletter* 4, no. 3 (1968); see also Lisa Davenport, *Jazz Diplomacy: Promoting America in the Cold War Era* (Jackson: University of Mississippi Press, 2009), 133.

116. Gene Lees, *Friends Along the Way: A Journey through Jazz* (New Haven, CT: Yale University Press, 2003), 253.

117. Bill Potts, liner notes to *Washington Concerts: Charlie Parker with Quartet and the Orchestra*, by Charlie Parker (saxophonist), Blue Note Records 7243 5 22626 2 5, recorded at Howard Theatre, Washington, DC, October 18, 1952, and March 8, 1953, and at Club Kavakos, Washington, DC, February 22, 1953, released 2001.

118. David Lightman, "Racial Barriers Fell Slowly in Capital," McClatchy News Service, January 16, 2009.

119. Marvin Caplan, "Eat Anywhere!" *Washington History*, 1 (Spring 1989): 31. See also Marvin Caplan, *Farther Along: A Civil Rights Memoir* (Baton Rouge: Louisiana State University Press, 1999).

120. Maurice Jackson, "50 Years after the March, the Fight for Equality Isn't Over: Addressing Income Disparities in Income and Housing is Next for the District," *Washington Post*, August 23, 2013, A16.

121. Caplan, "Eat Anywhere!" 26.

122. Ibid., 34.

123. John Kelley wrote in his *Washington Post* column that the list appears to have grown out of the sermon by Rev. A. Powell Davies of All Souls Unitarian Church on February 1, 1953, when Powell said that he would not "knowingly eat a meal in any restaurant in the District of Columbia that will not serve meals to Negroes" and called on "all who truly believe in human brotherhood" to join him. John Kelley, "D.C. Restaurant List Is a Relic from a Painful Past," *Washington Post*, October 5, 2011. Started in 1951, the list was constantly updated, in the end listing sixty establishments.

124. Dwight D. Eisenhower, "Annual Message to Congress on the State of the Union," United States Capitol, Washington, DC, February 2, 1953.

125. Dwight D. Eisenhower, "Annual Message to Congress on the State of the Union," United States Capitol, Washington, DC, January 5, 1956.

126. Penny M. Von Eschen, *Satchmo Blows Up the World: Jazz Ambassadors Play the Cold War* (Cambridge, MA: Harvard University Press, 2004), 63. See also Ingrid Munson, *Freedom Sounds: Civil Rights Call Out to Jazz and Africa* (New York: Oxford University Press, 2007), 1–2.

127. Terry Teachout, *POPS* (New York: Houghton, Mifflin, 2009), 314, 336.

128. "Satch Blasts Echoed by Top Performers: Nixes Tour, Raps Ike and Faubus," *Chicago Defender* 53 (September 28, 1957): 1–2.

129. "Satchmo Tells off U.S.," *Pittsburgh Courier*, September 28, 1957.

130. David Margolick, "The Day Louis Armstrong Made Noise," *New York Times*, September 23, 2007.

131. Brad Snyder, *Beyond the Shadow of the Senators: The Untold Story of the Homestead Grays and the Integration of Baseball* (Chicago: Contemporary Books, 2003), 285.

132. Quoted in ibid., 286; see also Frederic J. Frommer, *The Washington Nationals 1859 to Today* (Lanham, MD: Taylor Trade Publishing, 2006), 69.

133. See Thomas G. Smith, *Showdown: JFK and the Integration of the Washington Redskins* (Boston: Beacon Press, 2011), 178–84.

134. "Jail Sentence Started Him on Music, Satchmo Tells 1600 Lorton Inmates," *Washington Post and Times Herald*, July 3, 1957. For a look at Armstrong's own life in prison, see chapter 5, "Jail," in Thomas Brothers, *Louis Armstrong's New Orleans* (New York: Norton, 2006), 74–109.

135. These concerts are further explored in Maurice Jackson's forthcoming book *Halfway to Freedom: African Americans and the Struggle for Social Progress in Washington, D.C.*

136. Walter Cronkite, in *CBS News Special: SINATRA*, executive producer, Don Hewitt, originally aired November 17, 1965, 10:00 PM; excerpted in the HBO documentary miniseries *Sinatra: All or Nothing at All*, directed by Alex Gibney, 2015. For an interesting take on the social and political views of Sinatra, see Quincy Jones, *Q: The Autobiography of Quincy Jones* (New York: Random House, 2001), 180–85, 194–96, 282–83.

137. "Ella, Sinatra, Basie, Quincy Jones Send Inmates," *JET* 28, no. 16 (July 29, 1965): 54.

138. Leroy F. Aarons, "Stars Visit Prison-and It's a Near Riot," *Washington Post*, July 15, 1965; and "Only Invited May Watch Show," *Washington Post*, July 10, 1965, B2.

139. Monroe Anderson, "The Young Black Man," *Ebony: The Black Male*, August 1972, 132.

140. Alan Bunce, "Breaking Down the Color Barrier Producer Topper Carew Uses TV to Help Shape Values," *Christian Science Monitor*, February 2, 1988.

141. Michael Kernan, "That Summer Thing," *Washington Post*, August 19, 1984.

142. Wallace Roberts, "Black Arts for Black Youth: An Interview with Topper Carew," *Saturday Review*, July 18, 1970, 47–48.

143. Arthur Blackman, Ken Freidus, David Robinson, and Florence Shelton, "Interview with Topper Carew," *Harvard Educational Review* 39, no. 4 (December 1969): 112.

144. Juan Williams, "Roads from the Riots: How the Events of '68 Changed Three Lives," *Washington Post*, April 3, 1988.

145. Rusty Hassan, "Jazz Radio in Washington: A Personal Retrospective," *Washington History* 26 (2014): 77.

146. "An Interview with Topper Carew," 46.

147. Bunce, "Breaking Down the Color Barrier."

148. "Children Drum Up Interest in African Dance," *Washington Post*, January 30, 1969. See also Michael Kernan, "A Dancer's Homage: Heirs A Series on The American Family, A Dancer's Homage," *Washington Post*, January 19, 1977.

149. Kernan, "That Summer 'Thing.'"

150. Hollie I. West, "Blues Festival," *Washington Post*, November 9, 1970.

151. Hollie I. West, "Blues Festival at Howard," *Washington Post*, November 6, 1970.

152. Hollie I. West, "Blues Festival: Top Stars in 3-Day Event," *Washington Post*, October 9, 1970.

153. Lawrence W. Levine, *Black Culture and Black Consciousness* (New York: Oxford University Press, 1977), 5.

154. Quoted in Peress, *Dvořák to Duke Ellington*, 199.

155. Al Clarke, liner notes to *The "In" Crowd: The Ramsey Lewis Trio*, Chess Records MGAR S-9226, 1965, 33⅓ rpm.

156. Thomas J. Porter, "The Social Roots of African American Music," *Freedomways*, no. 3 (1971): 268.

157. Catherine K. Clarke, "Conversations with William (Billy) Taylor: The Jazz-Mobile Man," *The Black Perspective in Music* 10, no. 2 (1982): 182.

158. Taylor received a PhD from the University of Massachusetts in 1975. He also taught at Howard University, the University of Massachusetts, the Manhattan School of Music, and East Carolina University.

159. Taylor, *The Jazz Life of Dr. Billy Taylor*, 148.

160. Michael Eric Dyson, *Mercy, Mercy Me: The Art, Loves and Demons of Marvin Gaye* (New York: Basis Civitas Books, 2004), 66.

161. David Ritz, liner notes to *The Very Best of Marvin Gaye*, UTV Records 014 367-2, released August 20, 2001, 2 CDs.

162. Gil Scott-Heron, *The Last Holiday: A Memoir* (New York: Grove Press, 2012), 177.

163. Gil Scott-Heron, vocalist, "Washington, DC," by Gil Scott-Heron, recorded 1982, track A2 on *Moving Target*, Arista Records AL 9606, 33⅓ rpm.

2 Seventh Street
Black DC's Musical Mecca

Blair A. Ruble

The neighborhood around the intersection of Seventh Street and Florida Avenue, NW, was more than a crossroads for the city throughout the early decades of the twentieth century. It simultaneously was a hinge among different segments of one of the largest and most economically diverse urban African American neighborhoods found anywhere. To the north stood Howard University, with LeDroit Park located almost directly to the east. To the south, Seventh Street served as the focus for a vibrant African American working-class community. U Street, African American Washington's burgeoning high street, extended to the west. Numerous major African American institutions in the city were within a mile or two radius of this critical corner.

Whites always were present, too, in part because many lived nearby, in part because they passed through while moving around town, in part because they attended big league ballgames at Griffith Stadium, and in part because they were patrons of the area's many music and dance clubs. Whites also owned and ran businesses in the area. Lingering pockets of German and other immigrant social clubs—and a few residents—were left over from the era prior to the hardening of segregation. Greek immigrants opened shops in the area. By the 1930s a small Chinatown developed around Seventh and H Streets as Chinese homes and businesses were destroyed to make way for the Federal Triangle government office complex following World War I.

Jewish merchants created a particularly vibrant commercial district as one moved south toward the busy Northern Market that stood at Seventh and O Streets. Food stores, such as J. Meyerowitz's Capital Delicatessen, Ladinsky & Kaplan, Pomona Foods, and Isadore Schultz, were joined by several Jewish-owned department stores (William Hahn & Co., Hecht & Co., Kann & Sons, Morton's, and Lansburgh Bros.) along a stretch of Seventh Street roughly between D and K Streets. Marlo Furniture and Charles Schwartz & Son Jewelers, which grew into metropolitan chains with stores still in business around the region, started along Seventh Street. Hechinger Hardware, which would be a local staple into the 1980s, similarly thrived on Seventh Street after starting as a wrecking company in Southwest and a lumberyard in Northeast. Much Jewish community life revolved around the Adas Israel Synagogue at Sixth and I Streets, the Ohev Shalom Synagogue at Fifth and I Streets, and the Washington Hebrew Congregation at H and Eighth Streets.[1]

White businesses served a large African American clientele in a complex relationship that ranged from close friendship to tense hostility.[2] Many of the businesses destroyed during civil unrest following the 1968 assassination of Dr. Martin Luther King Jr. were white-owned, often by Jewish proprietors.[3] For the most part, Jewish and African American Seventh Street coexisted prior to 1968 much as black and white Washingtonians did in general, living segregated lives that rarely touched one another throughout the first half of the twentieth century.

Recalling her childhood along Seventh Street, longtime Washingtonian Flora Atkin offered a compelling account of how the Jewish and African American neighbors lived together in a reminiscence published by the Jewish Historical Society of Greater Washington following the 1998 opening of the MCI (later Verizon) Sports Arena at Seventh and F Streets. "Between 1924 and 1934," she recalled, "Seventh Street was a major black community. . . . It was THE black community. The whites who lived there lived above their stores. The blacks lived on the side streets mainly, and shopped in the Jewish-owned stores. Jewish entrepreneurs owned clothing, yard goods, notions, shoe, and hardware stores. The blacks had, to my recollection, small places that would be the equivalent of pinball machine arcades, record music stores of interest to Negroes, and food places."[4] Other reminiscences report closer relationships, particularly on a one-on-one basis, and many in the Jewish community lent important support to the civil rights movement. However close individuals may have been, though, institutional life remained firmly segregated by race and faith.[5]

The crossroads of Seventh and Florida stood at the heart of African American Washington despite the presence of whites and Asians nearby. Beyond immigrant merchants and their families, white visitors to Seventh Street near Florida Avenue remained, for the most part, just that: largely outsiders who came to watch a baseball or football game, to listen to music, to be otherwise entertained, or to make a profit. Reactions to one another remained highly individualistic. Some African Americans resented any white presence in the area while others developed cross-generational family friendships. Some white merchants took advantage of their African American clientele by rampant overcharging for household staples, while others easily extended credit and provided jobs. Many whites denigrated blacks, while others appreciated the creativity of African American musicians and writers. Some viewed their African American neighbors as fellow citizens. Very few Washingtonians, black or white, could escape the racism deeply engrained in a segregated city lorded over by a Congress dominated by southerners. For the most part, everyone appeared to live their lives within their own group as much as possible. The music and literature emerging from the neighborhood suggests, however, that a far more complex chemical reaction was taking place beneath the surface.

The area developed following the Civil War as a robustly diverse community that included residents of different races and economic classes. Slaves fleeing to Washington as "contrabands of war" during the hostilities had sought the protection of Union Army encampments such as Camp Barker located at Thirteenth Street between R and S Streets and the Wisewell Barracks at Seventh and P Streets. After the war, many newly freed African Americans remained in their wartime settlements, giving birth to several historically black neighborhoods around the city, including the area around Seventh Street.

The Freedmen's Bureau, established to help newly emancipated slaves, built its Freedmen's Hospital to serve the black community, and the bureau's commissioner, Maj. Gen. Oliver Otis Howard, established an integrated university, later named for him, just north of Boundary Street (later Florida Avenue) and east of Seventh Street. When the Compromise of 1877 brought Reconstruction to an end and ushered in a new period of segregation by the mid-1880s, these institutions solidified the neighborhood around Seventh and Florida as an energetic center of African American life. Simultaneously, a middle class and elite class developed within the African American community in response to economic opportunities found in the federal workforce as well as the uplifting impact of higher education now offered at Howard and at other African American colleges and universities around the country.[6]

The intersection of Seventh and Florida thus was a point of interconnection among a variety of groups, making it a vital focal point for the emergence of an energetic, rough-and-tumble music scene. Seventh and Florida crossed one another in an urban cultural and social wetlands, a contact zone in which "cultures meet, clash, and grapple with each other, often in contexts of highly asymmetrical relations of power, such as colonialism, slavery, or their aftermaths."[7] Such zones are the necessary proving grounds where the diverse becomes transformed into an intercultural resource. They are where accomplished cities become successful.

The Howard Theatre stood at the center of it all. The magnificent 1,500-seat theater first opened its doors at Seventh and T Streets on August 22, 1910. That event proved to be one of the highlights of the year's social calendar, with the usually acerbic *Washington Bee* recording that "the Howard Theatre is no doubt the finest theatre in the city . . . one of the prettiest theatres in the country." The *Bee* continued that "the private boxes were filled with ladies of society. The orchestra was monopolized with the social elite of Washington, gayly and gorgeously dressed in gowns fit for goddesses." Washington's own Abbie Mitchell—who later created the role of Clara in the Broadway production of George Gershwin's *Porgy and Bess*—was among the performers that evening.[8]

Manager Andrew J. Thomas, who ran the Howard between 1911 and 1918, launched the tradition of varied bookings, including vaudeville, musicals, road shows, stock company productions, and even a circus or two, that marked the house from its opening until the stock market crash of 1929.[9] Under Thomas's management—and that of the dynamic Shep Allen after 1931—the Howard served the community, offering performances by local musicians and dramatic plays by Alain Locke's Howard University Players. The Howard rightfully could claim to be the premier African American theater in the country before the Apollo Theater in New York's Harlem emerged as a stage featuring black entertainers in 1934.

The Howard was forced to close for two years at the height of the Great Depression, becoming temporary home to Elder Lightfoot Solomon Michaux's Temple of Freedom Under God (Church of God) in 1930 and 1931. Duke Ellington reopened the theater with a wildly successful three-week run beginning September 26, 1931. With "D.C.'s Dean of Showbiz" Shep Allen at the helm, the Howard hosted the most famous African American entertainers of the day.[10]

Photo 2.1 Shep Allen and newsboys
Howard Theatre manager Shep Allen, the tall man in the center, stands with a group of newsboys
(and a few girls) in front of the theater in 1936. "DC's Dean of Showbiz," Allen brought in the
top African American shows of the day, and virtually every major jazz figure played there.

For all of the Howard's significance for African American cultural life throughout the twentieth century, the theater was built and owned by whites, initially by the National Amusement Company and later Abe Lichtman, who owned a chain of movie theaters catering to African Americans, including the Lincoln Theatre down the street.[11] The fact that white-owned theaters catered to African American audiences was not noteworthy in and of itself. There are numerous examples of similar arrangements around the country. The Howard assumed particular importance within the African American community because its white proprietors hired and gave free rein to Thomas and Allen. While this decision may appear in retrospect to have been good business, such an arrangement was noteworthy at the time. Meaningfully for Washington, Thomas and later Allen ran the theater as if it belonged to the local community. Their understanding of African American Washington, in all of its complexities, helped to make the Howard an essential component of black DC from the moment the theater opened its doors in ways in which other white-owned entertainment establishments in the city and elsewhere were not. As the article about the Howard's grand opening from the *Washington Bee* suggests, the theater was a point of considerable pride for Washington's African Americans from the moment performers first set foot on its stage.

Neither Thomas nor Allen allowed himself to be confined by the constraints of segregation. Thomas—who also managed the Minnehaha movie house (later Ben's Chili Bowl) on U Street near Thirteenth—joined with Sherman H. "Uncle Dud" Dudley in 1914 to take over the American Theater on Pennsylvania Avenue downtown. Their effort to bring African American entertainment to the white business center proved short-lived, as few blacks ventured downtown where segregation made them feel unwanted. By the 1920s, however, they joined with other African American movie theater owners to establish the Colored Exhibitors' Association to cater to the needs of black movie audiences around the country.[12]

Dudley, who had begun his career as a vaudevillian in Texas, organized the Colored Actors' Union to help fellow African American performers while simultaneously expanding his chain of movie houses, bringing the new art form of film to African American audiences. He eventually operated nearly thirty theaters across the South, East, and Midwest. Following World War I, Dudley began promoting musicals in what became the first black-controlled theatrical circuit in the country, S. H. Dudley Theatrical Enterprises. Uncle Dud retired after the crash of 1929 forced him to sell many of his theaters. He died in Oxon Hill, Maryland, in 1940.[13]

Dudley's entrepreneurial efforts also included the Theater Owners' Booking Association (TOBA), which operated a loose association of major African American theaters—primarily in the Northeast and Midwest—that became known as the "Chitlin' Circuit." TOBA-associated theaters included the Apollo in New York, the Regal in Chicago, the Uptown in Philadelphia, the Royal Theater in Baltimore, the Fox in Detroit, and, of course, the Howard on U Street. At one point the association controlled bookings at eighty of the 107 theaters presenting African American performers around the country, making the neighborhood around Seventh and U streets the home of the headquarters for many of the organizations that served as a control center for national black entertainment.[14]

As important as the Howard Theatre was to African American Washingtonians, it was hardly the neighborhood's lone entertainment venue. By the late 1920s there were several major motion picture palaces catering to African American audiences—often offering live entertainment together with films—including the top-of-the-line Lincoln at Thirteenth and U Streets, Republic at Fourteenth and U, and Dunbar at Seventh and T. These three theaters were selling nearly 1.4 million tickets a year during the midtwenties.[15] The Lincoln Colonnade in the basement of the Lincoln Theatre, the Murray Palace Casino at Tenth and U Streets, the Scottish Rite Temple near Eleventh and R Streets, and the National Press Club a couple of blocks away were among the best dance halls in the city, opening their doors to over three thousand hoofers on a good night.[16]

Whites rarely went to see a movie at the big cinemas along U Street; they didn't have to since they had larger, more luxurious movie houses of their own downtown. Similarly, whites didn't venture into African American neighborhoods for meals. But whites sought out music in African American clubs because they offered a sound that did not exist in white Washington. To hear the legendary Jelly Roll Morton, for example, a music fan would have to go to Morton's club next door to the Minnehaha (in what today is Ben's Next Door); to hear Billie Holiday required a trip to one of the clubs along Seventh Street behind the Howard Theatre. For many whites, the crossroads of Seventh and Florida offered music that was different, better, and unavailable closer to home.

If someone liked the music being played all around the neighborhood, she or he could step into Max Silverman's Quality Music shop at 1836 Seventh Street, later known as Waxie Maxie's. The shop had no equivalent in white Washington. It was precisely for this reason that Ahmet Ertegun, the son of the Turkish ambassador, made his way across town during the mid-1930s to hear a sound he could find no place else.[17]

Sneaking out of the embassy at midnight, Ertegun caught a Cab Calloway show at a club along U Street one summer night in 1935. He was hooked. He began scouring DC for recordings of the great artists—Duke Ellington, Louis Armstrong, Jimmie Lunceford, Fats Waller, and Mary Lou Williams—whom he was hearing at the Howard Theatre,

Club Bengasi, Casbah, and Crystal Caverns. He became a regular denizen of Silverman's little record store near the Howard Theatre. Ertegun went on to establish Atlantic Records and to become one of the most successful record producers of American popular music during the last half of the twentieth century.

In a noteworthy 1927 study of the leisure activities of Washington's African Americans, Howard University sociologist William H. Jones recorded that the Oriental Gardens and the Andrew Thomas Cabaret along R Street and the Phoenix Inn opposite the Lincoln Theater on U Street offered superior cabaret performances, as did the city's largest cabaret, Cafe De Luxe, at Seventh and S Streets. The Dreamland Cafe and Paradise Cafe around the intersection of Seventh and T, Jones continued, provided less wholesome and more disorderly cabaret performances, with some of the "girls" allegedly offering more than drinks for sale in back rooms. The Night Club Bohemia in the basement of the Davis Drug Store at Eleventh and U Streets similarly failed to maintain standards and, according to Jones, "degenerated somewhat because of the demoralizing influences of a class of unscrupulous patrons." Meanwhile, "a number of probation officers have reported" that the Silver Slipper Club in the Pythian Temple building at Twelfth and U had become "the 'hangout' of a rather large number of their delinquent girls."[18]

White patrons who frequented the music clubs along U Street and Seventh Street were met with varying degrees of acceptance. At a minimum, they represented paying customers in an African American community that had been crippled economically by the segregation policies of the Woodrow Wilson administration and, later, by the Great Depression. African Americans created their own community spaces beyond white presence in churches, fraternal societies and sororities, pool halls, and barbershops. These institutions remained beyond the reach of white folk, places where African Americans could worship, make music, and converse among themselves.

U Street and Seventh Street sported many of the city's best billiard parlors—too many for Jones to count easily—that were, according to the professor,

> the harbingers of superstition and magic, since luck and chance play an important role in the activity performed. But they also are places where much liberal thought is promoted through discussion, disagreement, and the giving of information. The majority of pool hall patrons are persons who have wide experience, even though they have little formal education. They are men who traveled widely as porters, waiters, chauffeurs, etc. And one only needs to assume a sympathetic attitude to realize that here experience and ideas from the "ends of the earth" are assembled. The contacts of these patrons are truly cultural, though hardly intellectual.[19]

With names such as the Silver Slipper, the Poodle Dog, and the Idle Hour, such places combined casual mixing of classes with games, libations, and, at times, hot piano music.

Conversations that started in pool halls continued at the fourteen barbershops along U Street between Fourth Street and Florida Avenue to the east and Fourteenth and U Streets to the west, which similarly were important places for socializing. Informal social clubs, church halls, fraternal groups, sororities, and civic associations of all kinds sponsored entertainment for their members, rounding out a portrait of the neighborhood's vibrant street and cultural life.

Photo 2.2 Couple swing dancing

Swing dancing to the jazz rhythms of the 1930s and 1940s was popular in the many clubs and dance halls. Although William Gottlieb did not note where this couple was dancing, the photographer and reporter for the *Washington Post* documented the jazz scene in DC, where he was friends with most of the players.

Jones also reported that there were "play and amusement activities that do not receive the approval of either formal laws or public opinion, because they make for the demoralization of the community. Chief among these forms are the three vices: prostitution, gambling, and alcoholic orgies. These represent the illegitimate and unwholesome side of the play life of any community but constitute in no small degree means of socialization."[20]

Jones concluded his study by noting that "most Negro communities in Washington are not characterized by solidarity. They lack homogeneity of cultural types. Variety rather than uniformity prevails, and this interferes with the development of like-mindedness from which a strong set of public sentiments and attitudes could arise. The best Negro communities may represent uniformity in economic status but are characterized by pronounced cultural variations."[21] Churches, clubs, billiard parlors, and barber shops reflected the complexity of black Washington, offering the space in which identity formed.

The complexity of the communities and people colliding around the corner of Seventh Street and Florida Avenue inspired some of the most profound and enduring voices of early-twentieth-century America. The neighborhood's deep contradictions created a tense conflict between norms and attitudes that melded into an explosive and creative mix of class and background. Three local cultural figures in particular—the poet Langston Hughes, the novelist Jean Toomer, and the composer Duke Ellington—capture the area's inventiveness.

Hughes, Toomer, and Ellington were more or less contemporary products of the nation's nascent African American middle class, with personal stories tied by family to the neighborhood as well as to its churches, schools, and community life. Hughes's 1927 poem "Fine Clothes to the Jew," Toomer's *Cane*, and Ellington's homage in his memoirs to Frank Holliday's pool hall reflect the rough-and-tumble street life of Seventh Street with its rich and juicy language and musical tradition.[22]

Seventh Street was the space, both physical and metaphysical, in which Hughes, Toomer, and Ellington embraced the African American experience in all of its hues and classes. As Hughes recalled in his memoirs, *The Big Sea*,

> From all this [that of the "talented tenth"] pretentiousness Seventh Street was a sweet relief. Seventh Street is the long, old, dirty street, where the ordinary Negroes hang out, folks with practically no family tree at all, folks who draw no color line between mulattoes and deep dark-browns, folks who work hard for a living with their hands. On Seventh Street in 1924 they played the blues, ate watermelon, barbecue, and fish sandwiches, shot pool, told tall tales, looked at the dome of the Capitol and laughed out loud. . . . And I went to their churches and heard the tambourines play and the little tinkling bells of the triangles adorn the gay shouting tunes that sent sisters dancing down the aisles for Job. . . . Their songs—those of Seventh Street—had the pulse beat of the people who kept on going. . . . I liked the barrel houses of Seventh Street, the shouting churches, and the songs. They were warm and kind and didn't care whether you had an overcoat or not.[23]

In *Cane*, Toomer penetrates the heart of the matter in a passage from the 1920s about the Howard Theatre.

> Life of nigger alleys, of pool rooms and restaurants and near-beer saloons soaks into the walls of Howard Theatre and sets them throbbing to jazz songs. Black-skinned, they dance and shout above the trick and trill of white-walled buildings. At night, they open doors to people who come in to stamp their feet and shout. At night, road-shows volley songs into the mass-heart of black people. Songs soak the walls and seep out to the nigger life of alleys and near-beer saloons, of the Poodle Dog and Black Bear cabarets.[24]

The local and national struggle against the laws that supported racial segregation gained momentum during the 1920s and 1930s, attaining greater strength following World War II. The neighborhoods around Seventh and Florida slowly changed. A series of Supreme Court rulings made it possible for African Americans to live and work beyond the confines of their old community. Many middle-class patrons of the theaters, clubs, and stores began to move out of the neighborhood following the desegregation court rulings of the 1950s. White venues elsewhere in the city aggressively sought out bookings with top-flight African American performers. Physical decline set in as the area around the Seventh and Florida intersection was becoming among the District's poorest. The area's traditional middle class moved further out into formerly white areas while poor blacks displaced by urban renewal in Southwest Washington piled in on top of one another.[25]

By the 1960s the neighborhood was caught by the more general traumas washing across the city. The Howard Theatre's great run came to a close following the April 1968 outbursts of communal violence, despite fitful attempts to bring new life to the place throughout the 1970s.[26] The Howard's legacy found a form of permanence in the music of Ellington and the poetry and prose of Hughes and Toomer. Perhaps more significantly

Photo 2.3 Pearl Bailey at Crystal Caverns

Pearl Bailey and friends enjoy an evening at Crystal Caverns, now the Bohemian
Caverns, at Eleventh and U Streets. She got her start as an entertainer on U
Street and often appeared at the Caverns and other clubs in the area.

for Washington, it secured a special place in the hearts and memories of the performers
and local Washingtonians who frequented the theater.

Virtually every African American living in the city before the 1970s remembers the
Howard as an important place in their lives. Well into the 1950s, parents left children on
weekends as they ran errands, teenagers went on their first dates, and aspiring musicians
met their idols. The Howard remained part of the community as the famous and the
not-so-famous performers ate at the same modest eateries nearby and frequented the
same barbershops and beauty parlors around the corner while the theater was open.

District leaders understood that the abandoned Howard Theatre building stood as an
open wound in the psyche of longtime DC residents. The District government, together
with cultural institutions and private developers, undertook massive renovations for the
Howard Theatre to have it restored by the time of its centennial. The reopening, on
April 9, 2012, proved to be a grand day for the city, with several hundred—if not a couple
of thousand—Washingtonians showing up to see various officials cut the ceremonial
ribbon to mark the auditorium's rebirth.[27]

The proceedings that day began with an African incantation to the ancestors performed by a group that included neighborhood drummers who played every Sunday
at nearby Malcolm X Park. A cousin of the famous mid-twentieth-century American
contralto Marian Anderson sang the Lord's Prayer, and a well-known local pastor, the
Reverend Doctor Sandra Butler-Truesdale, was among the masters of ceremonies. Duke

Ellington's son and daughter were there to personify a link with the past. Washingtonians and others who made the reopening possible after literally decades of hard work were rightfully proud. Politicians such as Mayor Vince Gray, DC congressional delegate Eleanor Holmes Norton, councilmembers Jim Graham and Marion Barry had their says. But ceremonies are ceremonies. The beautiful spring day—with temperatures in the seventies cooled by a steady breeze—belonged to the people in the street.

Like New York's Harlem, New Orleans' Storyville, Memphis's Beale Street, and Chicago's Bronzeville, Seventh Street and its adjoining streets in the Northwest quadrant of Washington, DC, became one of the places where modern American—and not just African American—culture was born. Excluded by whites, African Americans of all classes created the dominant sounds of the United States of the twentieth century, and jazz was among them. The vibrant world that made Seventh Street so important a century ago was a product of a segregated social system that thankfully no longer exists. The life described by Ellington, Toomer, Hughes, and Jones is no more. Its protean legacy has become part of a more universal American culture, which returns in new forms to reinvigorate Seventh and Florida once more.

Notes

1. *Remembering Seventh Street: Personal Remembrances, Historical Advertisements, List of Jewish Seventh Street* (Washington, DC: Jewish Historical Society of Greater Washington, Lillian & Albert Small Jewish Museum, 1998).

2. Field research in the area before, during, and after the 1968 disturbances found considerable dependence on and hostility toward white-owned business establishments around the neighborhood; see Ulf Hannerz, *Soulside: Inquiries into Ghetto Culture and Community* (New York: Columbia University Press, 1969), 160–62.

3. The National Capital Planning Commission identified 201 (out of 250) nonresidential buildings along Seventh Street, between Mount Vernon Square and Florida Avenue, damaged during the disturbances, including ninety-three that were more than half destroyed. This corridor had a significant number of Jewish businesses; see National Capital Planning Commission, *Civil Disturbances in Washington, D.C. (April 4–8, 1968): A Preliminary Damage Report* (Washington: NCPC, May 1968), 9–12. Commentary about the racial composition of the owners of businesses burned in 1968 has remained contentious ever since; for a brief overview, see Keith Mulder and the D.C. History Curriculum Project, *City of Magnificent Intentions: A History of the District of Columbia* (Washington: Intac, 1983), 497. An oral history project about the 1968 disturbances found that many former business owners and their families remained bitter about their displacement more than four decades later; see Dana Lanier Schaffer, "The 1968 Washington Riot in History and Memory," *Washington History* 15 (Fall/Winter, 2003–2004): 5–33.

4. Flora B. Atkin, "Recollections of Seventh Street" (August 1998), in *Remembering Seventh Street: Personal Remembrances, Historical Advertisements, List of Jewish Seventh Street* (Washington, DC: Jewish Historical Society of Greater Washington, Lillian & Albert Small Jewish Museum, 1998), n.p.

5. Cultural Tourism DC, *What's the Story? A Deeper Look at the History of Greater Shaw in Washington, D.C. in the Context of the National African American Experience*, Conference Proceedings, December 7–8, 2004 (Washington: Cultural Tourism DC, 2005).

6. For further discussion of this history, see Blair A. Ruble, *Washington's U Street: A Biography* (Baltimore: Johns Hopkins University Press; Washington, DC: Woodrow Wilson Centre Press, 2010), 19–41.

7. Definition of "zone of contact" from Mary Louise Pratt, "Arts in the Contact Zone," *Profession 91*: 33–40, in David Bartholomae and Anthony Petrosky, eds., *Reading the Lives of Others* (Boston: Bedford Books of St. Martin's Press, 1995), 180–95.

8. Bettye Gardner and Bettye Thomas, "The Cultural Impact of the Howard Theatre on the Black Community," *Journal of Negro History* 55 (1970): 253–55.

9. Ibid.

10. Laura Bergheim, *The Washington Historical Atlas: Who Did What When and Where in the Nation's Capital* (Rockville, MD: Woodbine House, 1992), 249–50.

11. Marya Annette McQuirter, "Claiming the City: African Americans, Urbanization, and Leisure in Washington, D.C., 1902–1957" (PhD diss., University of Michigan, Ann Arbor, 2000), 94–102; and Stephanie Barbara Frank, "'If We Own the Story, We Own the Place': Cultural Heritage, Historic Preservation, and Gentrification on U Street" (MA thesis, University of Maryland, College Park, 2005), 65–69.

12. McQuirter, "Claiming the City," 112–115.

13. Loften Mitchell, *Black Drama: The Story of the American Negro in the Theater* (New York: Hawthorn, 1967), 67–68.

14. Tamara Lizette Brown, "Lingering Lights from America's Black Broadway: Negro Renaissance to the Black Arts Movement, African-American Theatrical Dance in Washington, D.C." (PhD diss., Howard University, Washington, DC, 2004), 10, 76–80.

15. McQuirter, "Claiming the City," 113–14.

16. William H. Jones, *Recreation and Amusement among Negroes in Washington, D.C.: A Sociological Analysis of the Negro in an Urban Environment* (Westport, CT: Negro Universities Press, 1927), 125–31. See also Marya Annette McQuirter, *African American Heritage Trail, Washington, D.C.* (Washington, DC: Cultural Tourism DC, 2003), 9.

17. David A. Taylor, "It All Began One Night Near U Street," *Washington Post*, January 7, 2007, www.washingtonpost.com/wp-dyn/content/article/2007/01/05/AR2007010501519.html.

18. Jones, *Recreation and Amusement*, 131–34.

19. Ibid., 136.

20. Ibid., 161–62.

21. Ibid. 162–63.

22. Langston Hughes, *Fine Clothes to the Jew* (New York: Knopf, 1927); Jean Toomer, *Cane* (1923; repr., New York: Liveright, 1993); and Edward Kennedy "Duke" Ellington, *Music Is My Mistress* (Garden City, NY: Doubleday, 1973), 14–17.

23. Langston Hughes, *The Big Sea*, vol. 13 of *The Collected Works of Langston Hughes*, ed. Joseph McLaren (Columbia: University of Missouri Press, 2002), 166–67.

24. Toomer, *Cane*, 50.

25. Ruble, *Washington's U Street*, 173–222; and Mark Opasasnick, *Washington Rock and Roll: A Social History* (Tinicum, PA: Xlibris, 2003), 24–50.

26. Gardner and Thomas, "Cultural Impact of the Howard Theatre," 260–62.

27. DeNeen L. Brown, "The Curtain Finally Rises on the Reborn Howard Theatre," *Washington Post*, April 9, 2012, http://articles.washingtonpost.com/2012-04-09/lifestyle/35454523_1 _howard-theatre-ellis-development-crowd.

3 Washington's Duke Ellington

John Edward Hasse

Once upon a time a very pretty lady and a very handsome gentleman met, fell in love and got married, and God blessed them with this wonderful baby boy. They held him in the palm of their hand and they nurtured him until he was eight years old and then they put his feet on the ground. He ran out of the front door, out across the street and somebody said, "Hey, Edward, up this way." The boy was me, incidentally. He got to the next corner and somebody says, "Hey, Edward, up there and turn left, you can't miss it." And it's been going on ever since.[1]

That's how Edward Kennedy "Duke" Ellington once described his start in life in his native city of Washington, DC. Both fanciful and characteristically oblique, his description also reveals his family pride and penchant for florid language, speaks to his sponge-like gift to absorb musical and life lessons from others, and suggests his self-confidence, sense of accomplishment, and exceptionalism. Many of these qualities result from his upbringing in a loving, close-knit family, his exposure to teachers who instilled racial pride, his learning from musicians who guided him, and his suffusion in the remarkable culture of black Washington.

Ellington became a jazz composer, orchestrator, bandleader, and pianist who led one of the greatest jazz bands, wrote more than 1,500 compositions, and became one of the twentieth century's greatest musicians. He used the term "beyond category" as the highest possible praise for others, and the phrase richly applies to Ellington, for he led one of the most singular musical careers in American history and left a brilliant legacy likely to endure for the ages.

Edward Ellington was born into one of the most difficult periods African Americans have experienced. Indeed, historians Rayford W. Logan and Constance Green have described the period from 1897 to 1901 as an extremely low point in the history of black Americans.[2] African Americans faced two basic facts of life during Ellington's boyhood: socially and politically, things were getting worse—most of all in the South but also in the North, and increasing numbers of them would make the fateful decision to leave the South and move north.

Photo 3.1 *Duke Ellington*
Duke Ellington, at age
26, already displays his
characteristic elegance and
self-assurance. Raised in a
warm and supportive family
in the first decades of the
twentieth century, Ellington
credited the good fortune of
finding mentors who were
role models and helped him
develop musically. He also drew
enduring life lessons from his
experiences in Washington's
schools, theaters, dance halls,
pool parlors, cafes, and clubs.

The downward spiral of justice and opportunity for African Americans that gripped the nation also affected Ellington's hometown. In Washington, equal treatment under the law had largely disappeared by the time of his birth. Control of many institutions lay in the hands of whites. Residential segregation increased during Ellington's first twenty years. In 1913 President Woodrow Wilson segregated the civil service throughout the nation, which hit especially hard in Washington, the nation's capital. Many African Americans lost their jobs; others were moved to dead-end, out-of-sight positions; and with photographs now required with applications, black people knew they would not be hired. In 1913, Booker T. Washington, the foremost African American leader of the day, wrote, "I have recently spent several days in Washington, and I have never seen the colored people so discouraged and bitter as they were at that time."[3]

And yet, when compared with rural and urban locales in the Deep South, Washington was a better place for black people. They avoided the sharecropping system, the Ku Klux Klan, and the worst of southern racial violence. In 1900 Washington had the largest black population of any American city, with 31 percent of the population African American. Racial segregation forced blacks to live separately from whites, as they did in most other places in the rural and urban South. But with a strong middle class, Washington's African American community developed viable businesses, respected churches, active social organizations, and even an opera company.[4] The community's "main street" was U Street,

NW, especially between Seventh and Fourteenth Streets. The neighborhood embraced a mix of occupations.[5]

The city was a leader in the education of African Americans, home to M Street High School (predecessor to Dunbar High School, which opened in 1916), the nation's first public high school for black students, and to Howard University, established in 1867, the most distinguished black university in the nation. The poet Paul Laurence Dunbar wrote in 1900 of Washington as having "a higher standard of culture among people of color than obtains in any other city."[6] The city, writes historian Harvey G. Cohen, was "a center of black musical and intellectual resistance to racism" and, despite racial problems, "probably the best place to be an African American at the turn of the century."[7]

Within this population, people drew strong class distinctions: the black populace was structured like a pyramid. At the top was a small aristocracy, comprising about sixty or seventy families—generally people of light skin color, who themselves or whose ancestors had lived in Washington for many years, who pursued "honorable occupations," and who had a certain amount of money and education.[8] Next was a middle class of government workers, professionals, and businessmen. The Ellington family just fit into this group. The largest and poorest section—most of the pyramid—comprised recent migrants from the South, many of whom lived lives of destitution and economic deprivation.[9]

Most people of color were aware of differences in hue among themselves, and thus Washington's black community recognized caste as well as class lines. "I don't know how many castes of Negroes there were in the city at that time," wrote Ellington, "but I do know that if you decided to mix carelessly with another, you would be told that one just did not do that sort of thing."[10]

"What one did with one's mind had a lot to do with one's station," declared Theodore Hudson, a retired professor of English from Howard University who grew up in a middle-class Washington family. "It was an era when you put your best foot forward, when you didn't go to movies, play cards, or listen to light music on Sundays. In polite black society in Washington, you didn't offend people. You couldn't say 'lie,' you had to say 'wasn't telling the truth.'"[11]

Decorum and propriety extended to musicians, too. Many Washington musicians, especially those Ellington would grow to admire, exemplified what Ellington would later call a "disciplinary climate."[12] Ellington's first biographer, Barry Ulanov, wrote of "a Washington pattern" among musicians. "It involved a certain bearing, a respect for education, for the broad principles of the art of music; a desire for order, for design in their professional lives."[13]

In Washington, many middle- and upper-class blacks expected their children to become achievers—for example, doctors or teachers. Jazz pianist Billy Taylor, who attended Dunbar High School, attested that career expectations and Washington role models yielded positive results.[14] Ellington's sister, Ruth, perceived that making a mark in the world "was a norm for that Washington black American middle class group" that Ellington grew up in.[15] Edward himself later declared: "The driving power was a matter of wanting to be—and to be heard—at the same level as the best."[16]

Duke Ellington came into the world as Edward Kennedy Ellington on April 29, 1899, in Washington, DC. He was the second child; the first had died in infancy. He would spend the first twenty-four years of his life—nearly one-third—in the nation's capital. During those years, his character and personality would take shape, largely as a result of his relationship with his parents, and he would choose the career to which he would devote his life. His parents and his experiences with community, church, and music would shape his character and ultimately his music.

His mother, Daisy Kennedy Ellington, was a beautiful, soft-spoken woman. Born in 1879 in Washington, DC, she came from a middle-class family and had completed high school, an unusual achievement at that time. Her father had been a District of Columbia policeman, a coveted job for a black man in those days. Daisy raised young Edward with love, praise, and encouragement and always treated him as someone very special, telling him, "Edward, you are blessed. You don't have anything to worry about. Edward, you are blessed." Edward would maintain this confident feeling of being favored for the rest of his life. The women in his family, he said, "pampered and pampered" him, spoiling him rotten. Finally, when he was eight, he said, his feet were allowed to touch ground.[17]

Edward's father, James Edward Ellington, had been born in Lincolnton, North Carolina, in 1879, the same year as Daisy. Like so many other southern blacks, before and after, he had migrated north hoping for a better life, settling in Washington, DC. James held a series of occupations from the late 1890s until about 1920. He worked first as a driver, then as a butler for the family of Middleton F. Cuthbert (1462 Rhode Island Avenue, NW), a prominent white physician with whom he enjoyed a close relationship. Cuthbert allowed Ellington to read in his extensive library, enabling him to continue his education. Sometimes Ellington got work as a caterer and a few times served as a butler for catered events at the White House. After World War I, he secured a job as a blueprinter at the Navy Yard. "He raised his family as though he were a millionaire," Edward Ellington would write later. "The best had to be carefully examined to make sure it was good enough for my mother."[18] As a domestic servant, James did not make a lot of money but sought to maintain high standards of behavior within his household.

Between 1898 and 1921, James and his family lived in fourteen different locations, all in Northwest Washington. Why the family moved so often has never been explained. Most of the Ellington family homes were situated in the near northside area now known as Shaw, and while "Shaw had a significant racial mix until early until the early twentieth century," writes Kathryn Schneider Smith, "around 1900, many white residents chose to move to new suburbs to the north, which were closed to African Americans."[19] The family's frequent moves could have been related to race or caste issues, to the parents' aspiring way of life, to noisy or difficult neighbors, or to another factor. Whatever the reason, Ellington left no mention of it.

In Ellington's day, the neighborhood consisted of pleasant middle-class homes. According to Rex Stewart, who lived in Washington from 1914 to 1921 and later would play cornet with the Duke Ellington orchestra, people who lived in Northwest "were the lighter complexioned people with better-type jobs, such as schoolteachers, postmen, clerks or in government service. . . . The southwest area . . . [had] the working class, the coal men, the fishmongers, the gamblers, pimps and sporting females."[20] Ellington's parents attended different churches: she the Nineteenth Street Baptist (Nineteenth and I streets, NW), at which many old-line families worshiped, and he the John Wesley African

Methodist Episcopal Zion Church (1615 Fourteenth Street, NW).[21] All indications are that they had a warm, close relationship with one another and with their son.

When he was seven or eight, attending Garnet Elementary School, his mother signed him up for his first formal training in music.[22] Edward studied for a time with a teacher who was named Marietta Harvey (née Clinkscales). No evidence survives, however, that the lessons had much effect. At that age, he showed far more interest in playing outdoors and watching baseball. Playing baseball on Sixteenth Street, Ellington would sometimes notice President Theodore Roosevelt ride by on horseback, stop, and watch the boys; as Roosevelt left, he waved to them and the boys would wave back. And big-league baseball excited him. "Washington was in the American league and every day I had to see the game," Ellington remembered. So he got a job hawking peanuts, popcorn, and candy at the baseball stadium, where the Senators team played. At first he was extremely self-conscious. "I was completely terrified at the Washington ballpark; it was like going on stage, stage fright. Everybody in the park was looking at me! All I wanted to see was the baseball game."[23]

Edward liked "putting on a show," at least for his family, and at a very young age revealed a theatrical flair by telling jokes, dancing, and playing the Jew's harp.[24] By the age of twelve, he was slipping surreptitiously into the Gayety Theatre (513 Ninth Street, NW) to watch the burlesque shows. "The shows were very good," he said, "and I made a lot of observations, on show business techniques, on the great craftsmanship involved, and on the rather gorgeous girls."[25] Throughout his life, in fact, Ellington constantly looked for lessons in his experiences.

No doubt without his parents' knowledge, at age fourteen Ellington began sneaking into Frank Holliday's poolroom (624 T Street, NW), situated next to the well-known Howard Theatre and only seven blocks from Ellington's home on Thirteenth Street. "It was not a normal, neighborhood-type poolroom. It was the high spot of billiard parlors, where all the kids from all neighborhoods came, and the great pool sharks from all over town." Waiters, porters, students, piano players, drummers, medical interns, gamblers, pickpockets—they all came to Holliday's. Here Ellington learned to appreciate "how all levels could and should mix." Railroad porters and dining-car waiters told of having just been in New York, Cleveland, and Chicago and whetted Ellington's appetite for travel.[26]

Rubbing elbows at Frank Holliday's poolroom with all levels of the black community, Ellington undoubtedly grew impatient with discrimination based on skin color, income, and occupation. And his parents maintained that all people were of equal worth, that no race was better than another one. "In our house," said his younger sister, Ruth, "while I was growing up, people of all colors were there. More whites than colored. My father was like that. [Duke] didn't talk about color. In our house, you didn't talk about color."[27] Duke Ellington said, "There was never any talk [at home] about red people, brown people, black people, or yellow people, or about the differences that existed between them."[28]

As part of his education, Ellington was taught pride in his race and responsibility to represent it well. His eighth grade English teacher, Mrs. Boston, emphasized, according to Ellington, that "everywhere you go, if you were sitting in a theater next to a white lady or something like that, or you were on stage representing your race, no matter where you go or what you do, you are representing your race and your responsibility is to command respect for that race. They taught that. I've always had that."[29] On another occasion, Ellington said, "They used to pound it into you, you go to the English class, that [race pride] was more important than the English."[30] Ellington and his peers grew up believing that, as Jacqueline Moore observed, "if they worked quietly behind the scenes to contradict negative images of African Americans, they could bring whites to accept them as equals without open conflict."[31] This belief became an abiding tenet for Ellington the rest of his life.

Besides making him feel privileged, well-fed, confident, special, and very loved, Ellington's parents also instilled a pride in the person he was and the achiever he might become. They taught him and Ruth that they could do anything, encouraged them, and instilled in them a positive attitude toward life.[32] With all this as a foundation, Ellington built a strong sense of self-confidence. With a reservoir of love, self-assurance, and racial pride, Edward Ellington, about to become a teenager, began to explore what his life's calling might be. As he would move from boyhood to young manhood, Ellington would show talent in several of the arts and would have to choose what he would make his career. His decision would not only chart his career path but also reveal a great deal about how he would solve problems.

As he proceeded through grade school and entered Garrison Junior High School in 1911, Ellington's piano lessons had faded into memory and he was now showing a flair for art. In 1913, as he prepared to enter high school, Edward might have gone to M Street High School, an academically oriented school.[33] Instead, he entered the neighboring Samuel H. Armstrong Technical High School to study commercial art. In the opinion of Mercer, Ellington's son, Armstrong was "a kind of rough high school. If you went there you were practically regarded as incorrigible."[34]

Music still tugged at Ellington, too. When Ellington was a youngster, piano sales were booming and in 1909, when he was ten, the sale of pianos hit an all-time high in the United States.[35] In 1913 Ellington and his mother, Daisy, vacationed in Asbury Park, an oceanside resort in New Jersey. There Ellington heard a pianist named Harvey Brooks, who inspired the teenager to take up playing piano again. Like many people his age, Ellington was drawn to the toe-tapping syncopated genre of ragtime. He began to go out and listen to sharp ragtime pianists, or, as he called them then, "piano plunkers."[36] "Oh, I was a great listener!" he recalled.[37] Washington bred many fine pianists—the unschooled ones such as Ralph Green, Shrimp Bronner, Lester Dishman, Clarence Bowser, Sticky Mack, Blind Johnny, and "the Man with a Thousand Fingers"; and the ones who read music, like Claude Hopkins, Roscoe Lee, Gertie Wells, Doc Perry, Louis Brown, and Louis Thomas. Because he could not read music very well, Ellington listened carefully to other pianists and tried to reproduce their ragtime, popular songs, and dance numbers.[38]

During Ellington's musically formative years, from the age of eleven through seventeen, he lived with his family a scant two and a half blocks from True Reformers Hall, a large, well-equipped public facility located at 1200 U Street, NW, in the heart of black Washington. "I played my first date at the True Reformers Hall, on the worst piano in the world," Ellington remembered. "I played from 8 p.m. to 1 a.m. and for 75 cents. Man, I snatched that money and ran like a thief. My mother was so proud of me."[39]

Even at this early stage, he began to compose music, though he started more by necessity than by design. During the summer of 1913, he took a job as a soda jerk in the Poodle Dog Café on Georgia Avenue. Ellington later recalled:

We had a piano player in the Poodle Dog who was one of the best when he was sober, but that wasn't often. When he got to where he couldn't play any better than I could, the boss would throw him out, take my place behind the soda fountain, and have me play piano. The only way I could learn how to play a tune was to compose it myself and work it up, and the first one was *Soda Fountain Rag*.[40]

The piece was also known as the "Poodle Dog Rag." Ellington attracted some attention with "Soda Fountain Rag," and soon he composed another piece, which he called "What You Gonna Do When the Bed Breaks Down?," a slow-dancing number he later termed "a pretty good 'hug-and-rubbin' crawl." The piece was never published or formally recorded, but its bawdy lyrics have been preserved:

Tried it on the sofa, tried it on the chair,
Tried it on the table, didn't get nowhere,
What you gonna do when the bed breaks down?
You've got to work out on the floor.

If you can't be good, be careful.
And if you can't be careful, name it after me.[41]

Ellington's teenage audiences, with their raging hormones, loved the song.

Until that point, Ellington's friends called him "Eddie."[42] But around 1913, in high school, his pal Edgar McIntree—whom Ellington described as "an elegant cat, a swinger of his day"—"decided since I was a pretty fancy guy, I was eligible for his constant companionship, I should have a title, so he called me 'Duke.'"[43] The name stuck, perhaps because it was short and memorable and because it fit with Ellington's aspirations. According to his cousin Bernice Wiggins, "He said, 'Mother, your son is going to be one of the great musicians in the world. . . . Someday . . . I'm gonna be bowin' before the kings and queens.'"[44]

After Ellington entered high school, McIntree pushed him into playing a number for the senior-class dance. He made a hit. From then on, Duke Ellington was in demand as a pianist at dances and parties. He quickly noticed that "when you were playing piano there was always a pretty girl standing down at the bass-clef end of the piano. I ain't been no athlete since."[45]

In the 1910s dancing in public was gaining respectability as new dance halls sprung up. By 1920 Washington was rife with dance halls for the outspread African American population. As cornetist Rex Stewart recalled: "I don't think there were many towns with more dance halls than Washington, excluding only maybe that fabled New Orleans scene. Starting with the then spanking new Lincoln Colonnades, there was Murray's Casino, True Reformer's Hall, Eye Street Hall, Stack O'Lee's in Foggy Bottom, Odd Fellows Hall in Georgetown, the Woodman's Hall in Anacostia, Eagle's Hall in the Northeast section, the Masonic Hall in midtown, and Convention Hall, plus at least ten or so smaller halls."[46] Soon Ellington would find himself part of this beguiling scene. For the dancers, the musicians would perform repertory ranging from cotillion dance tunes, popular songs, and waltzes to rags, blues, and the emerging jazz. Dance steps of the period include the waltz, tango, turkey trot, grizzly bear, Ballin' the Jack, one-step, fox-trot, two-step, and Texas Tommy.

A self-professed "constant listener and hanger-on," Ellington found new musical influences.[47] "Every time I reached a point where I needed direction," he reflected, "I ran into a friendly advisor who told me what and which way to go to get what or where I wanted to get or go or do."[48] One of those advisors or mentors was Oliver "Doc" Perry, a popular Washington bandleader who took Ellington in hand and taught him to read music. Perry and fellow pianist Louis Brown deeply influenced Ellington with their poise, manners, discipline, musical skill, and broad-mindedness. Soon Perry invited Ellington to fill in for him at Wednesday afternoon dances. And Ellington began filling in at clubs and cafes in black Washington.[49]

In 1916 Ellington entered and won a poster contest sponsored by the National Association for the Advancement of Colored People. He, however, turned down the prize—a scholarship to study art at the Pratt Institute in Brooklyn. Instead he decided to stay in Washington and pursue music. In about February 1917, three months shy of graduation, Ellington left Armstrong School. His departure from high school marked the beginning of his career as a professional musician. During World War I, he worked as a messenger for the Navy Department and then the State Department.[50] After the war, he worked with partner Ewell Conway in a business painting signs for dance halls and backdrops for the Howard Theatre. By night, Ellington performed music and cleverly found a way to capitalize on both lines of work. "When customers came for posters to advertise a dance, I would ask them what they were doing about their music. When they wanted to hire a band, I would ask them who's painting their signs."[51]

In 1917 or perhaps early 1918, Ellington took the next step on the road to becoming a full professional: he formed his own group and named it The Duke's Serenaders. At first, the Serenaders comprised two to four players: Ellington on piano, along with drums, banjo or guitar, and saxophone. The fluctuating personnel included Bill Miller, William Escoffery, or Sterling Conaway on guitar; Felix Miller or Otto Hardwick on saxophone; "Devil" Miller, Lloyd Stewart, or Sonny Greer on drums; and sometimes Arthur Whetsol on cornet or trumpet.[52] By March of 1918, Ellington took three additional steps toward independence and professionalism. First, he moved out of his parents' home and into an apartment of his own. Second, he got a telephone—at that time, still a luxury—in fact, two and one-half years before his parents did. And third, he bought a listing for himself as "musician" in the classified section of the telephone directory. That ad sparked a big increase in business. "The reason I was so successful," Ellington would recall, "I imagine, was because I put a one-inch ad in the telephone book alongside Meyer Davis and Louis Thomas who were the only other bands who advertised in the telephone book."[53] Davis, incidentally, was white and Thomas was black. Sometime around 1918, Thomas sent Ellington to play a solo piano job at the Ashland, Virginia, country club. Thomas took 90 percent of the fee as commission. Stunned by the possibilities, Ellington decided to serve as his own booking agent; besides booking his own band, he booked other bands as well.[54]

In July 1918, Ellington married his neighborhood sweetheart, Edna Thompson, and about nine months later, Edna delivered a son, Mercer. The marriage, however, was destined not to last.[55]

"I was beginning to catch on around Washington," Ellington wrote, "and I finally built up so much of a reputation that I had to study music seriously to protect it."[56] He found the ideal teacher: Henry Grant, who lived in Ellington's neighborhood. Ellington went to Grant's twice a week for lessons. Grant's activities covered a lot of ground: he taught music at Dunbar High School, conducted church choirs, gave solo piano recitals, played in a classical music trio, conducted a group of folk singers, helped found the National Association of Negro Musicians in 1919, and edited its magazine, *The Negro Musician*. For someone so well trained in European "classical" music, Grant was unusual: he didn't condescend to or scorn popular music.[57]

In July 1919, in Washington's stifling summer, armed white soldiers and sailors attacked unarmed black civilians, injuring dozens. Ellington's reaction to the brutality in his city went unrecorded, but the pain of it, along with the other events in his life, thrust him into adulthood and gave him a new worldliness. His people victimized by racial prejudice, Ellington chose now to deal with the larger world by outsmarting it, by playing the trickster, the sly fox, garbed in the sheep's clothing of charm. He would dazzle them with his manners, polish, style, and entertainment, all the time pursuing his own goals. And he would walk with pride, head held high, everywhere he went.

By 1920 he was playing for outdoor summer dances at New Fairmount Park and the Anderson Open Air Gardens. His little band also played for pre-performance supper shows at the Howard Theatre, which had opened in 1911 as Washington's first large theater for blacks and was the foremost African American theater in the nation. These pre-performance shows featured as many as five local bands, who competed for the applause of the audience to determine the most popular. The Howard's location at 620 T Street, NW, was special; the same block contained the Howard, Holliday's, and a popular corner: "The corner of Seventh and T streets was *the* hangout for Washington musicians," said Rex Stewart.[58] Ellington hung out on that corner, too. "Everybody," Ellington observed, "used to stand on the street corners then and try and look big-time." Later, "after work, musicians usually gathered at Industrial Café [2006 Eleventh Street, NW], where they would hold a general gab-fest and jam session. Every guy would try to tell a bigger lie than the last one."[59]

One subject of discussion had to be band battles. "Band contests were very popular in those days," recalled Ellington.[60] Stewart said, "One of the features at these [dance] halls was the battle of the bands . . . [and] my first awareness of this delightful phenomenon was at the Lincoln Colonnades. There were three bands, but the main battle was between Doc Perry and Sam Taylor. The third outfit was only a pick-up group with Duke Ellington on piano."[61]

Some of the band's engagements were at embassies, society balls, and private mansions in Washington, DC, and fox hunt balls and barn dances in Manassas, Warrenton, Culpeper, and Orange, Virginia, while others were at humble DC dance halls. Cornetist Rex Stewart, eight years Ellington's junior, asserted that "there was a dance somewhere every night. . . . Of course, you had to know what the social climate might be before venturing into a hall where you were not known, as the natives were mighty clannish in those days. Sometimes you might have to leave a dance without your overcoat, your hat or even your head! Ambulances were rarely seen in a colored neighborhood in those days, and the victim generally bled to death."[62]

If there was trouble, the musicians themselves were not necessarily safe. Stewart recalled peeking into an Odd Fellows Hall in Georgetown, probably in 1921, where Ellington was playing with a quartet for a Saturday night dance. The foursome sounded great to us kids because they played the popular tunes of the day, such as *It's Right Here for You, and If You Don't Get It, It's No Fault of Mine; Walking the Dog; He May Be Your Man, But He Comes to See Me Sometime.* We gaped over the fence, drinking in the bright lights, the pretty girls, the festive atmosphere, and the good music. . . . These dances always started sedately, but as the night wore on and the liquor flowed faster, the tougher element went into action, and the customary fight erupted. This time it was a real brawl, and the Georgetown toughs ran the band out of the hall. . . . The band [was] hotfooting it down Twenty-ninth Street [with Duke in the lead].[63]

In 1922 the Lincoln Memorial was dedicated on the National Mall. This monument, along with other changes made as a result of the resurrection of Pierre L'Enfant's original plan for the city, symbolized the expanding visions and hopes of Washington's white populace. To some in the black community, the new grand buildings may have heightened the pain of their declining fortunes. Even at the dedication of the memorial, blacks were forced to sit in a roped-off area across a dirt road. Ellington's reaction to this affront went unrecorded. The irony of shrinking black vistas beside expanding white horizons could not have been lost on someone as discerning as Duke Ellington. Characteristically optimistic, however, Ellington evidently chose not to dwell on the negative but to take what he could from his environment. Did the visual beauty of Washington influence him? Did the grand vistas stimulate in him not only a sense of order and proportion but also his own ambition?

Duke Ellington was doing well in Washington. He could have remained there and probably led a comfortable life as a dance-band leader and booking agent. But somehow that was not enough. He had the drive to excel, to rise to the top, and the top at the time was New York City. His dreams of New York had been fed not only by the stories Pullman porters told at Frank Holliday's but, more importantly, by musicians. "You know how guys stand on the corner," said drummer Sonny Greer, who would perform with Ellington for over thirty years. "[Ellington] and [pianist] Claude Hopkins, [saxophonist] Toby 'Otto' Hardwick, standing on the corner, they was talking some jive, they started talking about New York. [Ellington] said, 'Sonny can tell you about New York. He's from New York.' So I come in there and started that jive talk, that funny old talk, telling them cats about New York, painting a glorious picture about New York, and right away them cats were on me like white on rice."[64] Recalled Ellington, "It was New York that filled our imagination," listing dozens of musicians he and his musical buddies admired. "We were awed by the never-ending roll of great talents there. . . . Harlem, to our minds, did indeed have the world's most glamorous atmosphere. We had to go there."[65] In 1923 he made the consequential decision to move to New York.

By this time, he had completed his musical apprenticeship in the nation's capital and become an avid listener and absorber of other black pianists and black music generally, a decent pianist, a budding bandleader and composer, and a pleasing entertainer. He had by now established his personality. He was tied strongly to his mother, secure, self-confident, optimistic, prideful, aristocratic in demeanor, charming, well mannered, easy with people from all walks of life, religious, ambitious, clever, didactically oriented, street smart, shrewd in business, restive with categories, averse to writing while inclined toward

Photo 3.2 *Duke Ellington and Max Silverman*

On one of many trips back to Washington for an engagement, this time at the Howard
Theatre in 1942, native son Edward "Duke" Ellington poses with Max Silverman outside
the Quality Music Co. on Seventh Street, NW. Ellington spent his formative years in
DC, and when he moved to New York to further his career, he named his first band the
Washingtonians. Max Silverman's store, later called Waxie Maxie's, drew music fans from all
over the city, one of the few shops that carried an extensive selection of jazz recordings.

oral communication, a stylish dresser, and a growing individualist. His decision to leave
for New York proved that he was also a risk taker.

After leaving Washington, Ellington's relationship with his hometown was mostly
positive, but the city gave him some disappointments, too. Ellington and his band flopped
during their first attempt to make it in New York City. They returned to Washington for
a spell and then tried again. This time they made it, and Ellington proudly called his new
seven-piece band "The Washingtonians." They came, after all, from the nation's capital,
the city that had only recently been eclipsed by New York as the "undisputed capital
of black America." His gift, learned in Washington, for readily navigating between the
black world and the white would blossom further in New York, where interracial relationships were much more fluid than in the southern city of Washington, and where a
long-standing tradition of black–white musical interaction existed.

His parents continued to live in Washington until 1929, along with Ellington's much-
younger sister, Ruth, his only sibling, who was born in 1915, and Ellington's son, Mercer,
who was born in 1919 and who lived with his grandparents in Washington once his father

left for New York. In 1929 they all joined Ellington in a Harlem apartment. Though not documented, it is possible that, between 1924 and 1929, Ellington paid brief trips to Washington to see his parents, sister, and son. It is documented that after becoming successful at Harlem's Cotton Club, Ellington and his band played a Baltimore one-nighter in 1929 and another in 1930—but evidently did not perform in Washington.[66]

By the time of his parents' move to New York, Ellington's star was shooting skyward. In 1927 he had landed a prime job for his band at Harlem's Cotton Club, Harlem's most celebrated nightspot. To accompany the stage dancers, he composed a series of pieces—such as "The Mooche" (1928), "Black Beauty" (1928), and "Rockin' in Rhythm" (1931)—which broke new musical ground. By this time, Ellington was developing a unique sound for his band. Above all, the sound depended on the distinctive instrumental voices of his musicians. He hired and featured some of the greatest, most individualistic players, including the alto saxophonist Johnny Hodges, the trombonist Joe "Tricky Sam" Nanton, and the trumpeter Cootie Williams.

Ellington's compositions combined his musicians' instrumental voices in innovative ways. Most arrangers for big bands voiced instruments in sections—pitting, for example, the trumpet section against the saxophone section. Ellington voiced his instruments across sections, combining, for instance, the clarinet, trombone, and trumpet in an innovative fashion to create the ravishing opening of "Mood Indigo" (1930). As a composer, Ellington developed a personal approach to harmony and instrumental voicing. Unlike most other swing bandleaders, he composed most of his band's music.

After leaving the Cotton Club in 1931, Ellington embarked on nearly incessant touring the rest of his life, maintaining his apartment in Harlem as his home base. In 1935, Ellington's beloved mother Daisy died, a huge loss for the maestro.[67] His father, James, died in 1937. Both were laid to rest in Washington's Harmony Cemetery.

His touring brought him back to his birthplace dozens of times. His primary venue was the Howard Theatre: he returned twenty-three times to perform there. His engagement at the "new Howard" in September 1931 sparked this newspaper description:

> That ace of colored musicians, none other than Duke Ellington and his Cotton Club orchestra, together with 50 colored entertainers, opened the re-decorated and refurnished Howard Theater Saturday afternoon. Featuring Ellington's special arrangement of "Stardust," "Dinah," and his own composition, "Black and Tan Phantasy" [sic], the Duke and his company drew bursts of applause from a full house at the first matinee of the fall season. . . . The interior of the theater is now in bright red, gold and green, and the new seats and carpets match in color. There is also a new steel curtain.[68]

Because many of his Howard engagements lasted a full week and featured multiple performances per day, his shows at the Howard numbered in the hundreds.

Among his fans at the Howard were two teenaged brothers, Ahmet and Nesuhi Ertegun, sons of Mehmet Munir Ertegun, Turkey's second ambassador to the United States. Ahmet, the younger of the two, asserted that he got his musical education during frequent visits to the Howard; later he would cofound Atlantic Records and become highly influential in taking black American music to a wide audience. On at least one occasion, in 1942, Ellington was invited by Nesuhi Ertegun, then nineteen, to come to the Turkish Embassy to jam and have dinner.[69] This grand mansion, which also housed the ambassador's residence, was probably the only place in rigidly segregated Washington where blacks and whites could sit down and have a formal dinner together. Ellington thought enough of the visit to mention it in an article he wrote for the *Norfolk New Journal and Guide*.

> I might write about an afternoon last February while we were playing at the Howard Theatre in Washington, DC. Our very good friend, Bill Gottlieb, a columnist on one of the Washington papers, came backstage to see us and brought with him an invitation from Nezuhu Ertigan [Nesuhi Ertegun], the son of the Turkish Ambassador to the United States (who, by the way, really has his boots zipped to the hip), to attend a "jam" session at the Embassy where we were all invited to "cut a Turkish rug." So we "jammed" until the "wee" hours of the morning—all in the cause of cementing Turkish-American good will with American "jam." But I can't write about that without the approval of the Department of State.[70]

His second-most-frequent Washington venue was the White House, with a total of seven visits, either to perform or be acknowledged. Prior to the term of Lyndon Johnson, Ellington's treatment by the White House was off-putting if not sometimes downright insulting, though Ellington never said anything publicly about it. In 1932 the black press carried stories that Ellington had been received at the White House by President Herbert Hoover. "Duke is the first colored entertainer ever to be received by the chief executive of the nation," the *Norfolk Journal and Guide* proclaimed with pride.[71] Such stories, however, were untrue. Accompanied by a "Welcome Home Committee," Ellington went to the White House, but Hoover refused to come out and meet him. The African American press accused Hoover of being afraid to be photographed with black visitors. "Hoover has covered more than half of his term and his record of never posing with a colored delegation is still intact," wrote Ralph Matthews in *The Afro-American* newspaper. "He does not know that only the jazz sent over the air nightly by such chaps as Ellington and his ilk have helped America endure the Hoover administration and weather the depression."[72] Undeterred, Ellington kept wanting to secure an audience with the president, and finally, on September 29, 1950, he presented the score of his new work, "Harlem," to President Harry S. Truman at the White House.[73]

As a master of indirection, Ellington was not one to publicly protest racial segregation. When confronted with a racial affront, he once said, "I took the energy it takes to pout and wrote some blues."[74] By the early 1930s, he had become a race hero to many African Americans. The *Pittsburgh Courier* wrote in 1931, "As one of the foremost citizens of America he has gained world-wide prominence not only for his race and profession, but has symbolized his genius in the musical world as one of the greatest and most unique tributes to the fine intellect of the Negro professionally. . . . Duke Ellington is a man of whom we should all be proud."[75] But he did not use his prominence to agitate openly for racial justice. True to his upbringing, he preferred to rise above racial indignities, or circumvent them, to "command respect" for himself and his race through his many accomplishments. He composed works that in effect asserted "black is beautiful" long before that phrase became popular in the 1960s. These works included celebrations of black history and culture—"Black Beauty" (1928), "Echoes of Harlem" (1936), "Harlem Airshaft" (1940), *Black, Brown, and Beige: A Tone Parallel to the History of the Negro in America* (1943), the *Liberian Suite* (1947), *Symphony in Black* (1935), *Harlem* (1951), "My People" (1963), *La plus belle Africaine* (1966), and *Togo Brava Suite* (1971)—and compositions honoring African American cultural heroes, such as Martin Luther King Jr., in "King Fit the Battle of Alabam'" (1963) as well as "A Portrait of Louis Armstrong" and "A Portrait of Mahalia Jackson" (both movements of his *New Orleans Suite*, 1970).

President Kennedy's White House snubbed Ellington. In May 1962 Ellington was one of the featured performers at the First Annual International Jazz Festival, which was held in Washington. Ellington was given the keys to the city and driven up Pennsylvania Avenue; his party stopped in front of the White House, in expectation of a visit or a photo opportunity with the president. The *New York Times* reported, "President Serenaded," but that was untrue. Nobody came out to greet or pose with Ellington. Perhaps the president did not wish to be seen with a group of black men for fear of alienating southern voters.[76]

Things improved under Kennedy's successor, Lyndon B. Johnson. In 1965 the Ellington orchestra performed at the White House Festival of the Arts. During President Johnson's years in office, Ellington went to the White House seven times for official functions or to perform.[77]

Other Washingtonians of influence promoted and honored him. The leadership of the Voice of America (VOA), the international shortwave broadcasting service of the US government, realized that jazz was a powerful tool for presenting the best of American culture to people around the world. The VOA's Willis Conover often played Ellington recordings and periodically interviewed him; Conover used Ellington's recording of his signature tune, "Take the 'A' Train," as the theme song of his popular radio program. The *New York Times* praised Conover's typical "extended biographies in sound—10 hours with Duke Ellington, for instance."[78] The US State Department sent the Ellington orchestra on goodwill tours, beginning in 1963, to dozens of countries, where he typically found enthusiastic audiences, many primed by years of VOA broadcasts.[79]

On the evening of the inauguration of President Richard M. Nixon in January 1969, the Ellington orchestra performed at the Smithsonian's Museum of History and Technology (now the National Museum of American History), while Guy Lombardo's band played on the lower level.[80]

On the occasion of his seventieth birthday—April 29, 1969—Ellington was honored and feted at the White House. President Richard M. Nixon presented Ellington with the nation's highest civilian honor, the Presidential Medal of Freedom, at a star-studded ceremony. In a remark that became oft-quoted, Ellington said, "There is no place I would rather be tonight except in my mother's arms."[81] Nixon winningly declared, "In the royalty of American music, no man swings more or stands higher than the Duke." Ellington kissed Nixon twice on each cheek. "Four kisses?" asked the president. "Why four?" "One for each cheek," Ellington replied. Nixon was momentarily dumbfounded.[82]

This particular event may have seemed to Ellington rich in meanings, associations, and ironies as well as sweetness. As ovations go, it was the capstone of his career. The ten-block journey from his birthplace to this White House occasion took Ellington seventy years and about ten million miles of travel.

But two events earlier in the 1960s had shaken Ellington and changed his feelings toward his hometown. In 1960 Harmony Cemetery was closed and its thirty-seven thousand graves were transferred to suburban Maryland.[83] Officials told Ellington that he had

Photo 3.3 *President Nixon presents Ellington with the Presidential Medal of Freedom*
President Richard Nixon presents Ellington with the Presidential Medal of Freedom on
April 29, 1969, Duke's seventieth birthday, during a gala tribute at the White House.

to dig up his parents' graves or else lose them. According to Ruth Ellington, after that, her
brother "had a completely different feeling about Washington. It was as if Washington
had disinherited him." Mercer Ellington also recalled his father's unhappiness about this
incident.[84] Ellington had his parents' caskets transferred to Woodlawn Cemetery in the
Bronx.

Six years later, he received another slap in the face. On December 5, 1966, Ellington
returned to his hometown to perform his innovative and now-revered Concert of Sacred Music at the famous Constitution Hall. Reflecting traditional religious views of
sacred and secular music, however, the 250-member Baptist Ministers Conference of
Washington went on record as "refusing to endorse the concert." Some complained his
music was too "wordly." His publicist, Joe Morgen, said, "This is the first time a thing
like this ever happened to him. He's 67 and he's upset. This is his hometown, and these
are ministers criticizing him." The show went on, though the house was not much more
than half full.[85]

His last visit to his hometown was for a Georgetown University concert in February
1974, when he was very ill with lung cancer. Less than four months later, he was gone.
Ellington died in New York on May 24, 1974, just a few weeks after his seventy-fifth
birthday. He is buried next to his father and mother at Woodlawn Cemetery in the Bronx,
where Ellington had purchased fourteen plots for the Ellington family. Later his sister,
Ruth, and son, Mercer, would join him and his parents.

After Ellington's death in 1974, his star continued to rise. In 1995 New York City's
Jazz at Lincoln Center established the Essentially Ellington High School Band Contest

Photo 3.4 *Ellington and Band at Howard Theatre*
The Howard Theatre was a frequent venue for Duke Ellington and his band, seen
here on stage in the 1940s, and they usually played two or more shows a day.

to stimulate interest in his music among young people. But much of the recognition
of Ellington came from his native Washington. Western High School was renamed the
Duke Ellington High School for the Arts; a bridge over Rock Creek Park was named for
him; a statue of him was erected outside the newly restored Howard Theatre; a giant
mural of him decorates the side of True Reformer building; and a tiny triangle of land
at M and Twenty-First Streets, NW, has been named Duke Ellington Plaza. The Public
Broadcasting Service, headquartered in the Washington area, has broadcast two docu-
mentaries about him, and public radio presented several commemorative series during
his centennial year, 1999.

Elements of the federal government have taken the lead. In 1986 the U.S. Postal Service issued a commemorative stamp in his honor, and in 2009, the U.S. Mint honored
Ellington on a quarter—the first African American to appear by himself on a circulating
U.S. coin. Arguably the highest recognition in his hometown has come at the Smithsonian Institution's National Museum of American History, which in 1988 acquired about
one hundred thousand pages of his unpublished music, another one hundred thousand
pages of documents, and five hundred artifacts. The availability of Ellington's collection
greatly stimulated public interest in him and, by making his music much more available
for performance and research, sparked a rising valuation of his legacy. The collection has
drawn researchers from around the world and found its way into doctoral dissertations

and books, radio series, concert programs, and a half dozen Smithsonian exhibitions. Among the prized artifacts in the Ellington Collection is the symbolically potent Presidential Medal of Freedom he was awarded at the White House—a building his father had entered via the servants' door and Duke Ellington proudly entered through the visitors' entrance.

Notes

For their kind help with research, the author wishes to thank Theodore H. Hudson, Franz Jantzen, and Andrew Greene.

1. Duke Ellington, interview by Michael Parkinson on *The Parkinson Show*, BBC TV, 1973, courtesy the National Sound Archives, the British Library, as quoted in Stuart Nicholson, *Reminiscing in Tempo: A Portrait of Duke Ellington* (Boston: Northeastern University Press, 1999), 4.

2. Rayford W. Logan, *Betrayal of the Negro: From Rutherford B. Hayes to Woodrow Wilson* (New York: Collier Books, 1965), 74; and Constance McLaughlin Green, *The Secret City: A History of Race Relations in the Nation's Capital* (Princeton: Princeton University Press, 1967), 119–54.

3. Quoted in Green, *Secret City*, 173.

4. Harvey G. Cohen, *Duke Ellington's America* (Chicago: University of Chicago Press, 2010), 10–11.

5. Kathryn S. Smith, "Remembering U Street," *Washington History* 9 (Fall/Winter, 1997/1998): 35.

6. Paul Laurence Dunbar, "Negro Life in Washington," *Harper's Weekly*, January 13, 1900, 32.

7. Cohen, *Duke Ellington's America*, 10.

8. Green, *Secret City*, 141. While Green's description here is specifically about Washington's black population in the late nineteenth century, these divisions were largely still in place during Ellington's youth.

9. John Edward Hasse, *Beyond Category: The Life and Genius of Duke Ellington* (New York: Simon & Schuster, 1993), 31–32.

10. Edward Kennedy Ellington, *Music Is My Mistress* (1973; repr., Da Capo, 1976), 17.

11. Theodore Hudson, personal communication, December 12, 1992.

12. Ellington, *Music Is My Mistress*, 53–54.

13. Barry Ulanov, *Duke Ellington* (1946; repr., New York: Da Capo, 1975), 13.

14. Mark Tucker, *Ellington: The Early Years* (Urbana: University of Illinois Press, 1991), 24–25.

15. Ruth Ellington Boatwright, interview by Marcia Greenlee, Duke Ellington Oral History Project, Archives Center, National Museum of American History, Smithsonian Institution, August 18, 1989, 49.

16. Ellington, *Music Is My Mistress*, 45.

17. Ibid., 6, 15.

18. Ibid., 10.

19. Smith, "Remembering U Street," 33; see also Blair Ruble, *Washington's U Street: A Biography* (Washington, DC: Woodrow Wilson Centre Press; Baltimore: Johns Hopkins University Press, 2010).

20. Rex Stewart, *Boy Meets Horn*, ed. Claire P. Gordon (Ann Arbor: University of Michigan Press), 34.

21. Theodore Hudson, personal communication, December 12, 1992.

22. Tucker, *Ellington*, 23.

23. Duke Ellington, interview by Carter Harman, Carter Harman Interview Collection, 1964, Archives Center, National Museum of American History, Smithsonian Institution, as quoted in Nicholson, *Reminiscing in Tempo*, 14.

24. Tucker, *Ellington*, 23.

25. Ellington, *Music Is My Mistress*, 23.

26. Ibid., 17, 23. For additional information on Holliday's poolroom, see Rebecca Sheir, "The Location: The Pool Hall That Inspired the Father of D.C. Jazz," WAMU *Metro Connection*, August 16, 2013, http://wamu.org/story/13/08/16/the_location_the_pool_hall_that_inspired _father_of_dc_jazz/; and Richard Brownell, "Duke Ellington's Education at Frank Holliday's Pool Hall," *Boundary Stones* (blog), November 8, 2016, https://blogs.weta.org/boundarystones/2016 /11/08/duke-ellington%E2%80%99s-education-frank-hollidays-pool-hall. Two books shed light on African American railroad porters and their importance to black culture: Larry Tye, *Rising from the Rails: Pullman Porters and the Making of the Black Middle Class* (New York: Henry Holt, 2004), and Martha A. Sandweiss, *Passing Strange: A Gilded Age Tale of Love and Deception across the Color Line* (New York: Penguin, 2009).

27. Cohen, *Duke Ellington's America*, 9.

28. Ellington, *Music Is My Mistress*, 12.

29. Hollie I. West, "The Duke at 70: Honor from the President," *Washington Post*, April 27, 1969, K10.

30. Ellington, interview by Carter Harman, 1964.

31. Jacqueline M. Moore, *Leading the Race: The Transformation of the Black Elite in the Nation's Capital, 1880–1920* (Charlottesville: University of Virginia Press, 1999), 21.

32. Tucker, *Ellington*, 24.

33. Sandra Fitzpatrick and Maria R. Goodwin, *The Guide to Black Washington: Places and Events of Historical and Cultural Significance in the Nation's Capital* (New York: Hippocrene Books, 199), 88–89.

34. Mercer Ellington with Stanley Dance, *Duke Ellington in Person: An Intimate Memoir* (1978; repr., New York: Da Capo, 1979), 9.

35. Solomon Fabricant, with Julius Shiskin, *The Output of Manufacturing Industries, 1899–1937* (New York: National Bureau of Economic Research, 1940), 597.

36. Ellington, interview by Carter Harman, 1964, as quoted in Nicholson, *Reminiscing in Tempo*, 6.

37. Ellington, *Music Is My Mistress*, 26.

38. Ibid., 24.

39. Gwen Dobson, "Luncheon with . . . Duke Ellington," *Washington Evening Star*, April 23, 1971.

40. Sanford Socolow, "The Summer Job I Had as a Boy," *Esquire*, June 1958, 55, 66.

41. Brooks Kerr, telephone interview by the author, September 1, 1991.

42. Rex Stewart, *Jazz Masters of the Thirties* (New York: Macmillan, 1972), 81–82.

43. Ellington, *Music Is My Mistress*, 20; Ellington, press conference, April 29, 1962, Voice of America collection, Library of Congress, as quoted in Nicholson, *Reminiscing in Tempo*, 13. The name of Ellington's high school pal is spelled variously. In Ellington's *Music Is My Mistress*, it's McEntree; in Nicholson's *Reminiscing in Tempo*, it's McIntree; in Cohen's *Duke Ellington's America*, it's McEntry.

44. Bernice Wiggins and Juanita Middleton, interview by Mark Tucker, September 6, 1983, Oral History of American Music, Yale University Special Collections, #551, as quoted in Cohen, *Duke Ellington's America*, 16.

45. Ellington, *Music Is My Mistress*, 22.

46. Stewart, *Boy Meets Horn*, 33.

47. Tucker, *Ellington*, 44.

48. Ellington, *Music Is My Mistress*, x.

49. Tucker, *Ellington*, 45–46.

50. Ellington, *Music Is My Mistress*, 22.

51. Ibid., 32.

52. Tucker, *Ellington*, 51. Conaway's name also appears as Conway. He played both guitar and banjo.

53. Nicholson, *Reminiscing in Tempo*, 19.

54. Tucker, *Ellington*, 53.

55. Hasse, *Beyond Category*, 129–30.

56. Ellington, *Music Is My Mistress*, 33.

57. Tucker, *Ellington*, 61.

58. Stewart, *Jazz Masters of the Thirties*, 81–82.

59. Nicholson, *Reminiscing in Tempo*, 26, citing an article in *Swing*, May 1940, 10.

60. Ibid., 24.

61. Stewart, *Boy Meets Horn*, 33.

62. Ibid.

63. Stewart, *Jazz Masters of the Thirties*, 81. The band consisted of a saxophonist-leader named "Tobin," string bassist Otto Hardwick, and a drummer called "Stickamackum," or "Sticks."

64. Sonny Greer, interview by Stanley Crouch, January 1979, Smithsonian Institution Jazz Oral History Project, courtesy the Institute of Jazz Studies, Rutgers University.

65. Ellington, *Music Is My Mistress*, 35–36.

66. Klaus Stratemann, *Duke Ellington, Day by Day and Film by Film* (Copenhagen: JazzMedia, 1992), 25; and Ken Vail, *Duke's Diary: The Life of Duke Ellington, 1927–1950* (Lanham, MD: Scarecrow Press, 2002), 36. The visit to Baltimore was mentioned in the *Baltimore Afro-American*, December 14, 1929.

67. "Mother of Duke Ellington Is Buried in DC. Wednesday," *Afro-American*, June 8, 1935, 14.

68. G.E.V., unidentified newspaper clipping, evidently September 1931, in Duke Ellington Publicity Scrapbooks, Series 8, reel 1, page 9, Duke Ellington Collection, Archives Center, National Museum of American History, Smithsonian Institution. Ticket prices for this Howard engagement were: Matinee, orchestra 40¢, balcony 30¢; Evening, orchestra 60¢, balcony 40¢; Midnight, orchestra $1.00, balcony 75¢.

69. Carolyn Bell, "Nesuhi Ertegun, Hepcat: Son of Turkish Envoy Says Jazz Is U.S. Classic," *Washington Post*, August 29, 1942, B4.

70. Duke Ellington, "The Duke Takes Pen in Hand," *Norfolk New Journal and Guide*, August 1, 1942, 16. William Gottlieb wrote a column, "Swing Session," for the *Washington Post* and took many photographs of jazz musicians in Washington and in New York City. His photograph collection is now housed at the Library of Congress. For more on the Ertegun brothers' pioneering work in jazz, see John Edward Hasse, "How the Turkish Ambassador's Sons Jazzed Washington and the Nation," in *The Turkish Ambassador's Residence and the Cultural History of Washington, DC*, ed. Skip Moskey, Caroline Mesrobian Hickman, and John Edward Hasse (Istanbul: Istanbul Kültür University, 2013), 107.

71. "The Duke after White House Visit," *Norfolk Journal and Gazette*, October 31, 1931, 29; see also "Duke Meets Herb at White House," *Philadelphia Tribune*, October 15, 1931, 7; and "When the Duke Met Hoover," *Afro-American*, October 24, 1931, 23.

72. "Where's Hoover's Picture? As Usual the President 'Sidestepped' Being Photographed with Visitors of Color," *Cleveland Gazette*, October 10, 1931; and Ralph Matthews, "Looking at the Stars," *Afro-American*, October 10, 1931, 9.

73. Hasse, *Beyond Category*, 296–97.

74. George T. Simon, *The Big Bands*, 4th ed. (New York: Schirmer Books, 1981), 187.

75. "Duke's Home Town Pays Him Fine Tribute as He Returns with Band," *Pittsburgh Courier*, October 3, 1931, 18.

76. Cohen, *Duke Ellington's America*, 422–23.

77. Ellington, *Music Is My Mistress*, 428, 476; see also Edward Allan Faine, *Duke Ellington at the White House 1969* (Takoma Park, MD: IM Press, 2013).

78. Jack Gould, "Jazz on a 'Global Scale': Willis Conover Heard in Eighty Foreign Countries over Radio Broadcasts by 'Voice of America' Network," *New York Times*, October 21, 1962.

79. When Ellington turned seventy-five and was gravely ill, the State Department, Voice of America, and United States Information Agency went into high gear, offering photo exhibitions, radio programs, magazine articles, and film screenings to people around the world; see Cohen, *Duke Ellington's America*, 575.

80. ". . . And Dancing Through the Night: An At-Ease, Low-Keyed Nixon Goes Out on the Town," *Washington Post*, January 21, 1969, D1, D3. Lombardo led a popular dance (as opposed to jazz) band, one that many jazz musicians considered unhip or "square." It is highly likely that the two bandleaders greeted and spoke with each other, and no doubt Ellington turned on his usual charm.

81. Ellington, *Duke Ellington in Person*, 287.

82. George, *Big Bands*, 184; see also Ellington, *Music Is My Mistress*, 427.

83. "Workers Start to Clear 100-Year-Old Cemetery," *Washington Post*, May 24, 1960.

84. Cohen, *Duke Ellington's America*, 423.

85. Phil Casey, "The Duke Will Play Despite Rebuff," *Washington Post*, December 3, 1966.

Table 3.1. *Synoptic Timeline of Duke Ellington's Early Years in Washington, DC*

Year	National/World Events	Musical Events	Washington, DC, Events	Ellington Life Events
1899	US begins "Open Door" policy with China.	"Maple Leaf Rag" by Scott Joplin published, eventually selling over a million copies.		Duke Ellington is born on April 29 at his parents' residence, 2129 Ward Place, NW. Ellington's father begins work as a driver.
1900	Hawaii becomes a US territory. US population reaches 75 million.	Philadelphia Orchestra founded.	Washington has 87,000 black citizens (31% of the total population), the largest black population of any American city, yet they include only 400 teachers, 90 ministers, 50 physicians, 30 lawyers, and 10 dentists.	
1901	President William McKinley is shot; Theodore Roosevelt succeeds him.	Louis Armstrong is born in New Orleans.	McMillan Commission plans development of National Mall from Capitol to Lincoln Memorial.	James Ellington family moves to 1462 Rhode Island Avenue, NW.
1902	First US motion picture theater is established.	"Bill Bailey, Won't You Please Come Home" and "In the Good Old Summertime" are published.		Ellington family moves to 1104 23rd Street, NW.
1903	Wright brothers make their first airplane flight. W. E. B. Du Bois publishes his influential *The Souls of Black Folk*.	Enrico Caruso makes first recordings for the Victor Company. Columbia introduces first flat records.	The Washington Conservatory is established. Many Conservatory students would have connections with Ellington, including singer Ernest Amos, his high school music teacher.	Ellington's father begins work as a butler. Ellington family moves to 1812 20th Street, NW
1904	The St. Louis World's Fair is open from April to December.	"Meet Me in St. Louis, Louis" and "Give My Regards to Broadway" become hit songs.		
1905	First neon light signs are used.	"In My Merry Oldsmobile" and "Wait 'til the Sun Shines, Nellie" become hit songs.		Ellington enters Garnet Elementary School.
1906		"Anchors Aweigh" is published.	The District Building, on 14th Street and Pennsylvania Avenue, becomes the official City Hall.	Ellington begins taking piano lessons with Marietta Harvey (née Clinkscales), but ultimately quits. Ellington family moves to 420 Elm Street, NW.

(continued)

Table 3.1. *Continued*

Year	National/World Events	Musical Events	Washington, DC, Events	Ellington Life Events
1907	Oklahoma becomes a state.	"The Caissons Go Rolling Along" is published.	Construction of Washington National Cathedral begins.	Ellington family moves to 1532 Columbia Street, NW.
1908	Ford introduces the Model T. Jack Johnson becomes world heavyweight champion William Howard Taft is elected president.	"Take Me Out to the Ball Game" and "Shine On, Harvest Moon" are hit songs.	Union Station, largest in nation, is dedicated.	Ellington family moves to 2107 Pennsylvania Avenue, NW.
1909	The National Association for the Advancement of Colored People is established in New York City. Robert Peary reaches North Pole.	Piano sales hit an all-time high in the United States.	Orville Wright demonstrates flight for the federal government.	Ellington family moves to 1206 T Street, NW.
1910	Pennsylvania Station opens in New York.	Hit songs include "Down by the Old Mill Stream" and "Some of These Days."	Blacks make up 28.5% of Washington's population. The Howard Theatre opens at 620 T Street, NW. Ellington would see many of its featured performers and eventually would appear there himself.	Ellington family moves to 1805 13th Street, NW.
1911	Roald Amundsen reaches South Pole.	Songwriter Irving Berlin publishes "Alexander's Ragtime Band."	Smithsonian's Natural History Museum opens. National Park (later renamed Griffith Stadium) opens as home for the Senators baseball team.	Ellington enters Garnet Junior High School.
1912	Arizona and New Mexico become states. RMS Titanic sinks, killing 1,513.	Flat records replace cylinders. W. C. Handy's "Memphis Blues" is published.	Washington chapter of NAACP opens. Cherry trees planted in Tidal Basin.	
1913	Woodrow Wilson is inaugurated as president, moves to segregate civil service. Ford introduces moving assembly line.	The term "jazz" first appears in a San Francisco newspaper. Tango dancing craze sweeps the United States. Stravinsky's "Rite of Spring" causes near-riot in Paris.	Woman Suffrage Parade is held on Pennsylvania Avenue, NW.	Ellington's friend Edgar McIntree gives him the nickname "Duke." Ellington enters Armstrong Technical High School to pursue commercial art.

(continued)

Table 3.1. *Continued*

Year	National/World Events	Musical Events	Washington, DC, Events	Ellington Life Events
1914	World War I begins in Europe. Panama Canal opens.	W. C. Handy's "St. Louis Blues" is published.	Lincoln Memorial construction begins. Future Ellington cornetist Rex Stewart moves to Washington.	Ellington family moves to 1816 13th Street, NW. Ellington receives a D in his high school music class.
1915	D. W. Griffith's film *The Birth of a Nation* opens.	Jelly Roll Morton's "Jelly Roll Blues" is published. Ukulele becomes popular.	Carter G. Woodson founds the Association for the Study of Negro Life and History.	Duke's sister, Ruth, born in Washington.
1916	Einstein issues first theory of relativity.	President Wilson issues an executive order making "The Star-Spangled Banner" the national anthem.		Ellington turns down a scholarship to study art at Brooklyn's Pratt Institute so that he can stay in Washington and pursue music.
1917	US enters World War I. President Wilson begins second term. Russian Revolution.	Original Dixieland Jazz Band records the album *Livery Stable Blues*, the first jazz recording.	Population grows with an influx of war workers.	Ellington family moves to 1703 8th Street, NW. Ellington drops out of high school to begin his career as a professional musician, forming his own group, The Duke's Serenaders.
1918	World War I ends. Global influenza pandemic begins; during 1918–19, 20 to 40 million people die worldwide.	Irving Berlin's "Oh! How I Hate to Get Up in the Morning" is published. Worldwide record sales reach 100 million.		Ellington moves out of his parents' home to 1955 3rd Street, NW, obtains a telephone, and lists himself as "musician" in the telephone directory. He marries his neighborhood sweetheart, Edna Thompson.
1919	Prohibition ratified in United States by constitutional amendment. First nonstop transatlantic flight occurs. "Red scare" grips the United States	George Gershwin's "Swanee" is published. Cornetist Joe "King" Oliver moves from New Orleans to Chicago.	"Red Summer" race riots result in at least seven dead and hundreds injured.	Ellington begins booking his own dates and playing at high-class venues such as embassies and fox-hunt balls and does well enough that he can purchase a car and a house. Ellington's son, Mercer, is born. Duke Ellington family moves to 2728 Sherman Avenue, NW.

(continued)

Table 3.1. *Continued*

Year	National/World Events	Musical Events	Washington, DC, Events	Ellington Life Events
1920	Warren G. Harding is elected president. The United States grants women suffrage. First US commercial radio stations begin broadcasting.	Mamie Smith's *Crazy Blues* becomes first issued "race record."	Blacks make up 25% of Washington's population. The Howard Theatre becomes the center of Washington's black musical life, with multiple bands competing each night for applause. Duke's Serenaders often win these contests.	At the Howard Theatre, Ellington meets Juan Tizol, a Puerto Rican–born valve trombonist who would join Ellington's orchestra in 1929.
1921	Emergency Quota Act restricts immigration to the United States.	Revue *Shuffle Along* opens, first all-black Broadway show. James P. Johnson's virtuosic "Carolina Shout" is published.	The Phillips Collection opens.	Ellington plays "Carolina Shout" for composer James P. Johnson at Convention Hall. Johnson is so impressed that he and Ellington tour Washington's southwest district through the rest of that night.
1922		Kid Ory's Original Creole Band is the first African American jazz group to record. Louis Armstrong moves to Chicago.	At the opening of the Lincoln Memorial, blacks are forced to sit in roped-off areas across a dirt road. Lincoln Colonnade ballroom opens in basement of the Lincoln Theater.	
1923	President Harding dies, succeeded by Calvin Coolidge.	Both Louis Armstrong and Jelly Roll Morton make their first recordings. Player piano sales reach all-time peak in the United States.	Freer Galley of Art opens.	Duke Ellington's address is listed at 1212 T Street, NW, the address of his parents. Ellington moves to New York, initially to play alongside clarinetist Wilbur Sweatman and drummer Sonny Greer.
1924		George Gershwin composes "Rhapsody in Blue."	The Key Bridge, over the Potomac River, is opened. C&O Canal ceases operations.	

Table 3.2. *Ellington's Return Engagements in Washington, DC*

Year	Date	Venue	Purpose
1931	Sept. 26–Oct. 2	Howard Theatre	Stage show, perhaps his first DC performance since leaving for New York in 1923; broadcast most nights on WJSV radio[a]
	Oct. 10–16	Howard Theatre	Stage show
	Oct. 12	Masonic Temple	NAACP charity affair, played after his Howard show
1932	Jan. 16–22	Earle Theatre	Stage show with a whites-only audience, billed as "20 Entertainers from Harlem"
	Apr. 30–May 6	Howard Theatre	Stage show
	Oct. 28–Nov. 3	Fox Theatre[b]	Stage show for a whites-only audience
	Dec. 2–9	Howard Theatre	Stage show, "farewell performance, before sailing for Europe"
1934	Feb. 9–15	Howard Theatre	Stage show, with dancer Earl "Snakehips" Tucker
	Oct. 21	Earle Theatre	During Paul Ash's stage show, Ellington went onstage to play "Sophisticated Lady"
	Nov. 9–15	Fox Theatre	Stage show for a white-only audience
	Nov. 9	WJSV Studios	Benefit for Community Chest
	Nov. 30–Dec. 6	Howard Theatre	Stage show, a revue with "40 stars" alternating with the movie *Pursued*
1935	Oct. 18–24	Howard Theatre	Stage show, with the dancer Bessie Dudley
	Dec. 13–19	Fox Theatre	Stage show, for a whites-only audience
1936	Oct. 2–8	Howard Theatre	Stage show
1937	Oct. 1–7	Howard Theatre	Stage show, with a "cast of 40"
1940	June 2	Howard Theatre	DC's first swing concert, with MC Bill Gottlieb, *Washington Post* writer
	June 2	*Robert E. Lee* boat	Cruise on *Cross Keys*, a Potomac River boat, billed as "8:30 till dawn"
1942	Feb. 27–Mar. 5	Howard Theatre	Stage show
	Dec. 4–10	Howard Theatre	Stage show
1943	Mar. 5	Howard University	Award ceremony, where Ellington received trophy from students
	Mar. 7	Turner's Arena	Dance
	Oct. 6	Uline Arena[c]	Stage show, drawing 6,000 people
	Dec. 6	Uline Arena	Concert
1944	Dec. 3	Turner's Arena	Dance
1946	Mar. 17	Turner's Arena	Dance
	Apr. 19–25	Howard Theatre	Stage show, alternating with movie *The Spider*
	Apr. 20	Howard Theatre	NBC Radio broadcast
	June 6	Junior Police and Citizens' Corps	Two jam sessions: one at their outdoor arena, one at their offices
	June 6	Watergate[d]	Watergate's first concert by a black artist, drawing recording-breaking 11,000 people
1947	Feb. 21–27	Howard Theatre	Stage show, with singers Kay Davis and Al Hibbler
	June 13	Watergate	Concert
	Nov. 16	Turner's Arena	Dance

(continued)

Table 3.2. *Continued*

Year	Date	Venue	Purpose
1948	Mar. 26–Apr. 1	Howard Theatre	Stage show, alternating with movie *Dick Tracy Versus Cueball*
	Oct. 22–31	Club Ellington	Dinner-dance for opening at a night club named for Ellington
1950	Sept. 22–28	Howard Theatre	Stage show, with comic Dusty Fletcher
	Sept. 29	White House	Presentation of a copy of *Harlem* by Ellington to President Truman
1951	July 6–12	Howard Theatre	Stage show
	Oct. 21	National Guard Armory	Stage show, billed as "The Biggest Show of 1951"
1952	Oct. 3–9	Howard Theatre	Stage show, with a "giant revue"
1954	Feb. 12–18	Howard Theatre	Stage show, with the Flamingos
1955	Apr. 20	National Guard Armory	Benefit concert
	Sept. 15–22	Howard Theatre	Stage show, also including comedienne Moms Mabley
1956	Oct. 25	Constitution Hall	Concert with National Symphony Orchestra, featuring Ellington and his rhythm section only
1960	Feb. 5	National Guard Armory	Mardi Gras Ball, for Omega Psi fraternity
1961	Mar. 20	National Guard Armory	Ball, from 10 p.m. to 2 a.m.
1962	Feb. 4	Bolling Air Force Base	Dance, held in Officers Club
	Apr. 20–26	Howard Theatre	Stage show, with dancer Bunny Briggs; four shows a day
	May 31	NBC-TV studios	Interview for *Patti Cavern Show*
	May 31	Constitution Hall	"Symphonic jazz" concert, the kickoff of the First International Jazz Festival
	June 1	Coliseum	"Jazz at the Coliseum" concert, including Sonny Rollins Quartet, Cannonball Adderley Quintet, and others
	June 2	Cramton Hall, Howard University	Afternoon concert, including Thelonious Monk, Oscar Peterson, Dave Brubeck, Lionel Hampton, and others
	June 2	Cramton Hall	"Jazz for the Small Ensemble" concert (evening), including a 22-minute program by Ellington and his trio and featuring Sonny Rollins Quartet, Gerry Mulligan Quartet, and others
	June 3	Constitution Hall	Afternoon concert, also featuring Dave Brubeck, George Shearing, Gloria Lynne, and others
1963	Mar. 31	Bolling Air Force Base	Dance
1964	Mar. 22	Sheraton-Park Hotel	Black-tie dinner for White House Correspondents Association, with President Johnson, 2,000 others
	May 29	Washington Coliseum	Benefit concert, promoted by Capital Cab Company
	Dec. 13	Bolling Air Force Base	Dance

(continued)

Table 3.2. *Continued*

Year	Date	Venue	Purpose
1965	May 30	Shoreham Hotel	Concert for International Publishers Association
	June 4	White House	Attendance at a reception and an interview by Voice of America
	June 14	White House	White House Festival of the Arts, also featuring Gene Kelly, Charlton Heston, Marian Anderson, and others
1966	Mar. 20	Sheraton-Park Hotel	Second Annual Washington Jazz Festival, also featuring Billy Eckstine, Mongo Santamaria, and Oscar Peterson
	Apr. 24	Bolling Air Force Base	A dance, also featuring Washington vocalists June Norton and Jimmy MacPhail
	July 4–10	Carter Barron Amphitheatre	Nightly concerts, sharing the bill with Ella Fitzgerald
	Dec. 5	Constitution Hall	Concert of Sacred Music, criticized by Baptist ministers' convention
	Dec. 15	White House	Christmas dinner, also featuring Washington vocalists June Norton and Jimmy MacPhail
	Dec. 30	Willard Hotel	Dance
1967	Mar. 11	Statler Hilton Hotel	"Bal de Futur," dinner-dance for the Mental Health Association
1967	June 27	White House	State dinner honoring the king and queen of Thailand, during which Ellington performed "Take the 'A' Train"
	July 3–9	Carter Barron Amphitheatre	Stage show, with Ella Fitzgerald and Jazz at the Philharmonic bands
	July 6	Lorton Reformatory[e]	Special afternoon concert for 1,000 inmates
1968	Mar. 27	White House	State dinner for President William S. Tubman of Liberia, during which Ellington performed with his octet
	Nov. 9	National Guard Armory	Concert and presentation of a plaque by Mayor Walter Washington to Ellington
	Nov. 21	White House	A solo performance by Ellington and the beginning of a six-year term on the National Council of the Arts
1969	Jan. 20	Smithsonian Institution[f]	Inaugural ball for President Nixon, during which Ellington performed on second floor and Guy Lombardo on ground floor
	Apr. 29	White House	Ceremony and birthday celebration for Ellington, during which President Nixon presented Ellington the Presidential Medal of Freedom
	Aug. 25	Elks Lodge	Award ceremony to present Ellington the Lovejoy Order of the Elks
	Aug. 31	Constitution Hall	Concert
1970	Mar. 11	US Capitol	Press conference to announce fund-raising concerts on Mar. 14–15
	Mar. 14–15	National Presbyterian Church and Center	Concert of Sacred Music, one concert each day
	Oct. 2	Constitution Hall	Concert

(continued)

Table 3.2. *Continued*

Year	Date	Venue	Purpose
1971	Feb. 14	Bolling Air Force Base	Dance
	Apr. 20–26	Blue Room, Shoreham Hotel	Two shows nightly, at 9:00 p.m. and 11:30 p.m.
	May 10	Constitution Hall	Concert to benefit Wolf Trap Farm Park, also featuring Nancy Wilson
1973	Aug. 26	Sheraton-Park Hotel	Dance for the Zeta Phi Beta sorority
	Oct. 3	John F. Kennedy Center	Concert
1974	Feb. 10	Georgetown University	Two concerts
	Feb. 11	Hawthorne School	Sat in on Marian McPartland's jazz education class

[a] During this visit, Ellington went to Arlington National Cemetery to pay his respects at the grave of Lt. James Reese Europe, an important figure in the transition from ragtime to jazz, who was also educated in Washington's public schools.

[b] Later renamed the Warner Theatre.

[c] Later renamed the Washington Coliseum.

[d] The Watergate was a band shell on a barge anchored on the Potomac River near the Lincoln Memorial.

[e] Located in Lorton, Virginia, near Washington, DC.

[f] The event was held at the National Museum of History and Technology, later renamed the National Museum of American History.

4 Bill Brower

Notes from a Keen Observer and Scene Maker

Interview by Willard Jenkins

For the past forty-plus years jazz historian Bill Brower, a native of Toledo, Ohio, has been a true DC jazz community renaissance man. He has been a jazz journalist-critic, occasional broadcaster, an event technical producer, and a concert, festivals, and jazz event producer. We interviewed Bill one afternoon in his Northeast DC kitchen, a few short steps from a room packed with records, CDs, and books on jazz and various sundry subjects.

When did you arrive in DC and what brought you here?

Bill Brower: I came here in the summer of 1971 after a series of coincidences that involved Tom Porter, then dean of the Antioch Putney Graduate School of Education based in DC. I graduated from Antioch [College] in the spring of 1971. A friend of mine from the Antioch days, Archie Hunter, came through that spring and said, "Why don't we go to Brooklyn and hang out at the African festival?" I was on my way to Brooklyn, Archie's car broke down, and I decided to go to DC and hang out with Tom; I'd known him since I was a sophomore at Antioch.

Tom quipped, "You're in Dayton, the *New York Times* comes a day late, and there's no music. You need to bring your butt to DC." Long story short, when my then-wife came back from California, I said, "Hey, we're moving to DC."

What was your experience on the jazz scene in DC in your earliest days here?

My first real DC job was as a community organizer, and that actually led to one of my earliest jazz experiences. I was working for the Washington Urban League coordinating a group called Government Employees United Against Racial Discrimination that . . . had various anti discrimination task forces within federal agencies. One of them was the Black Deputy US Marshal's organization, and Wallace Roney Sr. was their representative. We'd have these weekly meetings to discuss basic strategies and mutual interests—some were legalistic, some were direct action.

Wallace took me home one evening and, when he came up to my apartment, saw my living room full of records. He said, "I've got a son who's involved in jazz." That's when [trumpeter] Wallace Roney Jr. was at Duke Ellington School of the Arts. And because Senior traveled a lot, he needed someone to work with Wallace Jr. Wallace's early band had Clarence Seay on bass, Marshall Keys on sax, Geri Allen on piano, and Eric Allen was playing drums. . . . Some of them were in college. . . . Chuck Royal (trombone) and Kevin Berthaud (guitar) were in that band. [Wallace] had a lot of young, really good players. That's why [Wallace Sr.] needed me, because Wallace Jr. was at Duke Ellington; Marshall is a little bit older, he might have been in college. It was some high schoolers and some college-aged folks. They were playing [places] like the Pigfoot, Harold's Rogue & Jar, GW's student pub, venues that sold alcohol—that's where Wallace was getting gigs. So my job was to be the adult, to collect the money, watch the band. Kind of chaperone-manager.

What was the scene here like overall when you first got to DC?

I started collecting records when I was in junior high school and continued in college. When I got to DC I actually stayed with Tom Porter, and he introduced me to a bunch of other collectors like Bob Daughtry, and there was a legendary cat named Thomas Paul, who worked for what became Olsson's Books & Records. The first place I remember was a record store up Connecticut Avenue south of the Washington Hilton Hotel and there were two partners, Bob Bialick and John Olsson.

At one point Olsson split off. Thomas Paul was like the jazz guy at Olsson's. I fell into a group of cats that collected records, like Art Cromwell. Thomas Paul was our connection; we were like record junkies, if I can draw that analogy and not seem too pejorative. This was when Olsson's was across from what is now a SunTrust Bank at Dupont Circle, in the Dupont Circle building. Later on it became Olsson's Books & Records. Richard Goines was also a jazz buyer for Olsson's. Eventually I went to work for Olsson's in 1982, at Nineteenth and L, and I had a helluva jazz section. I was the jazz buyer there, and Richard was the jazz buyer at the Georgetown store. I did that maybe three or so years, until just after the first Capital City Jazz Festival in 1985.

Did that record store work open doors for you in the DC jazz community?

Before I started working in retail I was already writing [about jazz]. I started writing around 1974, with the *Washington Post* as a stringer. That didn't last long, so I had to decide whether I was still going to write or not. I had a jazz column for the *Afro-American* that went on for years. I started a column for the *Journal* newspapers, all jazz oriented. Then I had a jazz column for the *Washington Informer*, one of the two African American newspapers in the city at the time. I was also the Washington correspondent for *Down Beat*.

What aspect of jazz were you writing about for these local publications?

It was a combination of things—who's coming to town, almost like jazz notes. I might write a feature on somebody, it might be record oriented, I might do a bunch of short record reviews; it was a variety of things, whatever I wanted to do.

Where was the jazz being performed in DC at that time?

You had some venues on Rhode Island Avenue, like Mr. Why's, Moore's Love and Peace, the Pigfoot, Blues Alley in Georgetown, the Etcetera Club on M Street, the One Step Down, the Top of the Foolery, Harold's Rogue & Jar on N Street south of Dupont Circle.

Were these clubs that would feature mainly DC-resident musicians?

On the Rhode Island Avenue side, in Northeast where most of the black clubs were, it was local musicians. Wallace played there. Davey Yarborough, tenor saxophonist, now the head of the jazz program at Ellington, and his wife, the singer Esther Williams, were at Moore's Love and Peace a lot—a lot of local cats played those places. Bill Harris's place, the Pigfoot, would occasionally have a national talent like Betty Carter or someone from his years in the music that he had a relationship with, but also a lot of the local cats. I remember a wonderful afternoon with the great poet Sterling Brown accompanied by blues pianist Sunnyland Slim at the Pigfoot. I think it was a fundraiser for WPFW. Top of the Foolery played mostly resident musicians; Marshall Hawkins and Bernard Sweetney played a lot, for example. One time Andrew White, the saxophonist, and John Coltrane,

Photo 4.1 *Saxophonist Byron Morris and Unity at Blues Alley*
Blues Alley is packed for a performance by saxophonist Byron Morris and Unity in November 2000. The popular club in Georgetown has been showcasing local and national acts since 1965.

Photo 4.2 *Sterling Brown*
As part of a fundraiser for radio station WPWF, Sterling Brown reads poetry at the Pigfoot, Bill Harris's jazz club just off Rhode Island Avenue, NE. A Washingtonian, Dunbar High School graduate, and Howard University professor for forty years, Brown influenced many "jazz poets," including Amiri Baraka.

anthologist, played 6 p.m. to 6 a.m., and Steve Novosel played his bass the whole time. Later Andrew released every note that was played, twelve albums' worth on his label, Andrew's Music. The Top of the Foolery was near George Washington University, on Twenty-Third Street on the north side of Pennsylvania Avenue.

What was the occasion for Andrew to play that marathon?

Because that was an Andrew White production [*laughs*]: "I'm gonna play twelve hours." That was the gig. He produced all of that, you know, like his book [*Everybody Loves the Sugar—The Book*, White's 794-page autobiography] is this big [*holds hands wide apart*].

The Etcetera was on M Street between Connecticut and Nineteenth Street. They were a short-lived club—maybe a couple of years—they were trying to compete with Blues Alley. I remember Sun Ra playing there. And they would also do gigs at lunchtime. They weren't focusing on Washington artists; they were bringing national or international artists.

When I first got here, Blues Alley's orientation was traditional jazz. By the time I started to write, at least by the middle to late seventies, Blues Alley was a six-night-a-week national club, which would be like Dizzy Gillespie, Ramsey Lewis, the Heath Brothers, McCoy Tyner. . . .

The One Step Down was famous for their jukebox, and on Friday and Saturday evenings they would bring in a Barry Harris or sometimes a working trio or working quartet, but often times they were bringing in soloists to work with local rhythm sections.

One Step Down and Blues Alley were ongoing; I don't remember a time until One Step Down closed when those clubs weren't active. The Top of the Foolery was active as long as I could remember, then at some point it became a parking lot on Pennsylvania Avenue over by George Washington University, around Twenty-Third Street.

When you arrived in DC, who were some of the more important and impactful musicians around town?

Andrew White, Buck Hill, Reuben Brown, the pianist, Marshall Hawkins—those guys, those circles. Of course, Charlie Byrd was still around and his club, which was on K Street, was just south of Blues Alley. Can't forget Shirley Horn. Harold Kaufman, a psychiatrist and amateur piano player, owned Harold's Rogue & Jar. Wallace worked there, and I also remember David Murray playing there with Bobo Shaw, just after David married Ntozake Shange. I have tapes from that gig.

Would you characterize DC at that time as having an active jazz scene?

Oh yeah, definitely for the size of DC. There was jazz a lot of other places; there was an Ed Murphy's Supper Club over there by the Howard University Hospital who developed a hotel, and he had a club that I remember Sun Ra playing. Then, later you had Woodies Hilltop Lounge almost across from Howard University on Georgia Avenue and Euclid Street. He would bring in singles like [Philadelphia saxophonist] Bootsie Barnes, different soloists who would pick up a rhythm section here. The great drummer Philly Joe Jones would sit in at Woody's, after hours, after he made a gig at, say, the One Step, playing drums and piano. There are a bunch of places that popped up, but the real constant has been Blues Alley. As long as the greats of the bebop and hard bop generations of musicians were still touring—like Max Roach, Diz, Sarah Vaughan, the Heaths and Nancy Wilson—that echelon of artists played Blues Alley. A peg below that in terms of commercial viability would be One Step Down. Then occasionally Harold Kaufman might get in the game, then Etcetera was trying to be Blues Alley, but it didn't last.

What was it about the DC jazz scene that has made documenting its history compelling for you?

I began to feel that over the years Washington's role in the development of jazz was not sufficiently acknowledged. John Malachi, the wonderful pianist, was teaching at Howard University; he wrote "Opus X" and was the piano player with Billy Eckstine, who as a youth moved to DC from Pittsburgh and attended Armstrong High School. Then I understood that [Charlie Parker's bassist] Tommy Potter was in DC, Eckstine was here, too. If you looked at the Earl Hines band, then you looked at the Eckstine band, you'd see this DC element in those bands. Those cats didn't just pop out of the air, what was going on here?

As I began to find out more about people who were taken for granted, then I started to connect more dots. And then when I started to do more things with Dr. Billy Taylor, it

sharpened my knowledge and interest. Dr. Taylor had great stories about DC, like checking out Jelly Roll Morton at the Jungle Inn (above where Ben's Next is), when Malachi was the intermission pianist for Morton. Bringing attention to Washington jazz history was an important part of Dr. Taylor's mission, particularly as he could see the end of his life. Taylor was a graduate of Dunbar High School. It's very clear to me that the program that he put together at the Kennedy Center and hired me for—*Jazz in DC*—he wanted to find ways to get people to look at Washington as an important center for jazz development.

How did your relationship with Dr. Taylor develop?

I first met him because I had an assignment from *DownBeat* to write about *Jazz Alive* [the NPR series Dr. Taylor hosted] and through that I met [series producer] Tim Owens, Wiley Rollins, and Dr. Taylor. To do that article I had to research his career and all the things he was involved with. Through the years, as I evolved more from being a journalist into concert production, I would encounter [Billy] at festivals and different projects I'd be working on.

What was the nature of this Jazz in DC production?

I curated eight concerts, November 21–29, 2008, for the Millennium Stage that were all themed. . . . Some years earlier, 651, an arts-presenting organization based in Brooklyn, New York, organized a project called Lost Jazz Shrines in which presenters in different cities around the country were to do programs about historic jazz venues. Nathea Lee, then director of the U Street Theatre Foundation, hired me to write the essay for the Lost Jazz Shrines booklet about Washington venues. In the process, I also developed a menu of ideas for public programs related to DC "jazz shrines." Initially, the only program that came of that was a concert of Ellington's sacred music at the National Cathedral on Ellington's one hundredth birthday. I went back to that menu for ideas when curating Jazz in DC.

That concert came about when the dean of the National Cathedral, Rev. Nathan Baxter, approached Maurice Jackson, a parent of children at the National Cathedral School for Girls and the St. Albans School for Boys, about the idea to commission a concert of sacred music. Jackson suggested that instead he and the dean reach out to the Smithsonian Institute Jazz [Masterworks] Orchestra about performing a concert of Duke Ellington's sacred music. His "Sacred Concerts" had only been performed live a few times before. The concert, titled "Duke Ellington—Hallelujah! A Sacred Concert," was performed at the National Cathedral on April 29, 1999. It featured vocalist Queen Esther Marrow, who had been "discovered" by Ellington when she was twenty-two and, like Pearly Bailey and Ella Fitzgerald, was born in Newport News, Virginia. The concert also featured Kevin Mahogany.

What were the eight concerts you produced for Jazz in DC?

They were themed around venues. I did one around the Howard Theatre, one on Abarts and the Hollywood, Bohemian Caverns, stuff around Seventh Street—Little Harlem and the Offbeat. . . . I'd give a brief talk about the venue and show some images that I'd collected and then there would be a performance. We did one devoted to Dr. Taylor's big band music, the only one that wasn't themed around a venue. We put together a band led by Charlie Young, the saxophonist and conductor, who pulled a bunch of music charts at the Library of Congress. Charlie went through it and was able to reconstruct charts; we also got Afro Blue involved. That was quite a concert! Bobby Felder (trombonist, arranger, composer, and educator) helped me a lot with that series. We did one featuring the music Charlie Byrd did at the Showboat Lounge.

Billy did a big concert around James Reese Europe. There might have been a couple of concerts at the Eisenhower Theater that were part of it, but we did these eight nights on the Kennedy Center's Millennium Stage during Thanksgiving week. That was a real opportunity to get paid to dig into [DC jazz history] and do some research and come up with the concepts for those concerts.

Since your earliest days observing the jazz scene here, what are some of the elements you've witnessed that have negatively impacted jazz in DC?

That's just business cycles more than anything. I always make a distinction between the culture and the business. Businesses go up and down for a variety of reasons and that's not in and of itself a way to judge whether jazz is dead or alive. I think the reason that One Step Down came to an end was because the [owner, Joe Cohen, and manager, Ann

Mabuchi] got old. They were having health issues and there were development options coming in there, so people make [business] decisions.

So it's your sense that those kinds of things run in cycles as opposed to that old "jazz is dead" canard?

I get sick of that discussion; I think it's shortsighted. Dig a little deeper, think a little bit deeper about what may be happening. It might be because a club is in an area that's going through a change and the club can't survive that change. I think it has more to do with urban development or redevelopment than it does "is jazz up or down." You could be a good businessperson or a bad businessperson; you could be getting old or it could be a demographic change or some other kind of change that would cause that business to run a cropper.

Conversely, what have been some of the more positive developments on the DC jazz scene that you've observed?

The fact that the music has moved to other platforms than clubs. I'd say that right now, for a community like ours, we have an embarrassment of riches. We have the Friday night jazz scene at Westminster Church, but you also had the Smithsonian Natural History with a Friday night jazz scene kind of in the same time period, and other churches trying to replicate that. Just the fact that jazz is not limited to the club platform has been a real important development.

Obviously WPFW is very important. The loss of WDCU had nothing to do with the music, it had to do with the state [the University of the District of Columbia] was in. I think at the point where we had two radio stations providing on-air jazz programming was really important. I can think of a whole set of individuals who were very knowledgeable—lay scholars, if you will—aficionados who used radio as a platform to share their knowledge, their collections with the community, that was very important.

What the Kennedy Center has done for jazz, what Strathmore has done to a lesser degree, Clarice Smith [Performing Arts] Center at the University of Maryland, George Mason University—all that is relatively new stuff. Library of Congress, Smithsonian—the institutional engagement is providing more platforms for the music.

You're not one who reacts negatively to the whole notion of jazz in the institutions and the evolution of jazz to the concert stage?

Not at all; I think jazz is a big house and it's important that there is something happening in every room, so to speak. I would hate for musicians to feel dependent or feel like they have to be funded to do what they do. I think it is a dynamic culture, basically a vernacular culture that has moved into more academic realms. I think that's why jazz is healthy, vibrant, and dynamic; that's what I love about it. I like joints and I like concerts and I think they all have a place, they all fit and that's what's good about the situation now. I wish that the musicians at the club level could be compensated better, but then that sort of self-selects. Cats will play the clubs for their own agendas until they say, "I can't do that anymore."

Talk about your work on the Capital City Jazz Festival.

The seeds of that lie with A. B. and Karen Spellman, as well as with WPFW. The center of [Capital City Jazz Festival] was Karen Spellman. I had known Karen through SNCC [Student Nonviolent Coordinating Committee] connections. I got to know A. B. Spellman through [poet] Gaston Neal. She did a concert as a fundraiser for WPFW. And how I got involved was, the Roneys [Wallace Jr. and saxman Antoine] were on the concert. It was the McLeans—Jackie and Rene—the Marsalis brothers, and the Roneys.

I did my first Antioch College co-op here in 1966. Through coincidence I got off the bus one day on Fourteenth Street and I saw this guy in a storefront fixing it up, so I went in there, and it was Gaston Neal, and that's how I met him. He was getting ready to open up the New School for Afro-American Thought. He was part of the black poetry movement with Larry Neal, Marvin X, Amiri Baraka. . . . At that point what Baraka was to Newark, Gaston was to DC Gaston got sidetracked because of some personal things and never got his work out there in publication . . . but at that time he was definitely a cultural visionary and a lot of music was coming through that New School for Afro-American Thought. And that first weekend when it opened, A. B. Spellman was a part of it and that's how I came to know him. Gaston was later a founder of the Listening Group, an organization of black men who started to gather in the early 1980s to meet, eat, and discuss jazz once a month. It still exists.

Then later A. B. and Karen were in Atlanta and they got married and he came to Washington with the NEA. A. B. had attended Howard with Baraka and had authored the now-classic *Four Lives in the Bebop Business*. A. B. used to shop at Olsson's. He would come in once a month and say, "Bill, what should I buy?" One time he came in and said, "We're thinking about doing a festival, we believe that it's important that Washington have a festival."

The Kool Jazz Festival had come to the Kennedy Center in '77 or '78, and they actually used the whole Kennedy Center. I was like an intern, it wasn't a paid position, and I worked on that. Part of what A. B. was referring to was "this city is still ripe for a festival, there's a new Washington Convention Center with a subway stop right there, I can't do it. I'm at the NEA, Karen is going to take the lead, and I want you to get with her to do this festival." Because of the relationship Karen had with WPFW around that concert she produced for them as a fundraiser, they were in the mix, so Bob Tyner, who was then the program director, was involved. Jeff Anthony was at the NEA working in the music program specifically around jazz, but he resigned at some point after we'd done [Capital City Jazz Festival] a couple of years and he became an important part of that.

The Cap City team, led by Karen, later went on from the Capital City Jazz Festival to do a lot of things in DC. That same core of people did the Black Family Reunion, organized by the National Council of Negro Women led by Dorothy Height, and also started the Adams Morgan Day Festival, on the production side. One of the board members of the Capital City Jazz Festival was Ralph Rinzler, who was like an external affairs guy for the Smithsonian. Ralph was a mandolin player and the originator of the Smithsonian Folklife Festival. That's how we wound up doing events at the Smithsonian as part of the Capital City Jazz Festival. Those events were inspired by House Concurrent Resolution 57 [1997]. The first festival we did, we honored Bill Harris, Roy Haynes, and Benny Carter, and we presented Marlon Jordan and the American Jazz Orchestra under Loren Schoenberg's direction and they played a work of Benny's in the National Museum of American History Flag Hall.

The first two Cap City Jazz Festivals were at the old DC Convention Center. We actually did a full festival three years—two at the Convention Center, with a sidecar at Duke Ellington High School the second year. And then the third year, 1988, we did a weekend at Howard University, and we did a week of stuff at the Old Post Office Pavilion—that was lunchtime stuff—and then the next weekend we did at George Washington University. That was a festival where we basically got in so much debt that we never mounted another full festival of that type. But we did do another event at the Smithsonian in 1989. That was the only thing that we did in '89. Roger Kennedy made that second Smithsonian event happen. We honored Ella Fitzgerald and Milt Hinton. Keter Betts, also a Cap City board member, was most important in that because he was the connection to Ella and The Judge (Milt Hinton).

The first festival (1985) that we did we opened up with Miles Davis and the Dirty Dozen Brass Band at the Convention Center. It was around Miles's birthday and we gave him a big cake; he played so long that people got tired. We wheeled out the cake and Miles cut it and gave it out to the audience. We did a lot of great shows. We did M'Boom and the World Saxophone Quartet, Little Jimmy Scott with Milt Jackson, Betty Carter, Tito Puente, and Paquito D'Rivera, and we had a Latin jam session with local

Photo 4.4 *Max Roach and M'Boom at the Capital City Jazz Festival*
Max Roach and M'Boom take the stage during the first Capital City Jazz Festival
in 1985. M'Boom was an all-percussion ensemble in which all members could play
any of the tempered and untempered instruments featured in concerts.

Latin cats. . . . We had Abdullah Ibrahim and Hugh Masekela. We had Miles's paintings, we did a Chuck Stewart photography exhibit, we had panel discussions. . . . Particularly when we first started we didn't have a lot for artist fees, so I added a lot of stuff like the jazz marketplace, panel discussions, films.

In 1988 we did "Love Supreme," a tribute to John Coltrane with Gary Thomas, Joe Ford, Hamiet Bluiett, Andrew White, Dave Liebman, a slew of saxophone players. . . . We did "Homecookin' Revisited," with the Kenny Burrell Jazz Guitar Band and the [Jimmy McGriff & Hank Crawford] Quartet. For "Homecookin'," we passed out copies of "Lift Every Voice and Sing" to the audience, but nobody sang it; McGriff always ended his concerts with that song. I was giving away copies of "Lift Every Voice" for years after that. During the week we did DC-resident artists at lunchtime at the Old Post Office Pavilion. The last weekend of the festival we did "The Composer's Art: Contemporary Voices" with Geri Allen, Henry Threadgill, and Henry Butler. . . . The crazy thing is that before we even did the first Friday night concert at Crampton Auditorium, we were at the bank getting a loan to be able to pay the musicians.

That Sunday we all met at Karen's house because we knew we had to refashion the festival in order for it to get done. That was probably one of the most emotional times I've had because that year, 1988, Karen was working on the Democratic National Convention and I was really running everything. I did production, a lot of the programming, publicity stuff, but Karen was the interface with the money and she was better able to negotiate a lot of things.

Keter Betts, the great bassist who had moved to DC, really helped us the year we honored Ella Fitzgerald and Milt Hinton. He had played with her for many years. We had to make a lot of difficult choices. . . . Given the amount of resources that we had, what we were trying to do was probably too ambitious and probably should have been more conservative in our programming. I don't regret one moment, though.

We did three full festivals and another year we only did the Smithsonian piece; I think that was the year we did the piece with Milt Hinton and Ella. Because we had debt that we had to pay off, we would do sessions like Monday nights at Takoma Station and [at] Trumpets for a while. And we did concerts at people's houses; if they had a grand piano we'd say, "OK, we'll get Henry Butler." We'd have him come and play and we'd charge $75 per person, with champagne and cake for an intimate evening.

As a legal entity, we went on for a few years after we stopped putting on big things, mostly as a way to try to pay down the debt. People had put up their properties to secure the bank loan. There are people, including me, that were emotionally crushed by the fact that we were unable to pay for what we proposed to put on the stage. But there were people who said, "We'll support you." Reflecting on that still makes me cry.

How did that festival work evolve into your concert and festivals production work?

I started working as a stagehand well before this. I used to write for the *Unicorn Times* late seventies to early eighties, which was like the *City Paper* except it came out once a month. Richard Harrington, later the *Washington Post* "pop" music maven, was the editor.

He called me one day and said, "I want you to go down to the corner of Seventh and E; there are two guys there who are doing some interesting stuff." I was writing mostly about the avant-garde for the *Unicorn Times*. When I was writing for the *Journal* or the *Afro-American*, I wrote more about mainstream and more about local activities and record reviews. I got access to any club I wanted and I was inundated with music. I wrote for *JazzTimes*, I wrote for *Musician*, a bunch of different publications.

Anyway, he sent me down to this place, which had been like a lunchtime spot. There were two people there, Bill Warrell, who would later establish the arts-presenting non-profit District Curators, and a guy named Earl Bateman. Bill Warrell wanted to start a loft, which was what DC Space essentially was. Bateman wanted to do a festival in '78.

Bateman wanted to do two nights of "avant-garde" music, both "classical" and jazz: Cecil Taylor, Anthony Braxton, World Saxophone Quartet, Sam Rivers, Marion Brown, John Cage, Phillip Glass, Steve Reich—kind of like a mix-and-match thing. I never wrote the article for the *Unicorn Times* because Bateman hired me to be the publicist for these two nights of music. He said he'd pay me $ 1,000 and 10 percent of all the recording and videotaping that would result. So I signed on for that. I got one check for $100, which bounced. The concert was at Constitution Hall and collapsed the first night.

Marion Brown opened, after which Bateman came out and said, "We have technical difficulties." The technical difficulty was there wasn't enough money in the box office to pay the next artist, so that delay went on for forty-five minutes or so. Then Bateman came out and said, "Ladies and gentlemen, the concert is over." And it was a cold, icy, rainy night, a chill-to-the-bone night. They put everybody out of Constitution Hall.

DC Space wasn't quite ready as a performance space, but that night Bill opened it anyway. Out of that came his relationship with Julius Hemphill, Oliver Lake, and David Murray. They said, "We're in DC, we might as well play somewhere," so that night is actually when DC Space opened. But I never made it over there.

There was a club nearby where I could catch a bus to get home, so I stopped in there to drown my sorrows. I'm sitting there and next to me is the stagehands' union shop steward of Constitution Hall, a guy named Jerry King. First he recognized me as one of the people who did that concert the stagehands weren't going to get paid for. I thought I was going to get $1,000 at the end of the concert, and I'm sitting there trying to add this all up. We ended up spending that evening there.

Some time later a guy in my apartment building, who was a stagehand at the Warner Theater, asked me if I wanted to make some money. He said come down to the Warner Theatre at 10:00, they needed some extra guys for the load out. At the end of the night I got paid in cash! When the guy paid me, he looked at me and said, "Don't I know you?" It was the same guy Jerry from that night at the Kung Fu Lounge! He said, "You wanna work tomorrow? Be here at 8:00 a.m., and bring a crescent wrench." I had always been around theater, but never as a stagehand. I was still writing and the two fit together great. At one point I was working at Olsson's twenty hours a week, working as a stagehand, and freelance writing.

When I got to the Capital City Jazz Festival, I already had production chops. We had been doing circuses, ballets, plays. . . . Bill Washington's Dimensions Unlimited and Cellar Door Productions were presenting all of the major concerts in the area. Dimensions

Unlimited produced all the black shows. So that's what we did at Constitution Hall: the Whispers, Gladys Knight & the Pips, whomever. . . . Sometimes two shows a night.

Later, during the Cap City Jazz days, Quint Davis and Tom Dent, from the New Orleans Jazz & Heritage Festival and Foundation, respectively, came to DC to do a workshop for people who wanted to produce festivals. Karen Spellman wanted to get involved with them as a way to better understand the festival we had. I also approached them about working at JazzFest and nothing was available. A year later I heard from John Washington, [a friend of a friend who] was on the New Orleans Jazz & Heritage Foundation board. He knew I wanted to work at the New Orleans Jazz & Heritage Festival and that's how I got to New Orleans. That led to twenty-three years. I learned a lot about production and New Orleans culture.

Throughout all this work in DC on jazz, how has the DC jazz audience evolved through the ensuing years?

I think the audience I first knew got older and a new one developed. Obviously, a big boon has been the redevelopment of U Street, which went down with the King riots. It didn't really come back until the subway was finished. When that happened a whole new U Street nightlife developed and with that nightlife came a whole new generation. The resurgence of U Street meant a new audience, a young audience. There was an audience that was a part of what Blues Alley was about and Harold's Rogue & Jar, Top of the Foolery. . . . That audience I encountered at those places was probably a little bit older than me. Now it's forty-some years later and most people in their eighties aren't going out to clubs; you might see them at Westminster, but they're not going out to clubs. So with the revival of U Street as a nightlife venue, not only did the Bohemian Caverns come back, you had Twins Jazz there, but also you had other places that feature some type of jazz at some point or another, that's when I saw a new audience.

The continuity that was broken up was the result of all of these socioeconomic things that have happened, and then with the demographic infusion—the city has changed. One of the reasons I was so excited to come to DC was because I was from Toledo, went to Western Reserve Academy in Hudson, Ohio, then went to college in Yellow Springs, Ohio, then I came to DC, and I was loving all the black culture. But then Chocolate City has changed. After the [post-MLK assassination] riots a lot of people left DC because they could leave and a lot of people stayed because they couldn't leave, and a lot of areas that were central to the black community at that time were on the decline: H Street, U Street, and everything related to that; so those areas came back with this whole gentrification process and with that has come new audiences.

One such development in recent years has been a kind of do-it-yourself attitude as far as presenting jazz, as exemplified by CapitalBop and what writer Gio Russonello and musician Luke Stewart are doing, something of a loft scene.

The new loft scene.

Do you see any correlation between what Bill Warrell did with DC Space and what's happening now with this new loft scene?

There were some other places also; there was another kind of jazz scene, almost like a Black Nationalist scene. Jimmy Gray—aka Black Fire—another important figure people overlook or forget about, was one of those programmers who came on WPFW. Another was Eric Garrison. They were scholars in their own right, they really knew the music. Jimmy Gray had been in the record distribution business and got out to start his own label. . . . There were some other kind of loft scenarios that featured musicians that Jimmy was working with, not so much the well-known New York cats DC Space presented, but musicians who were trying to and could play in that way.

I haven't patronized CapitalBop's events, but my attitude is, this new loft development is in a way repeating the past—cats playing for small money in environments that are less than what I think the music deserves, and I feel sort of like "been there, done that." But it is a new generation doing their thing. More power to them.

The one thing I think continues that District Curator tradition more directly is what Transparent Productions does. I think that [Transparent producer] Bobby Hill was kind of a part of what we were doing, "back in the day." God bless Bobby Hill and his team.

One of the things I did when we had Capital City Jazz Festival, I invited Tom Porter, Bobby Hill, and a bunch of other people to do a sort of programming focus group. Once we started Cap City Jazz everybody felt like "I could do that" because everybody has ideas about programming. And that's when I realized that, yeah, I had great ideas about programming but what you really needed was a business sense, which I didn't have. We made choices out of what our vision was, not how to stabilize and grow a festival. By the time I went to work in New Orleans on the festival, that's when I realized what I needed to learn.

I would say that Transparent Productions represents more of a continuum with what District Curators was about. District Curators evolved out of DC Space. Bill Warrell produced a series at the Corcoran. He presented Cecil Taylor, the Art Ensemble of Chicago, and Julius Hemphill's *Ralph Ellison's Long Tongue*—three nights at the Corcoran. That was the genesis of District Curators. The Corcoran series led to what we did with *Long Tongues*. Warrell went on to produce all kinds of music via District Curators.

Transparent Productions, because of the individual people involved—Bobby Hill, Thomas Stanley, Larry Appelbaum—all those individuals had the experience of DC Space, felt the void when it went off the scene, and created a vehicle to continue in that spirit. What Luke and Gio are doing I don't think has anything to do with DC Space. They're a new young generation creating their own space; they may reverse engineer and look back and see themselves as inheriting some kind of a mantle, but to me Transparent Productions is what DC Space spawned, there's a more direct relationship between what they're doing and what DC Space was. I'm not going to say what Gio and Luke are doing is not important. It is important. They're creating another beachhead, creating opportunities for people to play. . . . I think their [CapitalBop] website is amazing—what they've put together and how they relate that to what they do. I think their initiative is great.

How do you see these developments, like Transparent Productions, what CapitalBop is doing, impacting DC's cultural scene in general?

The beat goes on, I'm just glad they're doing it. The fact that oncoming cats are doing what they're doing, you have to have faith in that.

How does your work on the annual Congressional Black Caucus Foundation [CBCF] jazz day impact the DC jazz community?

It's become an event that people like to go to, people that don't otherwise necessarily attend the CBCF Annual Legislative Conference [ALC] come to that event. When that started it was just a panel discussion and a reception.

Detroit, Michigan's congressman, John Conyers, dean of the Congressional Black Caucus and known as the "Jazz Congressman," sent out a letter [saying] that he wanted to do some jazz stuff, and Cedric Hendricks was on his staff. And because I could write, I could program and I could organize production, I became a very useful piece of that puzzle. I started out working with that event as a volunteer in 1985 [and in 1992 became a producer of the conference.] . . . That's not a gig I was looking for, but I owe that opportunity to John Conyers.

After '92, because I was one of the producers, I was able to push the jazz piece even further. By this time I'd been working in New Orleans, at Jazz at Lincoln Center . . . my range of contacts had grown exponentially. I had much more experience in terms of production, and not just production nuts and bolts, but I had that concept of what it is to be a producer. So I was able to push it to another level.

When we first started doing the jazz event the record companies would underwrite the performance if we picked up the travel. Once the record industry died, it became a different game in terms of sponsorship and how to keep that afloat. For the Foundation, it's all about every event earning more in sponsorship than it costs because the ALC is a fundraiser for the overall work of the CBCF throughout the year.

It is very important that the Foundation has remained committed to the Jazz Issue Forum and Concert despite the changes in the sponsorship situation. So it's a free event during the ALC that has a high level of talent that the community can participate in. As the years have gone on just about the only high profile thing left for the community to be involved in with no charge is the jazz event. . . . Now it's an asset to the whole CBCF enterprise.

House Concurrent Resolution 57, declaring jazz "an American national treasure," resulted from the first CBCF jazz evening panel discussion in 1985. At the end of that session Jimmy Owens challenged Conyers to do something legislatively for jazz. He took on the challenge. While we were working on the resolution, I was still working as a stagehand. I was on the show call at the Kennedy Center for a Kabuki Theater run, and a Japanese stagehand pointed to an artist and said, "You see that guy there? In Japan, he's a living national treasure." Bingo, that's where that language came from! That next day I took what that guy said to me and finished drafting H.Con.Res.57.

What's your overall goal for the CBCF jazz day?

Just that it's important that an organization of that significance in the national African American community and the nation at large has seen fit to put a showcase around the music. It doesn't happen with the Urban League, it doesn't happen with the NAACP, nor with the black fraternities and sororities—it does happen at the Congressional Black Caucus Foundation Annual Legislative Conference. And the reason it happens is because John Conyers had that vision to add that piece as an issue discussion and it has evolved. Because of his stature he was able to create that space.

If there's a study or something done in the jazz community, I've tried to have a presentation about it to open up the issue forum because I know that much of that information is not broadly disseminated, even within those circles in the black community that claim they're interested in the music. So we say, "Let's do it there, let's bring together a panel of experts, let's elevate a discussion." It became more of a day; we went from an issue forum coupled with a concert to a two-hour block of prime time for the issue forum that is something of a town hall meeting on jazz. In the evening we have the concert and keep a humanities element in it by having a meet-the-artist discussion so that people who don't get into the issues forum still get to have some introduction to what people think about this music. We also present the CBCF Jazz Legacy Awards. This year we honored Dr. Larry Ridley and Bobby Watson. I'm all about preserving our stake, the African American stake, in this music. That's my agenda. This music came out of our experience, in our community, in the American context. Cedric and I are all about using that platform to keep that alive, that's what WE can do.

I'm disappointed that *JazzTimes*, *DownBeat*, and the rest of them don't pay any attention to this event, but I think they're gonna pay attention around HR2823 [Conyers's 2012 jazz support legislation]. The reason this bill was drafted is because John Hasse, curator of American music at National Museum of American History, met with Conyers to discuss the state of the Smithsonian's jazz efforts. Cedric called me with the idea that maybe it was time for some new legislation. I said if we're going to do a new bill, it can't just be about getting the Smithsonian more money.

Conyers is planning to introduce this new jazz legislation just prior to Jazz Appreciation Month (April), in conjunction with an event that the Smithsonian is organizing called Two Johns, honoring Congressman Conyers and John Coltrane, Conyers's favorite musician next to Charlie Parker, celebrating the fiftieth anniversary of Coltrane's "A Love Supreme." That will give us a piece of legislation with some teeth; it will direct agencies of government to spend money for preservation, education, and the promulgation of jazz.

5 Jazz Radio in Washington, DC

Rusty Hassan

Radio introduced me to jazz, as it has countless listeners over the decades. On New Year's Day, January 1, 1958, I was in my bedroom making a model airplane with the radio on. I'm certain I was in the seventh grade. The announcer featured the entire Benny Goodman 1938 Carnegie Hall concert. I heard the Goodman orchestra play "Let's Dance." The quartet with Lionel Hampton, Teddy Wilson, and Gene Krupa played "The Man I Love." Guest artists from Duke Ellington's orchestra, Cootie Williams, and Johnny Hodges played "Blue Reverie." Count Basie and Lester Young jammed on "Honeysuckle Rose." I was hooked. After I saved up enough, I bought the two recordings of the concert at the local Woolworths. My allowance shifted from buying plastic models of World War II fighter planes to vinyl LPs. I still have the third LP I purchased: *Diz 'N Bird*.

While rummaging through a closet, I found 78 rpm records that my mother had stored—Woody Herman's *Woodchoppers Ball* and *Jazz at the Philharmonic*. Intrigued that I liked her old records, she encouraged my interest in jazz by taking me to see a Lionel Hampton performance.

By the time I was in high school in the early sixties, I discovered Symphony Sid broadcasting on WEVD out of New York City. Sid was so influential in the 1940s jazz scene that Lester Young composed and recorded "Jumping with Symphony Sid." Today, Sid Torin is best known for the broadcast performances of Charlie Parker at the Royal Roost on the Savoy label. When I heard Sid he was featuring such recordings as "Ole" by Maynard Ferguson from *Maynard '61*, Oscar Brown Jr.'s vocal rendition of "Dat Dere" by Bobby Timmons, and Stan Getz doing "I'm Late, I'm Late" from Focus. Other New York announcers I heard during this time were Mort Fega, Ed Beech, and Billy Taylor.

My high school in Fairfield, Connecticut, had a small coterie of hipsters who listened to Jean Shepherd and jazz instead of the rock and roll of Murray the K and Cousin Brucie. During recess, we would talk about LPs such as *Miles Davis at the Blackhawk* or *Art Blakey's Jazz Messengers with Thelonious Monk*. Live performances were certainly on the agenda. Butch Fettig and I made our way to the city for the Daily News Jazz Festival at Madison Square Garden where we heard Sonny Rollins, Dave Brubeck, Carmen McRae, Chris Conner, and Maynard Ferguson. Shortly after graduation in 1963 Butch and I told our parents we were spending the weekend at each other's houses and drove across the state in my 1954 Studebaker to attend the Newport Jazz Festival. Willis Conover from Voice of America introduced Willie "The Lion" Smith, Thelonious Monk, Jimmy Smith, and John Coltrane. I can still conjure up "My Favorite Things" in my memory bank.

In the fall of 1963 I took my albums with me to Washington, DC, to attend Georgetown University. I soon discovered *The Album Sound* on WMAL-AM. Felix Grant had been broadcasting in DC since his discharge from the Coast Guard in 1945. Looking for a way to play jazz on air despite the station management's reluctance to give him a jazz show, in 1954 he devised the concept of the "album sound," featuring music from the recently introduced long-playing albums rather than 78 rpm singles. At that time, most jazz recordings were on LP. Although jazz and blues were staples of his programming in the fifties, by the time I started to listen to him he was introducing the blend of Brazilian samba rhythms and cool jazz known as bossa nova. He was on the air from 7:30 until midnight, Monday through Friday, followed by Bill Mayhew, who continued overnight with a blend of pop and jazz.

Through his interviews with artists performing in town, Grant introduced me to the DC jazz scene. I was soon hanging out at the Bohemian Caverns at Eleventh and U streets, NW, where I caught performances by John Coltrane and Miles Davis. I was at the Caverns when Ramsey Lewis recorded "The 'In' Crowd," which became a big hit in 1965.

I discovered the One Step Down on Pennsylvania Avenue NW shortly after it opened in 1963. It was a long, narrow room with tables on one side, booths on the other, with the bar in the rear. The attraction for me was the jukebox, which contained only jazz records. I hung out at the One Step for about a decade for the recorded music and ambience, when Ann Mabuchi came on board and convinced owner Joe Cohen to feature live performances. There was no stage. Tables were moved from the front end of the bar to accommodate a baby grand piano and drums. Ann booked such prominent artists as Benny Carter, James Moody, and Lee Konitz, just to name the alto saxophonists. The One Step Down was a favorite of fans and musicians until it folded in 2000.

It was serendipity that started my broadcasting career. One afternoon during my junior year I was drinking beer with friends when I noticed another student holding some jazz albums. To check out how hip he was, I asked to see what he had. He passed the hipness test and we talked about the music. He had just played the recordings on his radio show on the campus station, WGTB-FM, but he had to give up the program to take a class that was scheduled at the same time. Evidently I passed his hipness test because he asked me if I would take over his show.

I don't remember the exact date of my first broadcast. It was probably in January 1966, the beginning of second semester of my junior year. I remember being nervous, but I soon overcame my natural shyness as I began to share my love of jazz and introduce others to the music as I had been by Symphony Sid and Mort Fega. I have been broadcasting jazz over the Washington airwaves almost continuously ever since.

After I graduated from Georgetown in June 1967, I spent a brief period in Mississippi, where I met Mrs. Fannie Lou Hamer. She instilled in me a commitment to social justice that would be integrated into my love of jazz and blues. She also introduced me to gospel music through the recordings of the Staple Singers. Back in DC, I became a VISTA (Volunteers in Service to America) volunteer and kept my radio show on WGTB.

To be in Washington in 1968 was an incredible experience. Students at Georgetown demonstrated against the war in Vietnam and pushed for the abolition of ROTC. Students at Howard University struck for the inclusion of Black Studies in the Eurocentric curriculum and jazz in the music program, where Donald Byrd would become its first director. The assassination of Rev. Martin Luther King Jr. and subsequent riots dramatically changed the city for decades. The music I programmed reflected the times: "Ascension," by John Coltrane, and "Meditations on Integration," by Charles Mingus. As a VISTA volunteer, I became connected to a community organization in Adams Morgan called The New Thing Art and Architecture Center, where I met Sondra Barrett, who was teaching African dance to children. The New Thing, named after a term applied to avant-garde jazz, also sponsored photography, art, music, and karate classes. It held weekly jazz performances at St. Margaret's Episcopal Church on Connecticut Avenue, featuring such artists as Shirley Horn, Andrew White, Paul Hawkins, and Byron Morris. Morris was the first musician I interviewed on the air. I also interviewed New York saxophonist Noah Howard, who had come to Washington for a performance at the New Thing that didn't work out. But an on-air discussion with the director Topper Carew had a major impact on my broadcasting career.

After I had Topper on my show to talk about the jazz performances and other programs at the New Thing, he decided that the organization should have its own radio show. He sent out proposals to various stations, and WAMU-FM came up with airtime on Sunday afternoons. I helped to get the first shows on the air in July 1969. *The New Thing Root Music Show* kicked off what would be a golden age for jazz radio in Washington, DC, as jazz radio programming proliferated during the 1970s.

Sondra and I got married in August and went to Europe, where we heard performances by Miles Davis, Cecil Taylor, the Art Ensemble of Chicago, Archie Shepp, Duke Ellington, and Bill Evans. I interviewed Anthony Braxton and Leroy Jenkins and played pinball with Keith Jarrett between sets when he was performing at a Parisian club. We returned to the states in December with albums that I was eager to get on the air. In my absence, *The New Thing Root Music Show* was hosted by Eric Gravatt, who was the drum instructor for the organization, and Ralph Higgs, who taught karate. Gravatt soon left DC to work with McCoy Tyner and Weather Report. Brother Ralph, as he called himself on the air, handed over the mike to me when he got a show at midnight on Saturday.

When I resumed broadcasting on WAMU, the listening audience was beginning to shift from the AM to the FM band. For decades AM radio dominated the airwaves with Top 40 music programming, but there were also some commercial jazz shows, such as Felix Grant's on WMAL-AM. FM radio had a much clearer sound than AM but reached a smaller audience, partly because at that time fewer people had FM receivers. A couple of factors changed this. The FCC ruled that commercial stations could not simulcast all of its programming on both AM and FM. In the early 1970s college stations on FM attracted young listeners by featuring rock albums by The Doors, Cream, Jimi Hendrix, and many others that weren't getting played on commercial AM stations. The "underground" format would become a feature of commercial FM stations such as WHFS. Jazz programming benefited from this shift. Paul Anthony, for example, could play Miles Davis's "Bitch's Brew" on WRC-FM, whereas Felix Grant could not play such an extended cutting-edge piece on WMAL-AM. Washington also benefited from the addition of three new FM stations in the 1970s that featured jazz: WHUR, WETA, and WPFW.

Although the organization folded, I kept the title of *The New Thing Root Music Show* through the seventies. I was joined on WAMU by Gerald Lee and Russell Williams, two American University students who established a Saturday afternoon workshop called *Sound, Color and Movement*, later titled *Spirits Known and Unknown*. The workshop was intended to train African American students in broadcasting techniques, and among those who participated in the program were Vincent Muse, David Muse, P. W. Robinson, and the late Aaron Hiter. One highlight was a visit by Charles Mingus. Lee completed his legal studies and later became a federal judge. Williams became a professional sound technician for film and won Academy Awards for *Glory* and *Dances with Wolves*. He is currently a professor at American University.

In 1971 I met two professional broadcasters who would become close friends. Yale Lewis had a slight build, with keen features that reflected the Native American side of his heritage and a voice that rivaled Johnny Hartman. Ron Sutton carried the weight of an ex-football player. Sutton was working for WGAY where he had to play pop instrumentals by Mantovani but would slip in Clifford Brown with strings late at night.

Howard University obtained a commercial license in 1971, a gift from Katharine Graham when the *Washington Post* gave up WTOP-FM. WHUR would become the leading African American station in Washington through its Quiet Storm format in the late seventies, but it was also a jazz station through much of the decade.[1] Yale Lewis was one of the first announcers when the station went on the air in August. I visited Lewis in the trailer studio on campus with my daughter Aisha in my arms. Fortunately, she remained quiet during his announcements; a few days later he played the John Coltrane recording for which she was named.

Ron Sutton soon replaced Lewis in the evening slot and remained there until late 1977. Sutton and I would appear as guests on each other's shows, especially on Charlie Parker's birthday, August 29. During one of these shows, another WHUR announcer brought Geraldine Parker to the studio to talk about her marriage to Parker in the 1940s. On another occasion Sutton called me to hurry over to the station to join him in interviewing Sonny Rollins.

WGTB evolved into a free-form underground rock station while maintaining much of its jazz programming. W. Royal Stokes, a freelance writer for the *Washington Post*, had two shows. *I Thought I Heard Buddy Bolden Say* covered traditional jazz, while *Since Minton's* featured bebop and beyond. Stokes would later edit *Jazz Times* and publish four books on the music. Another programmer on the station was a Georgetown student named Ken Steiner, who got hooked on jazz while attending a Duke Ellington concert on campus and later became an Ellington scholar.

At Georgetown, meanwhile, WGTB was featuring a women's collective called *Sophie's Parlor* and health advice from the Washington Free Clinic. A free-form mix of Frank Zappa, Jefferson Airplane, and Bob Marley included a dose of radical politics. The gay-oriented show *Friends*, and the birth control advice provided on air, however, were too much for the university's Jesuit administration. The station was shut down for a few months in 1976 and finally ceased broadcasting on January 29, 1979. Father Timothy Healey, president of the university, sold the license to the University of the District of Columbia for one dollar.

In 1976 I participated in getting a new station on the air as part of the Pacifica Network that would play jazz, blues, and world music. But in February 1977 when Von Martin played "Take the 'A' Train" to open the WPFW-FM signal to the Washington airwaves, I opted to keep *The New Thing Root Music Show* on WAMU. I thought that jazz should be played on as many stations as possible. A number of my friends did get volunteer shows on the station. Ken Steiner came over from WGTB. Jimmy Gray did *Black Fire*, where he would "tell stories though the music" and rarely announce what he played. Saxophonist Byron Morris had a program named after Rahsaan Roland Kirk's "Bright Moments." Tom Cole started a Sunday morning show focusing on guitar music called *G-Strings* that is still on the air today.

About this time Ron Sutton introduced me to his neighbor, Jerry Washington, who had retired from the Air Force and was currently working for the United Planning Organization. Washington in turn showed me his collection of jazz and blues LPs. Although Sutton was employed by WHUR, he volunteered to do a show on WPFW with his friend Wash sitting in with him. One Saturday afternoon he could not make it to the station and Jerry Washington had to do the show on his own. This was so successful that Washington eventually became the host.

Jerry shifted the focus of the Saturday afternoon show to the blues and created a persona that was a brilliant mix of fantasy with a dose of reality that he called "the Bama." In African American parlance, a "bama" is someone from the country, unsophisticated in city ways and very likely to wear overalls. *The Bama Hour* would become the most popular show on WPFW. Jerry Washington would mix in philosophical and political commentary, discussions about what went down at the barbershop, and laments about fights he had with his girlfriend, Denise. Like most of his listeners, I bought into his stories. Since I knew him before he went on the air, I wondered when he broke up with his wife. Denise was a real person; Wash introduced me to her at a WPFW fundraiser at the Panorama Room in Southeast. But the on-air relationship and the stories were made up. Jerry Washington and his wife remained together until her passing, and he missed her terribly as a widower.

The Bama Hour was so popular that WPFW gave him another show featuring jazz on Sunday afternoons called *The Other Side of the Bama*. Now doing shows opposite each other, we developed a friendly rivalry. Wash would say, "If you don't like what I'm playing, turn the dial and listen to Hassan." Because he frequently played scratchy records on his show, whenever I played a recording with surface noise I would announce that it was from the Jerry Washington Collection of Classic Jazz.

Another friend who really blossomed as a personality on the WPFW airwaves was Nap Turner. I first met him when he was playing bass with Julie Moore Turner in a club at Fourteenth and Rhode Island Avenue, NW, when it was a rough neighborhood. His program on WPFW, however, focused more on blues vocals than jazz instrumentals, and soon he was singing at live performances. He called his show *Don't Forget the Blues*. Sometimes he read on air from the "Simple stories" by Langston Hughes, and his acting ability came through in the voices he used in portraying Jesse B. Semple.

A jazz enthusiast from Poland, Grzegorz Tusiewicz, introduced me to Willis Conover in 1977. Greg, as he preferred to be called, was involved in the jazz scene in Krakow and had met the Voice of America (VOA) broadcaster when he had toured Poland. Like countless other listeners throughout the world, Greg listened to the *Jazz Hour* religiously and had been thrilled to get an invitation to visit the VOA studios if he was ever in Washington. Greg, probably very much to Willis's surprise, took him up on it and then very graciously invited me to join him on the visit to VOA.

I remember that Willis Conover's office was jam-packed with LPs, stacks of tapes, and photographs of him with Louis Armstrong, Duke Ellington, and numerous other jazz greats. We chatted about the upcoming American debut of the pianist Adam Makowicz at the Cookery in New York, which Greg and I would attend. This was the beginning of my connection with the most famous jazz disc jockey in the world.

Over the next two decades I would run into Willis at clubs such as Blues Alley. I learned how he began broadcasting for VOA in 1955 and soon became known around the world because of the popularity of American jazz and the reach of the VOA shortwave broadcast signal. He was relatively unknown in the United States because the VOA was prohibited by law from broadcasting stateside. American jazz fans knew of him from his role hosting concerts at the Newport Jazz Festival. Before going to work for VOA, however, he had his roots in the Washington jazz scene.

Photo 5.1 *The Shirley Horn Trio*
The Shirley Horn Trio, including Charles Ables on guitar and Steve Williams on drums, welcomed guest Buck Hill on saxophone in a performance in 1989. A native Washingtonian, Shirley Horn chose to remain in her hometown despite tours that took her all over the world.

Willis told me that he had started broadcasting as a student before entering the army during World War II, and after the war he became a professional announcer playing jazz on such stations as WWDC in Washington. Because of his prominence in the jazz community, in 1951 drummer Joe Timer, pianist Jack Holliday, and saxophonist Ben Lary asked him to join them in forming a band. They felt that his name would help attract audiences. Billed as "Willis Conover Presents the Orchestra, Joe Timer, Musical Director," the group regularly featured guest artists, including such luminaries as Al Cohn, Zoot Sims, Lee Konitz, Stan Getz, Dizzy Gillespie, and Charlie Parker. Concerts were presented at Club Kavakos on H Street, NE, and the Willis Conover name did help draw an audience.

I asked him about one of these shows that I had heard of which featured Charlie Parker. It had been recorded by Bill Potts and released on LP in 1982, and one of the tunes on the album was titled "Willis," composed and arranged by Potts. Willis said that Bird's appearance then was a special treat for the musicians, who idolized him. His playing was in top form at a time when his lifestyle had become more and more erratic. Willis also told me that he was in the forefront in presenting performances before integrated audiences. A few years after this discussion, however, WPFW programmer Jamal Muhammed told me that he and Nap Turner had accompanied Charlie Parker to Club Kavakos, and they were the only African Americans at the performance. The color line was more likely to be broken on U Street than in the white sections of DC in the early fifties.

Willis told me that he was especially proud of helping to launch the career of Ruth Brown. He heard her perform at the Crystal Caverns, later called the Bohemian Caverns, at Eleventh and U streets, NW. He was so taken by her performance that he immediately contacted Ahmet Ertegun to persuade him to record her on his Atlantic label. Sons of the Turkish ambassador to Washington in the late 1930s and early 1940s, Ahmet and his brother, Nesuhi, had presented jazz concerts at the embassy before starting the label in New York. Her early hits were such that Atlantic became known as "The House That Ruth Built," parroting the line about Yankee Stadium.

In our conversations, Willis said that before he started broadcasting for the Voice of America, he made it clear to US Information Agency management that he wanted independent control over his programming. He didn't want someone telling him what music to play, and so he was hired as an independent contractor. The immense popularity of his show enabled him to stand up to interference when an employee would have had to back down. Intensely patriotic, he was especially proud of breaking down the barriers of the iron curtain during the cold war. He continued to broadcast the *Jazz Hour* up until shortly before his death from lung cancer in 1996.

In November 1977 the *Washington Post* noted the remarkable breadth and diversity of jazz radio programming in Washington. Much of the article focused on Yale Lewis and his Saturday night show *Jazz Plus* on WETA-FM but also mentioned my show as well as Russell Williams on WAMU, Byron Morris and A. B. Spellman on WPFW, and Ken Steiner, who had shows on both WGTB and WPFW.[2]

This strength of jazz programming on the air reflected the vibrant scene for performances in Washington. Major artists came through DC to play in clubs such as Blues Alley in Georgetown, Harold's Rogue & Jar on N Street near Connecticut Avenue, NW,

Pigfoot and Moore's Love and Peace around Eighteenth and Rhode Island Avenue, NE, and the One Step Down, in the 2500 block of Pennsylvania Avenue, NW. Musicians who came by the WAMU studios on a Sunday afternoon to be interviewed on my show included Art Blakey, Roy Haynes, Dexter Gordon, Eddie Jefferson, and Sun Ra.

I became close to Washington-area musicians who had international reputations but opted to remain in DC for personal or family reasons. Shirley Horn lived a few blocks from me in Brookland. Although she had recorded for a major label and had opened for Miles Davis at the Village Vanguard in the 1960s, she decided to stay in her hometown to raise her daughter. Her unique vocal styling and piano accompaniment eventually landed her a recording contract with Verve, and world tours followed, but she and her husband, Shep, continued to live in their house on Lawrence Street. Her increased income allowed her to build additions to her house, and she was especially proud when she could finally accommodate a grand piano in her home. She once joked that the DC government was threatening to deny her any more remodeling permits. As famous as she became, she continued to perform in local venues, remaining loyal to her DC friends and fans. This loyalty extended to musicians. She had the same rhythm section, Charles Ables on bass and Steve Williams on drums, for twenty-five years. She included her long-time friend saxophonist Buck Hill on some of her recordings. She was honored at a gala tribute at the Kennedy Center in 2004, and the National Endowment for the Arts declared her a Jazz Master in 2005.

Bill Harris, a friend and neighbor of Shirley Horn's, hosted backyard parties every Labor Day at his Hamlin Street home that would feature such prominent guitarists as Kenny Burrell and Jamaican Ernest Ranglin. He had been a member of the R&B group The Clovers in the early fifties and had recorded a solo jazz guitar album for Mercury. But it was his dream to move the backyard performances into a club, so when space became available at Eighteenth and Rhode Island Avenue, NE, he jumped at it. There were other clubs in the neighborhood, Mr. Y's and Moore's Love and Peace. Moore's featured a young couple, Esther Williams on vocals and Davey Yarborough on saxophone. Davey would become the jazz director for Duke Ellington School of the Arts. Bill Harris named his club Pigfoot after a Bessie Smith song, "Gimme a Pigfoot and a Bottle of Beer." The house pianist was John Malachi, who would conduct workshops and perform with featured artists such as Kenny Burrell and Leon Thomas. One of the workshop participants was George V. Johnson, who at the time drove a bus for Metro but would later sing with James Moody. Pigfoot lasted only a few years in the 1970s, but the impact it had on the DC jazz scene went well beyond the Northeast neighborhood. Bill performed at Charlie's in Georgetown in the eighties before he passed away in 1988.

I first met John Malachi in 1968, but his friendship with my wife's parents, Tom and Mary Barrett, went back to the early 1940s. Over the years he frequently performed at parties at the Barrett home. After guests left, Tom and John would work out songs on the piano and John would tell stories about his career. I was the "fly on the wall" watching the interaction between old friends and hearing tales I couldn't repeat on the air.

John grew up in Washington where he performed professionally in clubs on U Street while still in Armstrong High School. He and a friend from Dunbar High School, Billy Taylor, hung out at the Jungle Inn, where Jelly Roll Morton was the manager. In the early

Photo 5.2 *John Malachi*
John Malachi grew up in Washington
and played in local clubs before joining
Billy Eckstine and His Orchestra and later
becoming Sarah Vaughan's accompanist. In
DC he also taught at Howard University and
the Duke Ellington School of the Arts.

1940s he would accompany Pearl Bailey as her career was getting started. In 1944 he was recruited to be the pianist in the epochal Billy Eckstine Orchestra, along with Dizzy Gillespie on trumpet, Charlie Parker, Gene Ammons, and Dexter Gordon on saxophones, and Art Blakey on drums. Sarah Vaughan was the female vocalist. Many other important bebop artists such as Miles Davis and Fats Navarro passed through the band. In the early fifties John was Sarah Vaughan's accompanist. His decision to make DC his home base and not tour extensively may have limited his name recognition, but it certainly didn't diminish the love and respect his more famous peers had for him. Once when I went to hear him at a club at Fourteenth and Rhode Island Avenue, NW, he introduced me to Milt Jackson; I had missed Sarah Vaughan, who had come by to hear him a week earlier. Dexter Gordon introduced him to his audience at Blues Alley. Sometimes fans from overseas would come up to John and ask for his autograph.

In the 1980s he taught at both Howard University and Duke Ellington School of the Arts. One of his students at Howard was Geri Allen, who later recorded a song with Charlie Haden and Paul Motian that she dedicated to him, "For John Malachi." He would attend my jazz history classes at American University and engage students with stories about his work with Billy Eckstine and Sarah Vaughan. During an interview on my show in February 1987, he talked about the time in 1944 when the Eckstine orchestra was touring Florida and Charlie Parker asked him to stay behind after a performance. He said the two of them worked on changes on "Cherokee" for hours. This would be the basis for Parker's masterpiece "Ko-Ko," recorded on November 26, 1945, the day I was born. As John was leaving the studio I thought, I have to get more of these stories on tape. Two day later he died suddenly from a heart attack. Fortunately, I have that show and others with him on tape, but it is the memory of the late-night conversations with John and Tom Barrett that I will always treasure.

Roger "Buck" Hill told stories through his saxophone rather than verbally. Like John Malachi, Buck had attended Armstrong High, the same school Duke Ellington had attended decades earlier. He became a professional musician as a teenager in the 1940s,

Photo 5.3 *Roger "Buck" Hill*
Nicknamed the "Jazz Postman" and the "Wallin' Mailman," Roger "Buck" Hill chose
to keep his day job working for the US Postal Service while playing local clubs nights
and weekends. He also recorded on the Muse label and with Shirley Horn.

performing at the U Street clubs and the Howard Theatre. After military service in the early 1950s, he continued to perform in the competitive jazz environment, frequently going head to head in tenor battles with Sonny Stitt or Charlie Rouse. He could have made a living as a touring musician, but Buck decided a "day gig" in DC worked best for his family and took a job with the US Postal Service. William Claxton photographed him in his uniform holding his saxophone, captioned "The Jazz Postman." He performed locally at clubs such as the Showboat and recorded with guitarist Charlie Byrd.

In 1978 drummer Billy Hart wanted to pay back those who helped him get started with his career and arranged for Buck to record for the Danish Steeplechase label and perform in Europe at the North Sea Jazz Festival in 1981. Recordings for the Muse label followed, the first of which, *Capitol Hill*, featured the legendary pianist Barry Harris. He also appeared as a guest artist on Verve recordings by Shirley Horn. After he retired from the postal service in 1998, jazz gigs continued until he was well into his eighties. In June 2013 I was honored to serve as cohost with Ellen Carter at a tribute to him at Queen's Chapel United Methodist Church, where numerous musicians paid homage to the "Wailin' Mailman" at an event organized by bassist Cheney Thomas. Buck did not perform but sat back and listened to the fond words and music from others who had performed with him for decades.

I met Charlie Byrd through his long-time drummer, Chuck Redd. I was always curious about why his classic 1962 *Jazz Samba* album, featuring Stan Getz and the hit "Desafinado," was recorded at All Souls Unitarian Church on Sixteenth Street. Charlie said he had heard Brazilian music on Felix Grant's show, but during a State Department–sponsored tour to Brazil with Keter Betts and Buddy Deppenschmidt in 1961, their interest was really sparked by the music they heard there. Brazilian composers such as Antonio Carlos Jobim and Luiz Bonfa were blending jazz with samba rhythms, and the percussionists in his group were particularly eager to record the music when they returned to the states. Charlie played the recordings he brought back for Stan Getz, who liked what he heard and convinced Creed Taylor at his label, Verve, to make a record. When a New York session didn't pan out, they decided to do it in DC, probably at the Jewish Community Center at Sixteenth and Q streets, NW, where Charlie and his group performed regularly. But there was a bus stop right outside the recital hall and the noise would disrupt any recording. All Souls Unitarian Church, further up Sixteenth Street, had a hall with excellent acoustics and no traffic noise. *Jazz Samba* was recorded at the church on February 13, 1962, with Stan Getz on tenor, Charlie Byrd on guitar, his brother Gene on second guitar, Keter Betts on bass, and Buddy Deppenschmidt and Bill Reichenbach on drums and percussion. The album was released in April and soon "Desafinado" was a hit, introducing the bossa nova to American listeners.[3]

Keter Betts, originally from Port Chester, New York, settled in the Washington area in the early 1950s. Before working with Charlie Byrd, he had toured and recorded with Dinah Washington and then had a long association with Ella Fitzgerald. When he was not traveling with Ella, he performed extensively in DC. Keter was undoubtedly one of the best teachers about jazz, really engaging an audience of students in focusing on what to listen to in a performance. He was a great storyteller and recounted being on tour once with Ella Fitzgerald when, in an airport, they encountered a mother holding a crying infant. Ella went over and sang a lullaby to the baby, who soon stopped crying and fell asleep.

One of the most fascinating characters in the Washington jazz scene is saxophonist Andrew White. I met Andrew and pianist Harry Killgo at performances at St. Margaret's Episcopal Church in 1968. Harry was accompanied by his young son, Keith, on drums. Within a few years Keith Killgo was a member of Donald Byrd's Blackbyrds while he was at Howard University.

By this time Andrew had already had a multifaceted career, performing on electric bass with Stevie Wonder while he was at the same time the principal oboist with the American Ballet Theater Orchestra and performing on saxophone at his jazz gigs. He also played electric bass with the Fifth Dimension and recorded with McCoy Tyner and Weather Report. When he performs, he is notorious for his high-water pants that show off his multicolor socks, his outrageous sense of humor, and his incredible performance on his saxophones. I once arranged for him to give a lecture on improvisation at the Smithsonian, and his explanation was perhaps a bit beyond what was necessary for the lay audience, but his jokes made the discussion a hit for all involved. Today he runs Andrew's Music out of his house on South Dakota Avenue in Northeast. The core of his business is the sale of transcriptions of solos by John Coltrane, Charlie Parker, Eric Dolphy, and Coleman Hawkins. He has transcribed every recorded solo by John Coltrane, including those on bootlegs. Also for sale in his catalog are LPs of his performances, CDs of sessions recorded at the One Step Down, his own eight-hundred-page autobiography,

Photo 5.4 *Saxophonist Andrew White*
Saxophonist Andrew White has also played
electric bass and oboe with groups as varied
as the American Ballet Theater Orchestra,
the Fifth Dimension, and Weather Report.
In addition to his many local appearances,
he runs Andrew's Music, where he sells
transcriptions of performances by such jazz
greats as John Coltrane and Charlie Parker.

Everybody Loves the Sugar, and numerous publications about jazz and other music genres.
All of this is handled by mail order. He has no website, does no email blasts, and he is not
on Twitter or Facebook. Yet music students from all over the world continue to order
the transcriptions.

The expansion of jazz programming in Washington continued in the 1980s. WAMU
added a daily overnight show hosted by Carlos Gaivar. I had been offered the slot but
opted to continue my weekly show, now called *Jazz Sunday*. I had been employed as
a union representative for a few years and decided to continue that career rather than
jump into broadcasting full time. The station also added to the jazz programming on
Saturday. *Spirits Known and Unknown* continued with its workshop concept for young
African American announcers, and in 1980 *Hot Jazz Saturday Night*, with Rob Bamberger,
premiered and is still on the air today. In the early years Bamberger had five hours to
explore early jazz, with an hour of Duke Ellington to start. The show is now three hours.
Bamberger's scholarly and entertaining approach examines the recordings of a particular
artist such as Bix Beiderbecke or Teddy Wilson, focusing on the recorded output of a few
years. It is undoubtedly the best show for jazz up through 1945 in the country.

By 1980 Paul Anthony was a veteran broadcaster. He got his start in broadcasting as a student at Georgetown University on WGTB before my arrival. In the 1970s he established himself professionally doing voice-overs for commercials, the weather on television, and jazz shows on WRC-FM and National Public Radio. He convinced the management of WGMS, the classical music station in Washington, that it should air jazz, America's classical music. For a decade he broadcast a show on Saturday nights on a commercial station where his ratings were good and the advertising book solid. In 1990 new owners decided Bill Evans did not mix with Beethoven and dropped jazz. Anthony went on to Sirius satellite radio until the merger with XM.

National Public Radio also played a major role in getting jazz on the Washington airwaves. NPR offered programs such as *Jazz Alive*, Marian McPartland's *Piano Jazz*, and *Jazz Set*, which were aired on WAMU. I served on a program selection panel with Dr. Billy Taylor, where we discovered we had some personal connections. My wife's mother, Mary Barrett, and Dr. Taylor were in the same Dunbar High School class of 1940. He and my father-in-law, Tom Barrett, shared a close friendship with John Malachi. After Dr. Taylor became artistic director for the jazz program at the Kennedy Center, he did a show for NPR in which his trio would perform with an artist such as Jackie McLean and discuss the guest's career between musical performances. I would delight in taking Tom Barrett to hear someone like Harry "Sweets" Edison perform with Dr. Taylor, then eavesdrop on the conversation after the show.

In 1980 a new station came on the air to replace WGTB at 90.1 on the FM dial. The University of the District of Columbia designated the station as WDCU-FM, but it was soon known as Jazz90. The first announcers were Faunee Williams, who hosted the morning drive-time show, and Gwen Redding, who was heard in the afternoon. By mid-decade the lineup included Bill McLaurin, Whitmore John, Steve Metalitz, Tim Masters, and later Candy Shannon. Steve Hoffman hosted a blues show and Ernest White did public affairs.

In the *Washington Post* on August 22, 1986, Jeffrey Yorke did a short profile of Felix Grant and also listed other jazz radio shows. The programs on WDCU were included along with Paul Anthony's on WGMS. Among the WPFW programmers were Art Cromwell, Jerry Washington, Tom Cole, John Zimbrick, Miyuki Williams, and Larry Appelbaum. WAMU programs were Rob Bamberger's *Hot Jazz Saturday Night*, my *Jazz Sunday*, and Marian McPartland's *Piano Jazz*. By then WAMU had begun to cut back jazz programming. The overnight show and *Spirits Known and Unknown* had been dropped, and most of the musical offerings were bluegrass and folk.[4]

Yorke's profile of Grant focused on his Saturday afternoon show on WRC-AM, mentioning his earlier thirty-year tenure as WMAL's nightly jazz authority. Not mentioned was the fact that when WMAL management first announced it was dropping his show in 1979, the outcry in letters and phone calls was so overwhelming that the station kept him on the air with a public apology, including advertisements on Metro buses. In 1983, just short of his thirtieth anniversary, the station dropped him permanently. At sixty-seven, he was evidently content to do a weekly show at WRC because, as Yorke pointed out, his other jazz activities took him around the world with visits to Europe and China.

In 1987 WRC dropped his show and shortly thereafter WAMU dropped mine. The ensuing letter campaign supporting my show did not change the decision of WAMU management. I had had a good run at the station, interviewing my heroes and even being honored by the proclamation of Rusty Hassan Day in 1984 by Mayor Marion Barry on the fifteenth anniversary of my show. But I was depressed until Edith Smith, general manager of WDCU, called, offering me airtime on Sunday afternoons. She added that I would start the same weekend as Felix Grant, who would be hosting a show on Saturdays. It was a real thrill to join the station at the same time as Grant. Congressman John Conyers (D-Mich.) had the debuts of our shows mentioned in the *Congressional Record*.

Although we had been colleagues for over twenty years, it was during the time we shared at WDCU that I really got to know Felix Grant. He was hip without being a hipster. His seemingly casual on-air presentation belied the hours of preparation. Ever the professional, he typed his playlists in advance and used a stopwatch to time his programs. Bill Mayhew once told me that in all of the twenty years at WMAL that they changed shifts at midnight, he never saw Grant not well dressed. The same was true at WDCU. There were no casual Saturdays at Jazz90 for Mr. Grant.

He was hospitalized in April 1989, the week he was to dedicate the plaque on the US Postal Service building that was on the site of the birthplace of Duke Ellington. His research had determined the location. Diagnosed with cancer, Grant was undergoing chemotherapy while continuing to do his show. He once told me he was hoping to celebrate fifty years of broadcasting jazz on the air and that doing his show kept him alive. His on-air presentation gave no indication of what he was going through. His professionalism would not permit him to sound anything other than his old self while broadcasting. Ever the gentleman, he would leave a thank you note in my box for the times I filled in for him. He almost made it to fifty years, passing away in 1993.

Grant's legacy has been preserved by the University of the District of Columbia. In 1988 he donated his sound recordings, interview tapes, books, photographs, posters, and other material as a first step in creating a jazz archive at the university. The Felix E. Grant Jazz Archives has become a major research center for the study of this American art form. Other contributors to the collection have included Herb and Will Friedwald, Paul Anthony, and Royal Stokes.

The decade of the nineties was one of friendly rivalry between WDCU and WPFW. The stations frequently would be cosponsors of performances. I met long-time WPFW programmer Jamal Muhammed at a concert at Fort DuPont, where we both introduced Ahmad Jamal. We became close friends, and I enjoyed his stories about hanging out at the stage door of the Howard Theatre with his childhood friend Nap Turner in order to see Charlie Parker, or about the time he spent on Rikers Island incarcerated with Ike Quebec.

WDCU lacked the strong broadcast signal of WPFW, but it established its jazz identity in the Washington community. The station broadcast performances from the university auditorium, including the annual battle among the bands of Howard University, University of Maryland, and the University of the District of Columbia. It sponsored jazz cruises where Jazz90 listeners could hear Sarah Vaughan, Joe Williams, Clark Terry, Jay McShann, Benny Carter, and Phil Woods, and it cosponsored performances by Wynton Marsalis at Lorton and the DC Youth Center to enable the incarcerated to hear great music.

The years I spent at WDCU were among the best in my broadcasting career. The friendships and camaraderie that I had with fellow announcers Faunee Williams,

Whitmore John, Candy Shannon, Gwen Redding, Bill McLaurin, Tim Masters, and Felix Grant were especially rewarding. I hosted concerts with Wynton Marsalis and Sonny Rollins. On a station-sponsored cruise, I hung out with Jay McShann, Clark Terry, and my friend Yale Lewis. I interviewed Albert Murray. My favorite show, however, was with a retired letter carrier, cab driver, and pianist who played only for family and friends, my wife, Sondra's, father. On August 6, 1995, I interviewed Thomas Barrett on his eightieth birthday. He spoke of his early years in West Virginia, playing piano in houses of prostitution as a teenager; hopping a freight train to Washington, DC, where he played professionally on U Street; meeting his wife, Mary, at a Hot Shoppe; his friendship with John Malachi and what a thrill it was to have Billy Eckstine's band perform at the army camp in Louisiana where he was stationed in 1944; service in the Pacific. We played his favorite recordings by Jimmie Lunceford, Count Basie, and Clifford Brown, and he explained why he loved Bill Evans. Not too long after the show, Askia Muhammad from WPFW told me how much he learned from the interview.

Unfortunately WDCU became a victim of the District of Columbia's budget woes. The university sold the license to C-SPAN to close a budget gap for $13 million. There was some community opposition to the sale, but not enough to stop the sale, and the station went off the air in 1997.

I was soon asked to become a substitute host on WPFW, filling in for such programmers as Rick Bolling and Guy Middleton. This led to a permanent slot. I was now on the air with my friends Jamal Muhammed, Tom Cole, Miyuki Williams, Larry Appelbaum, Hassan Ali, Nap Turner, and Askia Muhammad. Over the next few years other WDCU programmers joined me on WPFW, including Faunee Williams, Candy Shannon, Steve Hoffman, and Tim Masters. WHUR veteran Robyn Holden also joined the family of volunteer announcers broadcasting jazz and blues.

Since 1997 WPFW has been the only station broadcasting jazz in Washington, with the exception of Bamberger's show on WAMU. WAMU now focuses almost entirely on talk and public affairs. WETA has been featuring European classical music since WGMS changed format. Neither of these NPR affiliates broadcast jazz offerings from the network such as *Piano Jazz* or *Jazz Set*. WPFW has been on a rollercoaster of internal management problems for the past fifteen years that the volunteer announcers have always managed to work around and continue to play music. But in December 2012 the station manager abruptly dropped all of the daytime jazz shows to expand the talk and public affairs programming. My show was shifted from Monday evening to late Thursday night. The programming for jazz remains strong with such announcers as Brother Ah, a musician who has performed with Thelonious Monk, John Coltrane, Sun Ra, and Peggy Lee, and Willard Jenkins, a jazz journalist who collaborated with Randy Weston on Weston's autobiography. The daily blues show at noon survived the changes, and an hour of jazz has been inserted in the afternoon. The community response has been strong, and it remains to be seen if other daytime jazz shows will be restored. WPFW faced other challenges in 2013, but new managers and their positive attitude instill the programmers with confidence that the jazz shows will continue.

In the March 2013 issue of *JazzTimes*, Giovanni Russonello wrote about jazz radio finding itself at an existential crossroads, with technology upending the media landscape and public funds drying up. The situation at WPFW is but one example of the crisis confronting jazz radio across the country. Russonello notes the explosion of music on the internet and the change in listening habits through downloads and online music services. His suggestion that WPFW embrace its niche audience and invest in event programming is solid advice and exactly what on-air hosts Miyuki Williams and Robyn Holden have been urging station management to do.[5]

How people listen to music has changed dramatically. Downloads to iPods are convenient, but background and appreciation for the music is lacking. An informed announcer on the radio provides the names of the soloists and tells stories about the music, conveying what Whitney Balliett called and Larry Appelbaum named his show: *The Sound of Surprise*. Washington, DC, is fortunate to have WPFW still broadcasting the music with knowledgeable programmers. I feel fortunate that I am still on the air attempting to educate and entertain listeners with the music I first heard on the radio as a kid. Radio is still the best way to discover jazz.

Notes

I want to thank Aaron Johnson, jazz musician, former DC resident, and PhD candidate at Columbia University, for providing me with pertinent *Washington Post* articles. Johnson interviewed me for his thesis on jazz radio, and our conversation was immensely helpful in jogging my memory for this article.

    1. Marc Fisher, *Something in the Air: Radio, Rock, and the Revolution that Shaped a Generation* (New York: Random House, 2007), 205–9.
    2. Hollie West, "Smooth Sounds: The Rising (Air) Waves of Jazz," *Washington Post*, November 29, 1977, B9.
    3. David Adler, "Stan Getz and Charlie Byrd: Give the Drummer Some," *JazzTimes*, June 2004, 19.
    4. Jeffrey Yorke, "Jazz Spots on the Radio Dial," *Washington Post*, August 22, 1986, Weekend 6.
    5. Giovanni Russonello, "Up in the Air," *JazzTimes*, March 2013, 29.

6 Legislating Jazz

Anna Harwell Celenza

The State Department has discovered jazz.
It reaches folks like nothing has.
—DAVE AND IOLA BRUBECK, *The Real Ambassadors*

When contemplating the connections between Washington, DC, and jazz, names such as Duke Ellington, James Reese Europe, Shirley Horn, and Billy Taylor come to mind. But there are others, less famous but still important, who have influenced the course of jazz in the United States over the past half century. What happens in the US Congress affects the arts community in more fundamental ways than most people realize. Beyond direct public funding, a wide range of political decisions made in Washington influence how music is produced, preserved, and perceived by audiences in the United States and abroad. In the realm of jazz, especially, politicians and policy advocates such as Adam Clayton Powell Jr., J. Bennett Johnston, and John Conyers Jr., have worked alongside some of the nation's finest musicians to make sure that jazz remains an integral facet of America's cultural identity.

The Jazz Ambassadors

The US government's involvement with jazz began during a period of ideological crisis: the Cold War. As political leaders in Washington, DC, struggled to present the nation as a model of peace and equality to foreign entities, civil rights struggles at home offered a strikingly contradictory image. By 1950 politicians regularly declared race as the "Achilles' heel" of American foreign policy, and in 1954 President Dwight D. Eisenhower decided to take action.[1] Frustrated by the stereotype of Americans as "a race of materialists" with no "worthwhile culture of any kind" and determined to debunk Soviet accusations concerning America's race problem, Eisenhower went in search of a home-grown, cultural product that could be exported around the world as proof of American innovation and diversity.[2] Jazz is what he found. Thanks to the distribution of Victory Discs (or V-Discs) and broadcasts via Allied Radio and Voice of America during World War II and the reconstruction era, jazz was part of a global cultural craze by the mid-1950s, and legislators

Photo 6.1 *Duke Ellington*
in the Soviet Union
Duke Ellington greets a delighted fan
during a trip to the Soviet Union in 1971.
Ellington and his orchestra traveled more as
jazz ambassadors than any other group, on
trips that could last for months at a time.

in Washington soon realized the benefits of promoting the genre and its most talented practitioners as symbols of freedom and American ingenuity.

Rep. Adam Clayton Powell Jr. of New York was the first to suggest to President Eisenhower and the State Department the idea of using jazz as a Cold War tool. Although Eisenhower's easy embrace of jazz seems hypocritical, given his noncommittal reaction to the early events of the civil rights era, his acute sense of expediency quickly superseded his well-documented condescension toward African Americans.[3] Recognizing the symbolic importance of an American genre firmly tied to black culture, Eisenhower went to the Senate in August 1954 and requested special appropriations in the "cultural and artistic fields."[4] Eisenhower wanted to add music to his arsenal of weapons against communism, and for the first time in American history, congressional leaders entered into conversations about the legislation of jazz.[5]

The result of these conversations was the development of a State Department program called Jazz Ambassadors, which, from 1956 through the late 1970s, sent the nation's finest musicians around the globe, from Iran, Pakistan, and Iraq to Greece, Cairo, the Congo, and the Soviet Union. As a *New York Times* reporter noted in 1955, the Eisenhower administration, with help from legislators, turned jazz into America's "Secret Sonic Weapon."[6] But not everyone in Congress was pleased with the proposal, and right from the start, implementation of the Jazz Ambassadors program met with resistance. After much discussion, Dizzy Gillespie was chosen as the first "ambassador" to go on tour, a decision that distressed Sen. Allen J. Ellender of Louisiana. "I have never heard so much noise in all my life," he said. "To send such jazz as Mr. Gillespie, I can assure you that instead of doing good it will do harm, and the people will really believe we are barbarians." Rep. John Rooney, a New York Democrat, concurred. Still, the Jazz Ambassadors program proceeded as planned.[7]

Gillespie first toured the Middle East, where he made appearances in Iran, Syria, Pakistan, and Lebanon before moving on to Turkey, Yugoslavia, and Greece in Eastern Europe. As Penny Von Eschen has noted, careful calculations went into planning the tour's itinerary, which moved along "the Eisenhower administration's conception of a 'perimeter defense' against the Soviet Union 'along the Northern Tier,' extending from Turkey to Pakistan."[8] This tour proved so successful that on August 1, 1956, the Eighty-Fourth Congress agreed to extend the special appropriations that had been designated for the President's Emergency Fund and formalize them into the President's Special International Program.[9] These new funds paid for an additional Gillespie tour, this time to South America, where he promoted American culture by performing for audiences large and small, from spontaneous exchanges with local fans to formal events with high-ranking officials. Yet, despite Gillespie's success, critics in Congress raged on. For example, the Senate Appropriations Committee added a stipulation to its appropriations bill banning the use of funds for future foreign tours by "jazz bands." Although the stipulation was later excised from the final version of the bill, continued resistance to the Jazz Ambassadors program by some members of Congress affected the content of the program and its reception by the American public. In April 1956 a group called the White Citizens Council of Alabama denounced jazz, claiming it was part of a "plot to mongrelize America."[10]

Angered by the battles in Congress and the racism still prevalent throughout the United States, Gillespie coauthored an article for *Esquire* when he returned home, titled "Jazz Is Too Good for Americans," in which he highlighted the sharp contrast between attitudes of members of Congress like Ellender and Rooney and the enthusiastic crowds he encountered abroad:

> Jazz, the music I play most often, has never really been accepted as an art form by the people of my own country. . . . To them, jazz is music for kids and dope addicts. . . . As an American, I'm deeply sorry that they [foreign countries] have beat us to the punch in exploiting so fully a music we originally created. Most of all—and this is the really great irony—I'm disappointed that the enormous upswing in jazz enthusiasm abroad has been accompanied by a decline in several major areas of jazz interest here at home.[11]

Toward the end of the article, Gillespie made a case for continuing the tours, explaining that "this lionizing of American jazzmen overseas has had a great effect on our morale." He suggested that instead of cutting back on the Jazz Ambassadors program, Congress should allocate more funds for tours and advocate for stronger jazz appreciation programs in the United States, "taught to school children at all levels of their education."[12] Although Congress would not embrace such an education program for many years to come, it did note how effective jazz had proven to be in the realm of cultural diplomacy and consequently continued to approve funds for additional tours featuring Benny Goodman and his band in 1956 (East Asia), the Dave Brubeck Quartet in 1958 (Eastern Europe, the Middle East, and South Asia), and Louis Armstrong & His All-Stars in 1960–61 (Africa).

Photo 6.2 *Dizzy Gillespie in Zagreb*
Dizzy Gillespie tries out a motorcycle in Zagreb in 1956, one of the stops on the first Jazz
Ambassadors trip, which took Gillespie and his band to the Middle East and Eastern Europe.
The young man behind Gillespie is Nikica Kalogjera, a local musician and composer.

Armstrong had been asked to participate in an earlier tour of the Soviet Union in 1957
but declined due to his disappointment with the Eisenhower administration's refusal to
enforce court-ordered desegregation of schools in Little Rock, Arkansas. "The way they
are treating my people in the South, the government can go to hell," said Armstrong.
"It's getting so bad, a colored man hasn't got any country."[13]

Gillespie sympathized with Armstrong's point of view. After his Middle East tour, he
admitted that, even though he was proud of his effectiveness "against Red propaganda,"
he was insulted by the State Department's attempts to "brief him" beforehand about
American race relations: "I've got 300 years of briefing. I know what they've done to us,
and I'm not going to make any excuses."[14]

Dave and Iola Brubeck also took note of the disconnect between the message promoted by the Jazz Ambassadors abroad and the reality of everyday life at home. As lyricist
Iola Brubeck explained, although "the entire jazz community was elated with the official
recognition of jazz and its international implications," the country's race problem continued. In an effort to draw public attention to this issue, the Brubecks joined forces with
Armstrong in 1961 and produced a musical titled *The Real Ambassadors*, which offered
a critique of the hypocrisy still inherent in the government program. Using satire as a
means of criticizing the State Department's handling of the Jazz Ambassadors program,
the musical also celebrated Armstrong's key role as a musical diplomat and defender of
the civil rights movement. *The Real Ambassadors* was recorded in 1961 and performed

live at the 1962 Monterey Jazz Festival. Received with great critical acclaim, the musical reinvigorated the public's appreciation for the Jazz Ambassadors program and set the stage for the most active jazz ambassador in US history, namely, Washington, DC, native Duke Ellington.[15]

Ellington as Ambassador

Duke Ellington and His Orchestra toured for the State Department more than any other ensemble, and their participation marked a new chapter in the Jazz Ambassadors program. In 1962 the Kennedy administration laid down new guidelines for the State Department tours in a report that justified the payment of "high salaries to outstanding artists . . . on the basis of extraordinary artistic talent" and recommended that performers interact with foreigners offstage so that young people, especially, have the opportunity to meet the performers and, when applicable, exchange skills and stories with them.[16]

Ellington's first tour began in the fall of 1963 with a three-month journey that took him and his band to a range of nations, mostly in the Near and Middle East. Their itinerary started in Syria, then continued on to Jordan, Afghanistan, India, Ceylon (now Sri Lanka), Pakistan, the region now known as Bangladesh, Iran, Iraq, and Lebanon. As Harvey G. Cohen explains in *Duke Ellington's America*, the band was originally scheduled to perform in Turkey, Cypress, the United Arab Republic, Greece, Egypt, and Yugoslavia, too. But the final leg of the tour was canceled due to the assassination of President Kennedy.[17] The publicity put out by the State Department for Ellington's tour described the musician as a symbol of the best in American culture. To borrow a phrase from cultural historian Reinhold Wagnleitner, Ellington's first State Department tour showed Congress and the State Department that jazz didn't need propaganda to succeed; "it was the propaganda that needed jazz."[18] This is perhaps most clearly shown in the numerous articles about Ellington that appeared in local papers, side by side with reports of official American support of the civil rights movement.

Jazz in the White House

Shortly after Ellington returned from his first tour as jazz ambassador, Dizzy Gillespie set his sights on a new residence in Ellington's hometown—namely, the White House. Although Gillespie embarked on his presidential campaign in jest, his underlying message was completely serious: American politics needed new energy. The chorus to Gillespie's 1964 campaign song, a rewrite of the Jon Hendricks tune "Salt Peanuts," said it all:

> Your politics ought to be a groovier thing.
> Vote Dizzy! Vote Dizzy!
> So get a good president who's willing to swing.
> Vote Dizzy! Vote Dizzy!

Gillespie promised that, if elected, he would rename the White House "the Blues House" and appoint a stellar cabinet: Duke Ellington as secretary of state, Max Roach as defense secretary, Peggy Lee as labor chief, and Miles Davis as director of the CIA. All joking aside, the impetus for his campaign was to address the issues at stake in 1964 and raise money for civil rights organizations such as CORE (Congress of Racial Equality) and the Southern Christian Leadership Conference. Gillespie touted his experience as a jazz ambassador as proof of his foreign policy competence. His candidacy became a regular topic in the media, and even after he pulled out of the race, talk show hosts and journalists continued to comment on the symbolic connections between jazz, American democracy, and the nation's foreign policy.

Gillespie didn't make it to the White House, but Ellington did, albeit not as president or secretary of state. On April 29, 1969—Ellington's seventieth birthday—he was invited to the White House and presented with the Presidential Medal of Freedom. He was the first jazz musician ever to receive such an honor. In his remarks, Richard Nixon referenced not only Ellington's talent but also his success as a cultural diplomat: "When we think of freedom, we think of many things. But Duke Ellington is one who has carried the message of freedom to all the nations of the world through music, through understanding—understanding that reaches over all national boundaries and over all boundaries of prejudice and over all boundaries of language."[19] After receiving the Presidential Medal of Freedom, Ellington was sent on numerous diplomatic tours by the State Department. Between his trip to Burma in 1970 and his tour of Asia in 1972, he performed in over forty countries on four continents under State Department auspices. Yet, despite his success, change was in the air. The Vietnam War, Watergate, and the energy crisis caused many politicians in Washington to call into question the financial commitment required for the government's continued sponsorship of the tours.[20] Consequently, the State Department sought new ways to offset the program's cost while simultaneously reaching out to new audiences. Beginning in the 1970s the tours were outsourced to a private entity, Festival Productions, under the directorship of George Wein, founder of the Newport Jazz Festival. Ellington's final tours were under Wein's management, as were those of other top performers: Miles Davis, Lionel Hampton, Earl Hines, Rahsaan Roland Kirk, Charles Mingus, Oscar Peterson, and Sarah Vaughan. Although the tours were now shorter, they still proved effective, and State Department officials praised the participants for being "superb representatives of the United States in every way."[21]

Defining Jazz through Legislation

Despite the continued success of the Jazz Ambassadors program, some policymakers in Washington voiced concern over the changes privatization brought to the program. Was the government's commitment to jazz growing less focused? Would the image of jazz as a specifically American genre be maintained by private investors? In an effort to preserve the importance of jazz as a symbol of American identity, on February 28, 1973, Rep. Robert C. Wilson of California introduced a joint resolution (H.J.Res.395) to establish a national music of the United States. The purpose of the bill was to declare "the national music of the United States to be jazz." But the measure failed to pass, and Congress's support of jazz began to wane. In 1978 the Jazz Ambassadors program was downsized dramatically and transferred from the State Department to the newly formed US International Communications Agency. Although National Endowment for the Arts funding was earmarked specifically for jazz in 1982, in general, discussions of the genre all but disappeared in Congress for more than a decade.

Rep. John Conyers Jr. of Michigan is largely responsible for reinvigorating jazz appreciation among Washington politicians. On September 25, 1986, he proposed "A concurrent resolution designating jazz as an American national treasure" (H.Con.Res.396). The goal of the bill was to ensure that jazz, "a rare and valuable American treasure," would be "preserved, understood and promulgated." As the title of this resolution indicated, it was concurrent with a Senate resolution (S.Con.Res.170) introduced by Sen. Alan Cranston of California on October 15, 1986. Although neither resolution gathered enough support for passage in 1986, Conyers and Cranston refused to give up. In 1987 they introduced revised versions in the House and Senate (H.Con.Res.57 and S.Con.Res.23), both of which passed unanimously under the general title of the "Jazz Preservation Act." For the first time in history, jazz was officially recognized as a national treasure, "an indigenous American music and art form, bringing to this country and the world a uniquely American musical synthesis and culture through the African-American experience."[22]

But the legislation of jazz required more than simply stating its value as a national treasure. In a 1990 congressional bill sponsored by Sen. J. Bennett Johnston of Louisiana, then chair of the Senate Appropriations Subcommittee for the Department of the Interior, the secretary of the interior was asked "to conduct a study of the feasibility of establishing a unit of the National Park System to interpret and commemorate the origins, development, and progression of Jazz in the United States" (S.2846). Because New Orleans was seen as the ideal location for the proposed national park for jazz, Louisiana representative Lindy Boggs introduced a similar resolution in the House. After much debate, the House and Senate passed both bills, which called for the establishment of the Preservation of Jazz Commission. The commission was charged with overseeing the congressionally mandated study, which proved to be divisive in the greater New Orleans community. In general, some in New Orleans were troubled by the commission's definition of the origins of jazz as strictly African American.[23] Local jazz historian Al Rose even went so far as to argue that the "myth of jazz's African origins" was blocking recognition of the contributions made by other ethnic groups.[24] Consequently, when the commission's report was submitted one year later, all ethnic categories were removed from the definition of jazz. In 1993, Louisiana representative William J. Jefferson and senator J. Bennett Johnston introduced the New Orleans Jazz National Historic Park Act into the House and Senate (H.R.3408, S.1586). After much debate, it was eventually voted into law as an amendment to the California Desert Protection Act of 1994, with no references to the music's African American origins.[25] References to the African American roots of jazz were also absent in a second legislative action that year, S.J.Res 182, a "joint resolution to designate the year 1995 as 'Jazz Centennial Year.'"

In response to these changes in the legislature's definition of jazz, Representative Conyers reintroduced H.Con.Res.57 in 1997, "expressing the sense of Congress respecting the designation of jazz as a rare and valuable national treasure." This resolution, which attempted to reinsert recognition of "the African-American experience" into the origins of jazz and describe the genre as "a unifying force, bridging cultural, religious, ethnic, and age differences in our diverse society," was passed on to committee and then abandoned.

The decision of the 105th Congress not to vote on this last resolution reveals how attitudes toward jazz began to change in Washington's political circles after the Cold

War. Instead of defining jazz as an art form rooted in African American culture, Congress began to describe the genre as an art form "indigenous to the United States" that "incorporates and transcends differences of nationality, religion, language, culture, socioeconomic status, and race."[26] Consequently, Representative Conyers and his colleagues Charles Rangel, Frank Pallone Jr., and Eleanor Holmes Norton began to seek new ways of recognizing the African American contribution to jazz. Since 2002, various concurrent resolutions in the House and Senate have noted the contributions of individual African American jazz musicians: Lionel Hampton, Dinah Washington, William "Count" Basie, Duke Ellington, Shirley Horn, Miles Davis, Jon Faddis, and Lena Horne.[27] In the case of Duke Ellington, the bill not only honored his life and work but also recognized "the Duke Ellington School of the Arts in Washington, D.C., on the occasion of its 30th anniversary" and pledged support for "the annual Duke Ellington Jazz Festival to be held in Washington, D.C.," which has been running successfully since 2005. In August 2017 the Duke Ellington School of the Arts reopened after a three-year, $170 million renovation.

Most recently, on March 26, 2015, Rep. Conyers introduced the National Jazz Preservation, Education, and Promulgation Act of 2015 (HR 1682) to the House of Representatives. Building on the 1987 version of H.Con.Res.57 (as opposed to the failed 1997 version), the 2015 bill calls for the establishment of a National Jazz Preservation Program at the Smithsonian, expansion of jazz education in the public school system, and the resurrection of a Jazz Ambassadors program modeled on the one launched by the State Department in 1956. Conyers first proposed a version of this bill in 2011, and each year since then he has secured numerous co-signers, but it has never been brought up for a vote. Instead the bill has been referred to the Subcommittee on Higher Education and Workforce Training where, as of September 2017, it still resides.

Over the last sixty-five years, decisions made in Washington have facilitated the establishment of jazz as an important element in America's cultural identity. And as the definition of jazz according to Congress has changed, so too has the genre itself, which appears to grow more inclusive, both at home and abroad, with each generation. One can even see the influence of the US Congress on a more local level, as was demonstrated by the establishment of the HR-57 Center for the Preservation of Jazz and Blues, a nonprofit performance venue and education foundation that was located on H Street in Northeast Washington, DC. Founded in 1993 as "a place where aspiring musicians gather," HR-57 paid tribute to the value of cultural legislation. But, like other nonprofit venues, a lack of funds eventually forced HR-57 to close in August 2014.[28] Let's hope that future jazz venues in the capital find the support they need. As Representative Conyers so aptly explained in presenting his most recent bill to Congress, the federal government has an important role to play when it comes to jazz. By preserving the past and creating a new generation of jazz musicians and fans, US legislation will help to ensure that this uniquely American musical genre lives on.[29]

Notes

1. "Achilles Heel" from Sen. Henry Cabot Lodge, in Thomas Borstelmann, *The Cold War and the Color Line: Race Relations in the Global Arena* (Cambridge: Harvard University Press, 2001), 76.

2. Frank Ninkovich, "U.S. Information Policy and Cultural Diplomacy," *Foreign Policy Association: Headline Series* 308 (1996): 24; see also Penny M. Von Eschen, *Satchmo Blows Up the World: Jazz Ambassadors Play the Cold War* (Cambridge: Harvard University Press, 2004), 4.

3. Von Eschen, *Satchmo Blows Up the World*, 5.

4. President Dwight D. Eisenhower to the President of the Senate, Estimate No. 82, 83rd Congress, 2nd Session (July 27, 1954), 511.00/7-2354, Foreign Relations of the United States, 1952–1954, vol. II, pt. 2, National Security Affairs, Document 363, U.S Department of State, Office of the Historian, https://history.state.gov/historicaldocuments/frus1952-54v02p2/d365. See also Von Eschen, *Satchmo Blows Up the World*, 4.

5. Music Advisory Panel (November 15, 1955), 2, ser. 5, box 12, fol. 12, Bureau of Educational and Cultural Affairs Historical Collection, J. William Fulbright Papers, University of Arkansas at Fayetteville; and Von Eschen, *Satchmo Blows Up the World*, 58.

6. Felix Belair Jr., "United States Has Secret Sonic Weapon—Jazz," *New York Times*, November 6, 1955, 1.

7. Von Eschen, *Satchmo Blows Up the World*, 40.

8. Ibid., 32.

9. For a contemporary report on the renewed funding, see Ross Parmenter, "U.S. Helps Out. Bill Passed to Make Cultural Tours a Branch of Our Foreign Policy," *New York Times*, August. 5, 1956, 7.

10. Von Eschen, *Satchmo Blows Up the World*, 26.

11. Dizzy Gillespie and Ralph Ginsberg, "Jazz Is Too Good for Americans," *Esquire*, June 1957, 55.

12. Ibid., 140.

13. Mary L. Dudziak, *Cold War Civil Rights: Race and the Image of American Democracy* (Princeton, NJ: Princeton University Press, 2000), 66. See also Von Eschen, *Satchmo Blows Up the World*, 63.

14. Fred Kaplan, "When Ambassadors Had Rhythm," *New York Times*, June 29, 2008, www.nytimes.com/2008/06/29/arts/music/29kapl.html?pagewanted=all&_r=0.

15. Penny Von Eschen, "The Real Ambassadors," in *Uptown Conversation: The New Jazz Studies*, ed. Robert O'Meally, Brent Hayes Edwards, and Farrah Jasmine Griffin (New York: Columbia University Press, 2004), 189–203.

16. Harvey G. Cohen, *Duke Ellington's America* (Chicago: University of Chicago Press, 2010), 423–34.

17. Cohen, *Duke Ellington's America*, 411–13.

18. Reinhold Wagnleitner, *Coca-Colonization and the Cold War: The Cultural Mission of the United States in Austria after the Second World War* (Chapel Hill: University of North Carolina Press, 1994), 210.

19. Richard Nixon, "Remarks on Presenting the Presidential Medal of Freedom to Duke Ellington," April 29, 1969, available at Gerhard Peters and John T. Woolley, *The American Presidency Project*, www.presidency.ucsb.edu/ws/?pid=2026.

20. Von Eschen, *Satchmo Blows Up the World*, 249.

21. Penny Von Eschen and Curtis Sandberg, "Enter the Newport Jazz Festival," *Jam Session: America's Jazz Ambassadors Embrace the World*, online catalogue for touring photography exhibition, http://www.meridian.org/jazzambassadors/newport/newport.php.

22. For a detailed discussion of the Jazz Preservation Act of 1987, see Jeff Farley, "Jazz as a Black American Art Form: Definitions of the Jazz Preservation Act," *Journal of American Studies* 45, no. 1 (2011): 113–29.

23. Michael Eugene Crutcher, *Tremé: Race and Place in a New Orleans Neighborhood* (Athens: University of Georgia Press, 2010), 87–89.

24. Preservation of Jazz Advisory Commission, Public Hearing Report, August 24, 1991, 66.

25. S.Amdt.1626: "To establish the New Orleans Jazz National Historical Park in the State of Louisiana" to S.21 "California Desert Protection Act of 1994."

26. Rep. Eleanor Holmes Norton, "H.Con.Res.501—Honoring the life and work of Duke Ellington, recognizing the 30th anniversary of the Duke Ellington School of the Arts, and supporting the annual Duke Ellington Jazz Festival," introduced September 28, 2004, http://beta.congress.gov/bill/108th/house-concurrent-resolution/501.

27. H.Con.Res.363 (2002), S.Con.Res.101 (2002), H.Con.Res.144 (2003), H.Res.778 (2004), H.Con.Res.501 (2004), H.Con.Res.300 (2005), H.Res.894 (2009), H.Res.641 (2012), H.Res 839 (2015).

28. Perry Stein, "Musicians Want to Make D.C. a Jazz Mecca Again. but Can the City's Jazz Be Saved?" *Washington Post*, April 16, 2016, https://www.washingtonpost.com/local/musicians-want-to-make-dc-a-jazz-mecca-again-but-can-the-citys-jazz-be-saved/2016/04/16/e95aeb76-00ad-11e6-9203-7b8670959b88_story.html?utm_term=.38dbb0c0d5e9.

29. Rep. John Conyers Jr., H.Con.Res.1682, National Jazz Preservation, Education, and Promulgation Act of 2015, https://www.congress.gov/bill/114th-congress/house-bill/1682?q=%7B%22search%22%3A%5B%22jazz%22%2C%22jazz%22%5D%7D; and Rep. John Conyers Jr., HR 2823, National Jazz Preservation and Education Act of 2011, https://www.congress.gov/bill/112th-congress/house-bill/2823.

7 The Beautiful Struggle

A Look at Women Who Have Helped Shape the DC Jazz Scene

Bridget Arnwine

When groundbreaking jazz drummer Viola Smith penned "Give Girl Musicians a Break!" for *DownBeat* magazine in 1941, it is quite possible that she was unaware of how far-reaching the article would be. During Smith's era, groups like the International Sweethearts of Rhythm and the Hour of Charm Orchestra entertained the troops while male musicians served in the armed forces and answered the call to war.[1] The all-female bands were not just casual stand-ins, however; they were good. Really good.[2] When the war ended, the all-female bands were gradually cast by the wayside in favor of the return to normalcy that was the promotion of male instrumentalists and the oversexualization of female "maisies."[3] With professional opportunities dwindling ever quickly, female performers often turned reluctant homemakers and caretakers.[4]

Nearly eighty years after Smith's article was written and after female instrumentalists performed in front of sold out and enthusiastic crowds, female jazz musicians are still in pursuit of their break and questions about female instrumentalists' musical abilities still abound. For every Louis Armstrong and John Coltrane, there is a Clora Bryant and Vi Wilson whose stories are rarely told. That, in 2015, female jazz musicians would protest outside of one of the world's most reputable houses of jazz in pursuit of performance opportunities and orchestra jobs while women were inside running the organization's day-to-day functions is just one example of the complexities that often surround women in jazz.[5]

While female musicians the world over have sought out opportunities to assimilate into jazz's mainstream culture, Washington, DC, is one metropolitan area that has molded the careers of several of jazz music's most celebrated female voices. Though there are many such voices, the task of detailing the stories of DC's jazz heroines is daunting at best. Who are they? What do they have in common? Who are among the most celebrated or most unsung? Because the questions and, yes, even the answers are so broad, this chapter details the biographies of some of DC's most notable female voices. Divided into three sections, this chapter features the stories and accomplishments of artists such as Shirley Horn, Eva Cassidy, and Ruth Brown.

Washington, DC's, Darling Daughters

In the world of jazz, New York City has become the place where some of the biggest names in the music have jumpstarted their careers. Artists such as Miles Davis, Louis Armstrong, Thelonious Monk, Wynton Marsalis, and DC's own Duke Ellington are just a few of the musicians who left home in order to reach larger audiences with their music and to pursue greater professional opportunities in the Big Apple. When artists such as June Norton, Shirley Horn, and Eva Cassidy shunned the bigger stage in order to build their careers closer to home, their professional sacrifices spoke volumes. Such sacrifices revealed that it was possible for musicians to believe in the music, love the music, even, and want nothing more than to create it in a place they knew and loved. For these women, that place was Washington, DC.

There's no DC Jazz without D-u-k-e

> Sometimes when I hear his music, I have to readjust my thinking to say, "was I really with him?"
> —JUNE NORTON, radio interview with Felix Grant (October 19, 1985)

June Norton was born on October 19, 1924, in Alexandria, Virginia. During her early years, she pursued classical training in hopes of having a career in opera. It wasn't until she determined that a career in classical music may not be possible (due mostly to her race) that Norton decided to expand her training to include popular music.[6]

Based on DC's racial climate during the 1930s and 1940s, Norton's apprehension about a career in classical music was understandable. One notable example involves famed African American opera singer Marian Anderson. After a well-received performance (for President and Mrs. Roosevelt) at the White House, organizers worked tirelessly to schedule a monumental performance for the young prima donna. No African American had yet performed on the Washington, DC, Daughters of the American Revolution (DAR) Constitution Hall stage, but the success of Anderson's high-profile White House performance led some to believe that she should be the first. Unfortunately, it would take years before that performance would happen. In 1939 Anderson was denied an opportunity to perform there simply because of her race.[7]

A career as a classical performer may not have been a likely career for Norton, but she would go on to mature as a vocalist under the direction of the best instructor experience could afford her, Mr. Duke Ellington. In 1950 Ellington's road manager, Jerry Rhea, invited Norton—who had begun making a living as a singer around Washington, DC—over to the Howard Theatre to meet Ellington. "Jerry called me one evening and said, 'June I want you to catch a cab and come over here to the Howard Theatre. Duke wants to meet you.' I said, 'Duke who?' Cause he was the last person I thought would want to meet me."[8] During her time with his band, Norton made an indelible mark on Ellington early on, but she was unable to achieve commercial success on her own. When the two met, they hit it off. Her first meeting with Ellington lasted for hours as the two worked on music that saw Norton singing the bandleader's works in different styles and keys. "He said 'June, come here. Do you know this song? Can you sing it in this key?'

That went on, you know. About an hour later, we were still doing that. And then he'd say, 'ok let's go over to the harps,' and two hours later we were doing the same thing."[9] They went on to work together for most of 1950. She also sat in with Ellington's band on occasion throughout his later years. The two would remain friends for the rest of Ellington's life.

For much of the 1960s Norton continued to perform around Washington, DC. Representatives from an advertising agency, who eventually hired her to sing commercials on television, discovered her during a performance at the Flame Restaurant. She was the first black woman in the region to appear in TV commercials marketed to southern states. For Norton, that distinction resulted in multiple awards, including the 1962 Achievement Award from the National Association of Colored Women, a TV Personality of the Year Award, the 1962 Emphasis Award from the National Association of Market Development, and a Singer of the Year Award for 1962 from the YMCA.[10]

From the 1970s until her passing more than thirty years later, Norton stepped away from the limelight, settling instead for a new career as a counselor and a personal life. She earned a masters of music education degree from Antioch College's DC location, and she dedicated the remainder of her days to helping underprivileged youth and female prisoners. She also married Thomas C. Cuff, though the year of their union is unknown.

June Norton Cuff passed away on October 30, 2004. Though she preceded her husband in death, the two are buried near each other at Arlington National Cemetery.

The District's Prodigy

> Music is my life. Without it, I would perish.
> —SHIRLEY HORN, *Jazz Times* (May 2001)

When the 109th Congress passed H.Con.Res.300 in recognition of the late Shirley Horn, the honor served as an acknowledgment of her contribution to jazz music and, subsequently, American culture.[11] The pianist, composer, and vocalist had a career that spanned more than six decades. She recorded more than twenty-five albums as a leader and worked as a side musician for such artists as Stuff Smith, Charlie Haden, Toots Thielemans, and—one of her musical idols—Oscar Peterson. Horn passed away after suffering complications from diabetes on October 20, 2005. She was seventy-one years old.[12]

Born the oldest of Ernest and Grace Horn's three children on May 1, 1934, Shirley Valerie Horn was groomed for musical success early on. Her family wanted her to grow up to be a concert pianist, so she began taking lessons before she could read or write. Encouraged by her grandmother to take lessons, Horn began studying piano with a man named Mr. Fletcher when she was just four years old. He worked with Horn until she was an eager eleven-year-old in need of more advanced studies. By the time Horn turned twelve, her uncle Dr. I. B. Horn, a wealthy doctor in Washington, DC, contacted Howard University about starting a junior school of music as a means of furthering her musical education. Horn was eighteen when her uncle passed away, and thus marked the end of her studies with the Howard University Junior Music School.[13] His passing may have also marked the end of the Howard University Junior Music School.

Photo 7.1 *Shirley Horn*
Felix Grant and Shirley Horn at
the Indian Spring Country Club,
Silver Spring, Maryland, 1988.

Documentation surrounding the existence of the program following Horn's studies is difficult to find.

Despite winning offers to attend Juilliard and Xavier University, Horn stayed in Washington, DC. Some accounts suggest that her family couldn't afford to send her away, while others suggest that her mother didn't allow her to go. Whatever the truth is, Horn stayed home, married Charles "Shep" Deering when she was nineteen, had a daughter that the couple named Rainey, and she played. A lot.

Horn toured and gigged consistently. When she was home, she performed at clubs around DC, such as Olivia's Patio Lounge, The Place Where Louis Dwells, the Merry-Land Club, and Bohemian Caverns (the club formerly known as Crystal Caverns). Having studied classical music during her time at Howard University's Junior Music School, her club engagements were initially an opportunity to grow and learn jazz music.

She learned jazz sitting in on jam sessions with musicians who were making a living playing the music. She had developed an affinity for Erroll Garner, Oscar Peterson, and Ahmad Jamal; her proximity to DC's jazz clubs and performance venues afforded her the opportunity to hear some of the biggest names in jazz. She was eager to learn. The reality of Horn's vision, however, was that her presence was not always welcome. "'Buck [Hill] was the only person who was nice to me the couple of times they let me sit in,' Horn says. 'I didn't know anything about jazz, just what I had heard, and imitations of Erroll Garner didn't fit in with what the guys were doing then. Their attitude was, 'Let's bear down on her.' Which was the best thing for me trying to come out of the classical tradition. I was nervous, but I was stubborn.'"[14]

Although Stere-O-Craft Records signed Horn to a record deal in 1960, her first recording was as part of Stuff Smith's 1959 release *Cat on a Hot Fiddle*. When she made her debut recording, *Embers and Ashes*, the notoriously introverted pianist and singer opened the door to realizing her dreams: she was going to be a concert pianist after all. What Horn was not aware of is that, although her record received modest fanfare, people were listening.

A few months after the release of *Embers and Ashes*, legendary trumpeter Miles Davis contacted Horn about opening for him at the Village Vanguard in New York City. In fact, he told management at the Vanguard that if Horn didn't play, he wouldn't play. And so her rise began. The woman who some musicians perceived as an unwelcome addition to the jam session was now in demand.

Soon she signed with the more prestigious Mercury Records, where renowned trumpeter-turned-producer Quincy Jones oversaw two of her recordings: *Shirley with Horns* and *Loads of Love*. Although her record deal with Mercury ended due to "creative differences," Horn maintained in her later years that she was happy during her time at Mercury. "With Mercury, yes, I was very happy with them. There was no problems. I had complete artistic control, and there was Quincy there, who saw about me, you know, so there were no problems."[15] Her recordings for Mercury saw Horn serving primarily as a vocalist while Jimmy Jones and Hank Jones contributed on piano. Horn began to accompany her piano playing with vocals when, as a young performer, a club patron offered to give her a large teddy bear if she agreed to sing "Melancholy Baby." She'd led her own bands and created her own music ever since she was a young girl. Horn had accompanied her piano playing with her own vocals on her recordings; there's no denying her propensity for piano playing and leading her own groups. Despite her assertions to the contrary, it's not difficult to imagine that relinquishing control of the piano bench presented some challenges.

After leaving Mercury, Horn continued to play in support of her music, choosing performances that were closer to home. Something had changed for the career-oriented Horn: she was now a mother. "But when I said I'm going to stay home and take care of my baby, you know, and I had to do that; I mean, it was no other way for me. I mean, I couldn't live with myself, because I'd seen so many cases where, oh boy, it's sorry."[16]

In the years that immediately followed Horns's time with Mercury Records, she only released two recordings: *Travelin' Light*, released in 1965 on ABC-Paramount, and *Where Are You Going*, released in 1972 on Perception Records. Other record deals and live audio recordings came and went during this time, but Horn wouldn't return to prominence until she signed with Verve Records in 1987.

Her first recording for Verve was *I Thought About You*, featuring the members of her longtime trio, bassist Steve Ables and drummer Steve Williams. During her time with Verve, Horn released eleven more albums. She also received countless awards, including a Grammy Award in 1999 for Best Jazz Vocal Album for *I Remember Miles*—a tribute to the late trumpeter—five Washington Area Music Awards, an honorary doctor of music degree from the Berklee College of Music, and the 2004 NEA Jazz Master Fellowship and Award, the highest honor bestowed upon jazz musicians by the National Endowment for the Arts.

Horn would battle several health issues over the years. In 2001 complications from diabetes led to amputation of her right leg, hampering her ability to play the piano as she once had. No matter the challenges, Horn's will to perform never subsided. "I have to do it," she declares. "I think when I was born, it's like God said, 'Music!' and that was it. All my life, that's all I knew. It's in me, it's jammed up and it's got to come out."[17]

The Music Never Dies

> In some ways, the explanation for Eva Cassidy's popularity—all told, her records have sold about four million copies, according to Bill Straw, the president of Blix Street—is simple: she possessed a silken soprano voice with a wide and seemingly effortless range, unerring pitch and a gift for phrasing that at times was heart-stoppingly eloquent.
> —ALEX WARD, New York Times (August 12, 2002)

As the twentieth anniversary of Eva Cassidy's death neared, a photograph of the album cover for Nightbird—a recording that features a collection of songs Cassidy performed during a singing engagement at Blues Alley ten months before she passed away—was posted on the home page of the Blix Street Records website. Standing underneath the famous Blues Alley marquee that once bore her name, the image of Cassidy positioned just outside of the spotlight holding nothing more than a guitar is very fitting. She was highly self-critical and unsure of her place in the industry, which contributed to her limited number of live performances. That Cassidy's fame was preceded by her death was of little consequence: the shy singer probably would not have had it any other way.

Born on February 2, 1963, in Oxon Hill, Maryland, Eva Marie Cassidy was the third born of four children. Her parents, Hugh and Barbara Cassidy, met while Hugh was a young soldier stationed in Germany in 1961. The two married four months after meeting and moved to the United States the following year.[18]

After settling in Bowie, Maryland, with their young family, Hugh exposed the children to music. A skilled bassist, Hugh taught a nine-year-old Eva how to play guitar while the youngest child of the family, Dan, learned the violin. Together, they formed a family band that featured young Eva on lead vocals. As much as she enjoyed singing, she disliked performing in front of a crowd that much more. Later in life, she shifted her focus from lead to background vocals. That is, until she met producer Chris Biondi.

Cassidy's friend booked a recording session at Biondi's studio, hopeful that Cassidy would take advantage of the opportunity to sing. While she was there, Cassidy not only wowed Biondi, she also secured a lifetime engineer, promoter, and advocate who worked tirelessly to help bring Cassidy's talents to a wider audience. Cassidy and Biondi forged a musical relationship that soon turned romantic. Nevertheless, the two maintained a professional relationship that centered on promoting Cassidy's music.

Eventually the two determined that nurturing their professional relationship was more important; Cassidy's singing needed an audience. Biondi was determined to lure Cassidy away from her job working in a nursery. Cassidy worked hard in the studio, but record labels weren't biting. She enjoyed music and singing without suffering the burden of favoring genres or labels. For record executives, that made her a challenge to market and even more challenging to work with. It also fed her insecurities as a performer, but, strangely enough, it also fed her dogged defiance. For as shy and self-doubting as Cassidy could be, she was equal parts unfettered artist. She sang what she wanted, when she wanted, and how she wanted. Her demos often included an eclectic mix of music that perfectly represented her approach to music.

Through her association with Biondi, Cassidy had an opportunity to perform back-up vocals on hip-hop and go-go records. She performed lead and background vocals for such acts as DC go-go band EU (Experience Unlimited) and Bay Area rapper E-40. Soon she caught the ear of DC's second-most famous son: R&B and go-go pioneer Chuck Brown. It was with Brown that Cassidy found her voice; the duo released a recording of mostly jazz standards titled *The Other Side* that they performed all around Washington, DC.[19] The recording afforded Brown an opportunity to sing music that he'd always wanted to perform, while Cassidy had an opportunity to showcase her vocals. The seemingly odd pairing was a great success locally. The recording's success led Cassidy to step a little closer to the limelight. She began performing around town with her own trio and—with the help of Biondi and her manager, Al Dale—she worked to release her own music.

Live at Blues Alley and *Eva by Heart* resulted from the trio's efforts, although Cassidy wouldn't live long enough to appreciate their success. By the summer of 1996, Cassidy learned that a cancerous mole that she had removed from her skin three years earlier had resulted in cancer that metastasized to her organs and bones. By the time Cassidy learned of her diagnosis, she'd also learned of her eventual fate: she didn't have long to live. On November 2, 1996, Cassidy died due to complications of melanoma. She was thirty-three years old.

Although death typically signifies the end to all of our stories, for Cassidy, hers offered a new beginning. Cassidy's friend and fellow performer, Grace Griffith, found a label interested in signing Cassidy to that elusive record deal. Blix Street Records executive Bill Straw collaborated with Cassidy's parents to work out the terms of the deal. Straw sorted through some of Cassidy's recorded music and released an album titled *Songbird*.[20] The recording went on to achieve international acclaim and, as a result, so did Cassidy. At last count, Cassidy has sold more than 12 million albums posthumously.[21] No other female jazz artist from Washington, DC, has replicated Cassidy's success.

Thank You, Washington, DC!

Not every woman discussed in this chapter was born, raised, or remained in DC throughout their careers in the same way as June Norton, Shirley Horn, and Eva Cassidy. Some, like vocalist Ruth Brown, earned their start due to a chance encounter at a DC nightclub, while others still, like bassist/vocalist Meshell Ndegeocello, moved away from DC after establishing their love for music and developing their early sound, for Ndegeocello as part of DC's go-go music scene. In spite of the fact that these women aren't or didn't remain DC locals, one thing is clear: DC is forever part of their musical stories.

When Ruth Met Ahmet

I was in the hospital for a year. I'll never forget that: On my twenty-first birthday, Ahmet came down to Chester to see me in that hospital. And he brought me a book on how to sightread, a pitch pipe and a big tablet to write on, because I had a knack for writing lyrics.
—RUTH BROWN, *Rolling Stone* (April 19, 1990)

Born the oldest of seven children in Portsmouth, Virginia, on January 12, 1928, Ruth Weston grew up to become one of the biggest stars on the Atlantic Records label.

The young woman who counted performers like Billie Holiday, Sarah Vaughan, and Dinah Washington as inspirations got her start performing for the USO during her teenage years.[22] By the time she was seventeen, Weston ran away from home, moving to Detroit to make a life for herself with a trumpeter named Jimmy Brown. The two would soon marry, and the young, wide-eyed singer changed her last name from Weston to Brown. She had been performing around town and making a name for herself when she discovered the unthinkable: her husband was already married. Although the two separated, Brown held on to her new name. She'd done well for herself using the moniker, and she wasn't interested in changing that momentum, so she bloomed where she was planted and thrived as Ruth Brown. Although she married several more times later on in life, she performed as Ruth Brown for the rest of her life; the rest, as they say, is history.

During her time in Detroit, she caught the attention of well-known bandleader Lucky Millinder. He was so impressed with her singing that he hired her to front his orchestra. It wouldn't last. During an engagement in Washington, DC, a short time later, Brown served drinks to members of the orchestra. In Millinder's eyes, the act was egregious; he fired Brown for it and left her in DC to fend for herself.

Photo 7.2 *Ruth Brown*
Singer Ruth Brown so impressed Willis Conover by her performance at DC's Crystal Caverns in the 1950s that he convinced Ahmet Ertegun, the head of Atlantic Records, to record her. Her success as a rhythm and blues singer led to the quip that Atlantic was "the house that Ruth built."

Hearing about her misfortune, someone introduced Brown to Blanche Calloway, older sister to legendary performer Cab Calloway. At the time, the elder Calloway happened to operate one of DC's premier jazz clubs: the Crystal Caverns. Always in need of fresh talent, she negotiated terms that would allow Brown to perform at the Caverns long enough for her to raise money to leave town. Brown became quite the attraction during her time with the Caverns, and soon artists were making their way to the Caverns after their own gigs in order to hear her sing. During one such occasion, Duke Ellington stopped by with radio disc jockey Willis Conover and singer Sonny Til. Conover was so pleased with what he heard that evening that he called Ahmet Ertegun of Atlantic Records right in the middle of Brown's set.[23] After sending a couple of Atlantic's executives to hear Brown on his behalf, Ertegun signed Brown to the label, sight unseen.

Although her professional journey took her outside of Washington, DC, Brown went on to be one of Atlantic Records' brightest stars. Her success led Atlantic Records to be known as "The House That Ruth Built." Some of her biggest hits include "5-10-15 Hours," "So Long," "(Mama) He Treats Your Daughter Mean," and "Teardrops from My Eyes."

When her time with Atlantic fizzled in the early 1960s, Brown worked odd jobs and performed on weekends. She found herself thrust back into the limelight in the late 1970s when her good friend Redd Foxx helped her land a role in the musical *Selma*. Brown went on to have a second career in radio, film, and theater; her work eventually earned her a Tony Award for Best Actress and an induction into the Rock and Roll Hall of Fame in 1993.

Brown died on November 17, 2006, due to complications from a heart attack and stroke. She was seventy-eight years old.

Free Like a Bird

> *My responsibility is simply to be myself, to express myself as sincerely as possible, and to be funky.*
> —MESHELL NDEGEOCELLO, *Los Angeles Times* (October 24, 2002)

Michelle Lynn Johnson may not have been born in Washington, DC, but the DC music scene served as fertile ground for the youngster, who went on to be known by her adopted name: Meshell Ndegeocello (Ndegeocello means "free like a bird" in Swahili).

Born in Berlin, Germany, on August 29, 1968, Ndegeocello was the younger of two children born to the union of Jacques and Helen Johnson. Jacques, who was a saxophonist and the first African American to earn the rank of sergeant major in the US Army, exposed his children to music at an early age.[24] When recounting her early musical influences in a 2014 interview, Ndegeocello stated, "My dad's a musician, so that was always around me."[25]

Jacques would eventually move with his young family to the metro Washington, DC, area, where Ndegeocello and her older brother, Jacques Jr., developed musically. During the early part of her youth, she tried to learn clarinet. With her father's saxophone inclination as a model, the unfortunate reality was that she could not fully step into his shoes. Ndegeocello and woodwind instruments didn't connect. "The blowing thing is something that you either have a predilection for or not. And I don't have that thing . . . I couldn't do it."[26] There was an instrument that the youngster discovered was more her style: the bass. She began studying the instrument at the age of fourteen.[27]

Although she attended the Duke Ellington School of the Arts for part of her secondary education, Ndegeocello honed her musicianship in clubs around DC.[28] She earned a gig as a bass player for a go-go band called Prophecy while she was still in high school. She earned that gig after the band's regular bassist was a no-show for one of their performances. Before long, she was playing in other groups such as Little Benny and the Masters and Rare Essence.

Ndegeocello left Washington, DC, shortly after graduating high school, but the DC music scene left an indelible mark on her music and her artistry in general. Ndegeocello currently tours the world as a bandleader and side musician for musicians of all genres. She has worked with some of the biggest names in music to date, including Jason Moran, John Mellencamp, Madonna, Herbie Hancock, Chaka Khan, Marcus Miller, and Robert Glasper, to name a few.

The Future Is Rooted in the Past:
Dr. Billy Taylor's Heartfelt "Thank You"

> These days you don't hear what I heard when I was a kid: "Aw, she plays nice for a girl." And that's because we gave them a shot to do it.
> —DR. BILLY TAYLOR, *Jazz Times* (September 2012)

The year 1996 also marked a new beginning for the John F. Kennedy Center for the Performing Arts. That year pianist and educator Dr. Billy Taylor, in his capacity as artistic advisor for jazz at the Kennedy Center, founded the Mary Lou Williams Women in Jazz Festival. It was a festival dedicated to the celebration of female musicians. Taylor counted Mary Lou Williams as a friend and undervalued talent, and this festival was an opportunity to recognize the ability of female musicians by giving them a space that was theirs to play in. "When I first went to the Kennedy Center, I said, 'I want to do a women's jazz festival,'" Taylor recalled in a 2009 interview. "They said, 'Well, can you find enough women?' They had not seen, at that time, enough women in music to think they could sustain a festival. But I was able to identify a hundred women right there."[29]

For some, the success of the Mary Lou Williams Women in Jazz Festival signified that the jazz scene, particularly in Washington, DC, was rife with opportunities for women and men equally. So much so that in 2013 pianist Jason Moran, the new artistic advisor for jazz at the Kennedy Center, changed the name and scope of the Mary Lou Williams Women in Jazz Festival to the Mary Lou Williams Jazz Festival.[30] For others, like pianist Amy K. Bormet, performance opportunities for women were still rare and worthy of a created space. "In all honesty, women are not getting the opportunities they need to showcase their abilities," Bormet said during a 2014 interview with the *Washington City Paper*. "And that's why I started this festival, because I was frustrated by that. I really wanted to have space for myself, and the people I knew in the District who were not as well-known as they should be. People that have been here and been working, and sound amazing, and were not getting the kind of attention that I thought they deserved."[31]

Today musicians and singers such as Bormet, Janelle Gill, Jen Krupa, Sharon Clark, Christie Dashiell, and Akua Allrich are just a few of the women who are making great strides around Washington, DC. Just like those who laid the path before them, these women are forging quite a path of their own. Whether it's to sing a song on your own terms, like Eva Cassidy, or to nurture one's own prodigious talents, like Shirley Horn, playing like a woman on the music scene in modern-day Washington, DC, is to be dedicated to the music and your right to be part of it. DC's jazz scene for women is but a microcosm of the jazz scene for women around the world, but times are changing. In the words of award-winning vocalist Dee Dee Bridgewater, "There are so many young women now who don't have the fear that we used to have. We have come forward by leaps and bounds."[32]

Notes

1. Sherrie Tucker, *Swing Shift: "All Girl" Bands of the 1940s* (Durham, NC: Duke University Press, 2000), 38.

2. D. Antoinette Hardy, *International Sweethearts of Rhythm* (Lanham, MD: Scarecrow Press, October 1, 1998), viii and xiii–xiv

3. Tucker, *Swing Shift*, 49

4. Kristin McGee, *Some Like It Hot: Jazz Women in Film and Television, 1928–1959* (Middletown, CT: Wesleyan University Press, 2010), 144; and Tucker, *Swing Shift*, 49.

5. "Media Advisory: Jazz Musicians and Supporters Gather at Jazz at Lincoln Center to Call for Equal Opportunities for Female Musicians," Equal Rights Advocates, press release, n.d., www.equalrights.org/wp-content/uploads/2015/04/April-29-jazz-women-rally-media-advisory.pdf.

6. W. Royal Stokes, *The Jazz Scene: An Informal History from New Orleans to 1990* (New York: Oxford University Press, 1993), 74.

7. Russell Freedman, *The Voice that Challenged a Nation: Marian Anderson and the Struggle for Equal Rights* (New York: Clarion, 2004), 3.

8. Stokes, *The Jazz Scene*, 74.

9. Felix Grant, radio interview with June Norton, October 19, 1985, Washington, DC, WRC 980 AM, for broadcast on The Station of the Stars.

10. "Remembering June Norton: Sang with Duke Ellington, Broke TV Race Barrier," *Parkview, DC* (blog), January 23, 2015, https://parkviewdc.com/2015/01/23/remembering-june-norton-sang-with-duke-ellington-broke-tv-race-barrier/.

11. "Paying Tribute to Shirley Horn in Recognition of Her Many Achievements and Contributions to the World of Jazz and American Culture," H.Con.Res.300, introduced November 16, 2005, https://www.congress.gov/bill/109th-congress/house-concurrent-resolution/300/text.

12. "Jazz Legend Shirley Horn Dies at 71," CNN, October 22, 2005.

13. Shirley Horn, interview for the Smithsonian Institution Jazz Oral History Program and the "Sung and Unsung/Jazz Women" Symposium, transcripts, June 13, 1996, 16, Smithsonian Museum of American History website, http://amhistory.si.edu/jazz/Horn-Shirley/Shirley_Horn_Interview_Transcription.pdf.

14. Richard Harrington, "The Wonder of the Way She Sings," *Washington Post*, October 18, 1992.

15. Horn, interview, transcripts, June 13, 1996, 30.

16. Ibid., 78.

17. Richard Harrington, "Health Setbacks Can't Stop Shirley Horn," *Washington Post*, December 17, 2004.

18. Rob Burley, Johnathan Maitland, and Elena Rhodes Byrd, *Eva Cassidy: Songbird* (New York: Gotham Books, 2003), 12.

19. Steve Huey, "Eva Cassidy," AllMusic, n.d., www.allmusic.com/artist/eva-cassidy -mn0000168256/biography; and Richard Harrington, "Echoes of a Voice Stilled Too Early," *Washington Post*, November 17, 1996.

20. Dave McKenna, "The Story Behind the Gigs That Helped Launch the Legend of Eva Cassidy," *Washington Post*, December 10, 2015.

21. Ibid.

22. Robert Greenfield, *The Last Sultan: The Life and Times of Ahmet Ertegun.* (New York: Simon & Schuster, 2011).

23. Lee Jeske, "Q&A: Ruth Brown," *Rolling Stone*, April 19, 1990.

24. Michael Kabran, "Jacques Johnson: Old School." *JazzTimes*, June 1, 2006.

25. Melissa Locker, "Meshell Ndegeocello." *Believer*, September 2014, https://www.believermag .com/issues/201409/?read=interview_ndegeocello.

26. Ibid.

27. Teresa Witz, "Meshell Ndegeocello Breaks Step with Pop," *Washington Post*, June 19, 2005.

28. Ibid.

29. Michael J. West, "The Mary Lou Williams Women in Jazz Festival." *JazzTimes*, September 2012.

30. Michael J. West, "Jazz Set List, May 16–22: That Ain't Mary Lou!" *Washington City Paper*, May 16, 2013.

31. Michael J. West, "'The Scene Queen:' Amy K. Bormet Talks the Washington Women in Jazz Festival." *Washington City Paper*, March 14, 2014.

32. West, "The Mary Lou Williams Women in Jazz Festival."

8 No Church without a Choir
Howard University and Jazz in Washington, DC

Lauren Sinclair

Prelude: The Founding of Howard University

Howard University (HU), established by Congressional Decree in 1867, has always occupied a distinct niche as a coeducational university, with a uniquely diverse curriculum launched for the "education of youth in the liberal arts and sciences."[1] Founded by and named after Union general Oliver Otis Howard, an abolitionist who served as the first commissioner of the Freedmen's Bureau and the third president of Howard University (1869–74), Howard is noted for promoting African Americans' social ascent through educational opportunities.[2] Institutions like Howard were characterized by a dedication to progressive and critical discourse that included a central role of the church as a social, philosophical, musical core of the institution.

The profound division of the Union after the Civil War and the flailing efforts of Reconstruction influenced formalized and advanced education of black citizens at the time of Howard's founding. According to Howard history professor and native Washingtonian Rayford Logan, congressmen who advocated for African American participation in Reconstruction, "play[ed] a crucial role in the founding of Howard University."[3] In this way, Howard University's inception sprung from radical ideals on black equality.

Howard University and its surroundings in LeDroit Park became an epicenter of notable African American thought influences, philosophers, and social activists such as Frederick Douglass, philosopher Alain Locke, sociologist E. Franklin Frazier, and artist Lois Mailou Jones. The literary, political, and musical worlds intermingled in influential artistic and social work in Washington, DC—a city distinguished by its unique geographical and political setting.[4]

In his history of the university, Rayford Logan refers to the "quixotic" and religious founding ideals of the university.[5] Evolving conceptually within two months from a theological seminary to a liberal arts college, the university's nascent framework included the College of Arts and Science (established in 1868), School of Divinity (established in 1870), and the College of Medicine (established in 1868).[6]

Oratorio: The Founding of a Music Department and Community

Music as a formalized study at Howard had a slow and modest start. A choir was founded in 1874.[7] Music courses have been offered at Howard since 1870.[8] The music program was created in 1892 out of the Normal School (Teachers College) and struggled until the early 1900s due to underfunding, low salaries for faculty, and low enrollment.[9] A small and underresourced department, Music Studies faltered for years at Howard and produced few graduates, mostly due to limited opportunities for black classically trained musicians.[10]

Since the eighteenth century, churches were central in leveraging the intellectual, musical, and professional talents of black worshipers and community members.[11] The connection between black higher education and schools of divinity can be traced to 1804.[12] Informally and formally, churches and religious education performed an enduring role in black education, literacy, and professional development. Churches occupied a crucial role in promoting the education, performance opportunities, and careers of emerging black musicians who sought a stage to showcase their talents.

The music department emerged from the theology department in 1914.[13] Just as the concept of a divinity school generated a full university, the theology department gave rise to the study of music. The two fields remain closely intertwined at Howard University, where sacred and secular music blend frequently. As founder (in 1975) and current director of the Howard University Jazz Ensemble (HUJE), Fred Irby III explains, musical

Photo 8.1 *Yusef Lateef and Fred Irby*
Yusef Lateef (multi-instrumentalist) and Fred Irby III (trumpet) in 2001. Lateef was awarded the Benny Golson Jazz Master Award in 2001. Irby is the director of Jazz Studies at Howard University (1976–present).

studies emerged naturally from theology because in a black community "you can't have a church without a choir."[14]

The Howard University Andrew Rankin Memorial Chapel has a long history of hosting religious and secular musical concerts, such as the Howard University Concert Series, founded in 1934, and the annual Jazz Week concerts highlighting students, alumni, and community talent. Historically, the chapel has been a site of renowned musical performances by noted musicians such as opera stars Todd Duncan and Carol Brice, classical piano legends Raymond Jackson and Roy Tibbs, and jazz greats Clark Terry and John Malachi.

The Fine Arts building on Howard University campus is named after former Howard University music director Lulu Vere Childers, who joined the music faculty in 1905 and founded the Conservatory of Music in 1913 and the School of Music in 1918. She was the music director at Howard from 1905 until 1942, when she also served as director of the HU Choral Society. Under her direction, a music recital and lecture series blossomed, beginning in the 1920s. The concerts in the series drew big names, such as opera star Marian Anderson, a close friend of Childers, and attracted racially mixed audiences, a rarity in Washington, DC—typically a segregated city. The Music Department at Howard University was Childers's legacy, as she devoted her life's work to documenting the history of African American musical contributions.[15]

Development: Howard University's Classical Music Foundations

Under Childers's leadership, the Howard music school became a recognized conservatory and was admitted into the National Schools of Music in 1943.[16] The conservatory was staffed by a small number of part-time faculty who trained their students to become music teachers or church bandleaders. As the program gained stature, Howard University produced talented orchestral players (Langston Fitzgerald, class of 1966[17]), internationally recognized operatic singers (Jessye Norman, class of 1967), and composers (Adolphus Hailstork, class of 1963[18]).

The classical foundation of the music department at Howard played an important role in influencing the career directions of its students. Howard's early graduates in classical music are characterized by their progressive stylings, distinguished by the same creative force for which the later jazz program would be recognized. Hailstork's early training, for example, was marked by improvisation, and his music is often noted as "postmodern" with musical allusions "to figures and events in African American history."[19]

Black consciousness was featured in Hailstork's instrumental music, which "contain[s] subtle jazz rhythms or blues riffs."[20] According to Howard University professor emeritus Raymond Jackson, this stylistic interchange and genre co-evolution was common. Jackson notes that classical music is folk music and the influence and interchange between black classical composers and more modern composers who incorporate jazz music into their classical compositions are fluid.[21] Dr. Arthur Dawkins, director of HU Jazz Studies (1976–2005), concurs, suggesting that jazz is America's classical music.[22] Jazz musicians are influenced by classical music and vice versa: "For many composers a black experience has inevitably and necessarily involved a jazz experience."[23]

Divertimento/Intermezzo: From Classical to Jazz

From its beginning, the tension between classical music and jazz music has had class and racial underpinnings in the diverse yet often divided socioeconomic black communities of Washington, DC. Organizations like the Treble Clef Club, a group founded in 1897 by upper-class black female musicians and music appreciators in Washington, DC, who hosted salon style discussions and performances, actively discouraged topics and performances related to jazz. Billed as "the only high class musical entertainment that was given free in the city of Washington at that time," a member of the Treble Clef Club conveys the predominating elite sentiment regarding jazz in the early twentieth century:

> Jazz at that time was unknown and so determined were we that there should be no jazz on our program, we did everything we could to preserve good music. But alas, the Lafayette Players came to Howard Theater, and . . . Clarence Muse. . . . And imagine the disgust of one of our members . . . who went there and heard Muse singing "Yacky Hacky Hoolah." She was so incensed . . . she said, "The more I heard him sing it, the more I wanted to get under the seat. But imagine my surprise, next morning every house in town was playing 'Yacky Hacky Hoolah.'"[24]

The distaste for jazz came from a lack of training, according to Fred Irby III. People "didn't know how to listen to it—they couldn't hear its form or structure because they hadn't been taught how."[25]

Sentiment toward jazz began to shift in the latter half of the twentieth century, but black scholars and activists continued to problematize jazz's ascendant popularity and corresponding negative stereotypes along class lines in the black community. For example, Sterling A. Brown, Washington, DC, native and HU English professor and jazz scholar, lectured at the Monterey Jazz Festival alongside Duke Ellington in 1959. During his lecture "The Social Background of Jazz," Brown "pointed out that contemptuous stereotypes of jazz and its musicians have turned many middle-class Negroes against it."[26] In 1959 Brown commented that "the closest thing to jazz that ha[d] been played over the Howard University public address system [was] Paul Whiteman's version of 'Rhapsody in Blue.'"[27]

Many HU students yearned for authentic jazz studies and performance opportunities. One of the earliest and most reputed Howard University students who made the transition from classical to jazz is saxophonist Benny Golson. He attended HU beginning in 1947, leaving in 1950. Golson went on to tour with Bull Moose Jackson & His Buffalo Bearcats in 1951. When Golson arrived at HU, there were no jazz music classes, and jazz music was "frowned upon," "so he and his fellow classmates began to play together for no credit in the school jazz band. He also performed with the Howard Swing Masters and wrote music with them."[28]

Golson noted he "was disappointed at school because there were so many music rules." In an interview, he expressed a strong urge to "break the rules" and "question everything in college" because "so many of the lessons [he] was taught contradicted the ideas [he] had in [his] head."[29] Prior to the creation of a formal jazz program, music students at Howard initiated their own explorations of experimental and jazz music, starting their own improvisational groups and seeking opportunities to play music in the DC venues surrounding Howard.

Echoing Golson, Andrew White, the renowned saxophonist, found it difficult to reconcile the "dualistic nature" of his classical and jazz lives.[30] Born in Washington, DC, White studied classical oboe at Howard. He received prestigious accolades as a classical musician, including a scholarship to study oboe at Tanglewood in 1963. From 1968 to 1970, he was the principal oboe with the American Ballet Theater. At the same time, White was the bandleader and saxophonist with a group called the JFK Quintet, consisting of local and HU musicians. They played regularly at the Bohemian Caverns on U Street. White went on to play musical accompaniment with popular musicians, including Stevie Wonder and Otis Redding.

White experienced "some contention" trying to resolve what the HU administration perceived as competing interests between his commercial and classical musical career paths. He felt he was "a disappointment" to the HU administration because he was being groomed to be a classical music great, yet he had interest in both worlds.[31] White is also an influential jazz collector and scholar and the 2006 Gold Medal Honoree of the French society of Arts, Sciences, and Letters. He is also recognized for his opus of transcriptions of John Coltrane and Charlie Parker saxophone improvisations; his music publishing company, Andrew's Musical Enterprises Incorporated, hosts a catalog including the world's largest repository of saxophone transcriptions.[32] Today, under the leadership of Irby, HU hosts regular networking events and lectures given by accomplished professionals in the music business.

Due to the absence of formal jazz studies, many talented musicians began their formal musical studies preparing for careers as classical musicians, with an eye toward jazz on the side. Shirley Horn, a Grammy award recipient and 2005 National Endowment for the Arts Jazz Master, studied classical music and composition at the Howard University Junior Music School from age twelve to eighteen (about 1946–50). Horn switched her interest to jazz at seventeen and won a scholarship to Julliard but, due to financial constraints, decided to continue her studies at Howard University instead.[33]

Another classically trained Howard University graduate who played a major role in the jazz community in Washington, DC, was Charlie Hampton, the last bandleader of the Howard Theater (1964–70). Hampton joined the saxophone section of the Howard Theater in 1957 after studying classical clarinet at the school. Although he proclaimed that his desire to improvise was not encouraged in the classical music program at Howard, he applied his classical training to make a serious name for himself as "a skilled arranger, composer, and conductor who led bands in Washington for 40 years."[34]

Recapitulation: A Community and Legacy of Artistic Achievement

The Howard University music program's legacy boasts generations of notable musicians and an academic life that demonstrates commitment to progressive social issues and critical thought, often emboldened by thought makers, civil rights activists, and ideals beyond their time.[35] At its origin in 1905, Childers hired Roy Wilfred Tibbs, a piano faculty who was trained at Oberlin College, and Joseph Douglass, violin faculty and son of Frederick

Douglass.[36] Such faculty promoted musical excellence, made visible the talent of their students on the world stage, and confronted racist barriers to performance.[37]

Howard students were patrons of the arts, inviting up-and-coming jazz musicians to campus and frequenting local establishments that hosted all the greats. The "What Good Are We" Howard Social Club, founded in 1915, organized house parties with music provided by local budding musicians such as Duke Ellington.[38] The HU student newspaper, *The Hilltop*, ran articles publicizing special student rates at jazz clubs such as Abarts, where, in 1961, the performance schedule included Slide Hampton, Stan Getz, Dizzy Gillespie, Thelonious Monk, Max Roach, Miles Davis, Horace Silver, Art Blakey, John Coltrane, and many other big names.[39] Additionally, the HU music fraternity, Phi Mu Alpha, consistently brought musical artists, such as pianist and singer Les McCann and Nick Kirgo, to campus to perform and speak on the music profession.[40]

Howard had a tradition of musical activism and grassroots organizing intended to shine light on the achievements of DC-area musicians. Howard University faculty and students founded initiatives to share their art and support talented musicians in the District. Such outreach supported causes such as female empowerment. Gregoria Fraser Goins was on the music faculty and founding member of the Treble Clef Club (1897), "an organization of professional female musicians and music teachers [who] promote[d] concerts in Washington that emphasized the music of black composers and the history of black performers."[41]

Rhapsody: 1968: Jazz Studies Formalized at HU

Howard University is at an epicenter of the DC cultural and intellectual community. Musicians took a sense of pride in the institutional backdrop, which represented a high point for black culture and intellectual life. In his biography, Billy Taylor, a DC native, Dunbar High graduate, and jazz pianist and composer, describes his childhood neighborhood as a discursive annex of Howard University, which attracted noted figures such as poet Langston Hughes, historian Carter G. Woodson, and poet Amiri Baraka. Taylor gave lectures and concerts at Howard, appeared with the HUJE on campus and was recognized for his jazz activism and as a Jazz Master by the National Endowment of the Arts.[42]

Dr. Donald Byrd founded Jazz Studies at HU in 1968, a significant year for Washington, DC, the United States, and the international community. In addition to Dr. Martin Luther King Jr's assassination and the consequent riots combated by the National Guard on the streets of Washington, DC, the United States also waged a costly and conflicted war in Vietnam, the international community was settled into the Cold War, and many nations in Africa established their independence. In black colleges and in black academe, students demanded more Afro-centric courses.[43] Howard's campus shut down for three days after students demanded "that the University become more black-oriented."[44]

As part of a shifting institution in a changing city, Howard's jazz program gained ground quickly. Donald Byrd's career with the Blackbyrds lent acclaim to the burgeoning program. A trumpeter noted for being "one of the most knowledgeable people of Black music," he toured the United States with his band, which included his students and Howard graduates Keith Killgo (drummer), Kevin Kraig Toney (keyboard), and Allan Curtis

Photo 8.2 *Donvonte McCoy and Donald Byrd*
Donvonte McCoy (Howard '11) is a musician and educator. He is pictured in 2010 with
Donald Byrd (trumpet), founding director of Jazz Studies at Howard University.

Barnes (saxophone).[45] At Howard University, Dr. Byrd taught four courses per semester in addition to his touring and speaking responsibilities. A rising star of the intelligentsia, Byrd studied and taught law so that "he could teach himself and others how to protect their rights under the law."[46]

According to Keith Killgo, Byrd approached his band leadership professorially:

He'd constantly challenge you musically. He'd throw music in front of you and, whatever instrument you played, he'd make you go research all the cats that played it. Not only the jazz cats, but the classical cats, the blues cats. . . . So you'd become well-rounded. Then, once you'd read UP on them, he'd make you LISTEN to all their MUSIC! So that, when you were up there onstage playing, he could see your progress. You know, he'd definitely check on you on a daily basis to see if you'd done your homework. We'd have these all-the-way-down-to-the-ground kinda band meetings. But, though we hated it at the time, it made us the musicians we are today. We were basically rookies, and we learnt from the best in the business.[47]

Byrd recorded over forty albums and was nominated for three Grammy awards. He played and collaborated with many jazz greats of his time, including Charlie Parker, John Coltrane, Thelonious Monk, Miles Davis, and Dizzy Gillespie, just to name a few.[48] He is noted for his contribution to the musical genre by way of introducing funk and soul into jazz. While heading the Jazz Studies program, Byrd released his acclaimed album *Fancy Free*, a transitional album, paving a way from bop to free-form jazz.[49] Byrd left Howard in 1971 to focus on his musical career but continued to be active in academe, teaching at many universities, including Rutgers University and North Carolina Central University, where he chaired its Jazz Studies program.

Another noteworthy Howard University music graduate and faculty member for forty-three years was Dr. Doris Evans McGinty, born blocks from Howard University. Dr. McGinty served as Music Chair for eight years and wrote the liner notes for the HUJE every year from 1976 until her death in 2005.[50] She was one of the first American women to be awarded a doctorate in musicology from Oxford.[51] McGinty was awarded the Benny Golson award in 2002 for her role in supporting the Jazz Studies program and Jazz Ensemble at Howard.[52]

The Benny Golson Jazz Master Award has been granted annually since 1996 to honor Golson's living legacy. Recipients include multi-instrumentalist Yusef A. Lateef (2001), pianist Geri Allen (2005), saxophonist and oboist Andrew White (2008), and drummer T. S. Monk, the son of Thelonious Monk (2010).[53] Howard meant a great deal to Golson, and the institution values his legacy profoundly. Golson was conferred an honorary doctorate from HU in 2014, a moment that he calls "fantasy at its best," making him feel that his "life was [then] complete."[54] In 2016 the Andrew Rankin Memorial Chapel hosted the annual Benny Golson Prize ceremony, named after jazz saxophonist, renowned composer, and alumnus Benny Golson. The ceremony featured a performance by Afro Blue, Howard University's award-winning jazz vocal ensemble, founded in 2002 by professor Connaitre Miller. The a capella group, which performs regularly, emphasizes jazz instrumentation expressed through the voice.[55] Among their many accolades, Afro Blue has performed with the National Symphony Orchestra (2008), at the Apollo Theater in New York City (2013), for the Congressional Black Caucus Jazz Concert "Geri Allen and Friends" (2014), and for President and Mrs. Obama at the White House (2013).[56]

The Cramton Auditorium is another performance space on campus that has hosted a range of impressive musical performances since its opening in 1961. In its opening year, the Cramton Auditorium hosted the Inter-American Festival, featuring the Orquesta Sinfónica Nacional de México.[57] It has also hosted jazz greats, including a memorial concert for trumpeter Lee Morgan given by Freddie Hubbard and Donald Byrd in 1972 the day after Morgan had been murdered in New York City.[58]

In 1972 Cramton Auditorium also hosted a concert sponsored by the Left Bank Jazz Society of Baltimore, featuring Leon Thomas (vocals), Gato Barbieri (tenor saxophone) and a young Gil Scott Heron (poet-singer). The concert intended to bring together "third world politics, black power advocacy, and jazz."[59] Since its founding, the Cramton Auditorium has hosted convocations conferring honorary degrees to jazz greats including bandleader and vibraphonist Lionel Hampton and Ella Fitzgerald.[60] Other performers include Diane Reeves (vocalist), Frank Wess (saxophone), Teddy Pendergrass (vocalist), Roy Ayers (vibraphone), Alberta Hunter (vocalist), Bill Harris (guitar), and Andrew White (saxophone).[61]

Finale: Noteworthy Howard University Alumni and Faculty

Billy Eckstine, the famed singer, trumpeter, and noted bandleader of Billy Eckstein and His Orchestra, resided in Washington, DC, and attended Armstrong High, Duke Ellington

Photo 8.3 *Howard University Jazz Ensemble*
Howard University Jazz Ensemble, Japan, 2009.

High School, and Howard University. While a student at HU, he launched his singing career after winning an amateur contest at the Howard Theatre in 1933. Eckstine went on to record hits such as "Fools Rush In" and "My Foolish Heart" with greats like Sarah Vaughan.[62] Eckstine's band, which he led and assembled beginning in 1944, consisted of "a who's-who of bebop: for example, trumpeters Dizzy Gillespie, Miles Davis, and Fats Navarro; saxophonists Charlie Parker and Dexter Gordon; and drummer Art Blakey."[63]

While Howard University musicians and scholars constructively enriched the establishments and culture of Washington, DC, they also served as international cultural ambassadors. The Howard University Jazz Ensemble (HUJE) was formed in 1975 under Fred Irby III, a trumpeter who has impressed both the jazz and classical music worlds.[64] Under the leadership of Irby, HUJE has performed in at least eighteen foreign countries in Asia, Central and South America, Europe, and Africa.[65] Asked about the HUJE role in jazz diplomacy, Irby notes that, primarily, the musicians just want to play their music, share their art. The audiences receive them enthusiastically, particularly in Japan, as they have few occasions to hear jazz music.

A special Howard Jazz Repertory Orchestra performance in 1982 was devoted to the music of the 1940s Billy Eckstine's band in a "stunning performance" featuring pianist John Malachi, among others.[66] Malachi, a pianist, lived in DC and taught at the Ellington School of the Arts and at Howard University in the Jazz Studies program. Malachi got his start playing in clubs around Washington, DC; by age seventeen, he was playing at the Jungle Inn at 12th and U Streets, NW, which was managed by Jelly Roll Morton. Malachi accompanied famous vocalists such as Pearl Bailey, Sarah Vaughan, Billie Holiday, and Dinah Washington.[67]

In addition to his teaching responsibilities, Malachi was active in the local music scene as the house band leader at Pigfoot, a club owned by the legendary guitarist Bill Harris on Rhode Island Avenue in Northeast Washington, DC.[68] Malachi conducted afternoon workshops and jam sessions at Pigfoot, welcoming any aspiring local musician. Although he did not have an advanced degree, he was an outstanding music teacher.[69]

Malachi taught piano to a young Frank Wess, who was studying premedical sciences and musical arrangement at Howard University. At seventeen years old, Wess left Howard

University to join the pit band on alto saxophone at the Howard Theatre. He eventually took up the tenor saxophone and joined big-name acts, including Blanche Calloway, Billy Eckstine and His Orchestra (beginning in 1945), and the Count Basie Orchestra (on flute and sax, beginning in 1953).[70]

Malachi was also an influential teacher of jazz pianist Geri Allen, who was one of the first to receive a bachelor's degree in Jazz Studies in 1979 from Howard University, where she later taught music courses. According to Fred Irby III, as a student, beginning in 1975, Allen composed and performed songs on the first four HUJE recordings. She also recorded and performed her first compositions for jazz orchestra at Howard University.[71] Allen has been recognized for her work as an accompanist as well as for her solo work and compositions. She has been lauded as "one of the most exciting new voices in contemporary jazz."[72] Perhaps this is due to her great dexterity across genres, playing folk music with artists such as Charlie Haden, free jazz with Ornette Coleman, and "electro-acoustic" jazz with Steve Coleman.[73]

Most resoundingly, her music was influenced by her native Detroit, shown through her albums such as *Grand River Crossings: Motown and Motor City Inspirations* (2013) with "cadences of the Black Church and Motown . . . ever present."[74] On her 1992 album, *Maroons*, Allen includes a track titled "For John Malachi," composed in his memory. Allen recalled her time at Howard University as "a very special experience" surrounded by "a lot of people we could look at in terms of excellence and what would be required of us in the professional world."[75] She passed away June 27, 2017, and in her memory fellow musicians lauded her as "a divine prism of pure heart and artistry" (Esperanza Spalding, bassist), "a sage" (Terri Lyne Carrington, drummer), "a God" (Jason Moran, pianist), "Grace itself" (Dee Dee Bridgewater, singer), "an unassuming powerhouse" (Diane Reeves, singer), "a big hearted educator" (Vijay Iyer, pianist), and ample appraisals beyond.[76]

Keter Betts was another informally trained yet prodigiously influential music instructor at Howard University beginning in 1963. Betts played bass on over two hundred recordings but is perhaps best known for his years as the bassist for Ella Fitzgerald.[77] He also performed with Dinah Washington and with Charlie Byrd on his jazz samba album with Stan Getz. Betts was a devoted educator for over twenty-five years in Washington, DC, influencing countless students of music through his work at the Washington Performing Arts Society, Wolf Trap's Headstart program, and Prince George's County's Arts Alive program.[78]

Another prominent influencer of DC jazz society was Calvin Jones, who received his master's degree in Music Education from Howard University in 1970. He went on to found the University of the District of Columbia (UDC) Jazz Program and oversaw the founding and development of UDC's jazz archives. Jones, a trombonist, broke the color line as the first African American to play in the Washington Redskins Professional Band (1965–83) and the Ice Capades in Washington and was among the first African Americans to play in the pit orchestra of the National Theatre.[79]

The list of talented and influential musicians trained at Howard University is too lengthy to explore exhaustively here. Other notable Howard musicians include Greg Osby (saxophone), Gary Thomas (saxophone, flute), Roberta Flack (vocalist), DC native

Billy Hart (drums), Gregory Royal (trombone), Wayne Linsey (piano), and Wallace Roney Jr. (trumpet), among others.[80]

Coda

Through the HUJE and formalized jazz studies, Fred Irby III has created a lasting legacy built on a simple yet strikingly potent formula. First, he established ensembles "to get the kids playing the music." According to Irby, students get more information from listening and playing music, particularly big-band repertoire, than from reading about it. For the first twenty years of its program, HU hosted two jazz ensembles. Of course, the Howard Jazz Studies program has jazz history and theory courses but also emphasizes improvisation classes and jazz arranging. Further, there is an emphasis on professional development, with jazz scholars and professionals visiting campus to perform and host workshops about the music business. Over the years, artists and professionals such as Clark Terry, Frank Foster, Jimmy Heath, and Bill Hughes have imparted their experience and mentorship toward HU jazz students.[81]

HU built a strong program through student recruitment at some of the top jazz high school programs, such as McKinley and Cardozo High Schools in Washington, DC. Since 1976 the HUJE has released thirty-four recordings. The program persists, offering free concerts to the Washington, DC, community by talented students, alumni, community members, and musical professionals.

It is remarkable that this post-Reconstruction institution has been the incubator for some of the most interesting contemporary music and performing artists in the country and the world at large for the last hundred years. Given the financial, professional, and social barriers HBCU's continue to fight, the accomplishments of Howard University's faculty and students should be applauded as even more significant. Howard University is a triumph that arose from the detritus of slavery. Across the years, the institution has struggled against adversity to establish itself as one of the most enduring and exceptional institutions of higher education in the United States.

Notes

The chapter's title, "No Church without a Choir," is from my interview with Fred Irby III, August 4, 2016. This research was accomplished with the support of Joellen El Bashir, Curator, Manuscript Division at the Moorland-Springarn Research Center at Howard University. I also express gratitude to Andrew White, Rusty Hassan, and Fred Irby III for multiple interviews and sharing their experiences and expertise. Finally, I thank Timothy Macek, conductor of the Howard University Symphony Orchestra, who introduced me to the music of Adolphus Hailstork and the staggering talent of pianist Raymond Jackson.

1. From Section 1 of the Howard University Charter, signed by the Howard University Board of Trustees on January 29, 1867. President Andrew Johnson signed Howard University into Charter in 1867 with a mission of "preparing students for leadership and service to the nation and the global community." From "HU Self-Study Report, 1999," executive summary: www.howard.edu /msche/selfstudy. For exploration of Johnson's concurrent advocacy for racist laws and disenfranchisement of black Americans, see Rayford Whittingham Logan, *Howard University: The First*

Hundred Years, 1867–1967 (New York: New York University Press, 1969). "Howard was . . . unique in the number and diversity of its departments. No other predominantly Negro 'university' offered as comprehensive a curriculum as did Howard. . . . Howard alone has increased its comprehensive departments to a number sufficient to call itself a university." Logan, *Howard University*, 26.

2. Logan, *Howard University: The First Hundred Years*, 68.

3. Rayford Logan was professor of history at Howard University and wrote one of two histories of Howard University, his entitled *Howard University: The First Hundred Years, 1867–1967*, 18.

4. Blair A. Ruble, *Washington's U Street: A Biography* (Baltimore: Johns Hopkins University Press, 2010).

5. Logan, *Howard University*, 4, 11, 13.

6. E. Kennedy, "Academic Programs," in "HU Self-Study Report, 1999, www.howard.edu /msche/selfstudy/chapter06.htm.

7. Richard Harrington, "The Classical Muse," *Washington Post*, March 1, 2002, https://www .washingtonpost.com/archive/lifestyle/2002/03/01/the-classical-muse/8d534625-f036-478a-9faa -27e134a23186/?utm_term=.a3290f43e628.

8. T. Holmes, "Sweet Sounds of Success: The Department of Music Celebrates 100 Years of Musical Genius," *Howard Magazine*, Summer 2014, p. 14.

9. Walter Dyson, "Howard University, the Capstone of Negro Education: A History, 1867– 1940" (PhD diss., Howard University, Washington, DC, 1941), 131–32.

10. Logan, *Howard University*, 381.

11. Doris Evans McGinty, "'As Large as She Can Make It': The Role of Black Women Activists in Music, 1880–1945," in *Cultivating Music in America: Women Patrons and Activists Since 1860*, ed. Ralph P. Locke and Cyrilla Barr, 214–30 (Berkeley: University of California Press, 1997), 220; and Dyson, *Howard University*.

12. Rayford Logan refers to the first honorary degree conferred to an African American, Lemuel Haynes, a Revolutionary War veteran and prolific preacher, by Middlebury College. Logan, *Howard University*, 4.

13. Other news sources establish the beginning of the Music Department as much earlier, beginning in 1866. See "Musical Memorial at Howard University," *Washington Post*, May 13, 1896.

14. Fred Irby III, interview with author, August 4, 2016.

15. McGinty, "'As Large as She Can Make It,'" 220.

16. Howard University Department of Music "History and Mission," n.d., http://coas.howard .edu/music/mission/index.html.

17. Fitzgerald is a classically trained trumpeter who has accompanied jazz greats such as Charlie Haden. He returned to Howard to teach music and conduct the symphony orchestra from 1970 to 1976. See Penn State School of Music, "Langston J. Fitzgerald III," http://music.psu.edu /faculty/langston-j-fitzgerald-iii.

18. Hailstork studied composition at HU: James Reel, "Adolphus Hailstork," *AllMusic*, n.d. www.allmusic.com/artist/adolphus-hailstork-mn0001670031/biography; see also "Adolphus C. Hailstork (b. 1941): African American Composer & Professor," AfriClassical.com, n.d. http:// chevalierdesaintgeorges.homestead.com/hailstork.html [with interview transcript]; "Adolphus Hailstork: Biography," Music @ Howard, n.d., http://web.archive.org/web/20100807020813/ http://www.howard.edu/library/Music%40Howard/Adolphus-Hailstork/Bio.htm.

19. James Reel, "Adolphus Hailstork."

20. Ibid.

21. "Much classical music is folk music at second or third remove from the original folk source." Margaret Just Butcher, *The Negro in American Culture* (New York: Knopf, 1957), quoted in Raymond Thompson Jackson, "The Piano Music of Twentieth-Century Black Americans as Illustrated Mainly in the Works of Three Composers" (PhD, diss., Juilliard School, 1973; ProQuest Dissertations & Theses Global [302692971]), 5.

22. Dawkins, A. "Westminster Program Notes: Howard University Jazz Ensemble Tribute to Westminster DC Presbyterian Church: Jazz Night in Southwest, DC," March 12, 2015; and W. A. Brower, "Arthur C. Dawkins, Ph.D." n.d., accessed December 24, 2016, http://coas.howard.edu /music/huje/dawkins.htm.

23. Jackson, "Piano Music of Twentieth-Century Black Americans," 8.

24. "History of the Treble Clef Club Founded 1897," Gregoria A. Goins collection, Moorland Springarn, HU, Box 36-15, folder 149, p. 2–3.

25. Fred Irby III, interview with author, December 12, 2016.

26. Luther P. Jackson, "Race That Bred Jazz Lends It a Top Scholar." *Washington Post and Times Herald*, July 9, 1959.

27. Ibid.

28. M. Sims, "Benny Golson," *Howard Magazine*, Summer 2014, p. 23.

29. Marc Myers, "Interview: Benny Golson (Part 1)," *JazzWax* (blog), September 8, 2008, www .jazzwax.com/2008/09/interview-benny.html.

30. Andrew White, interview with author, December 23, 2016.

31. Ibid.

32. "Andrew Nathaniel White, III," Andrew's Music, http://coas.howard.edu/music/huje /AndrewWhite.pdf.

33. "Shirley Horn Biography—Took to the Piano Early, Career Sparked by Miles Davis, Focused on Being a Homemaker," Brief Biographies, Net Industries, accessed December 25, 2016. http://biography.jrank.org/pages/2965/Horn-Shirley.html.

34. Matt Schudel, "D.C. Jazz Band Leader Charlie Hampton, 75, Dies." *Washington Post*, August 26, 2005, www.washingtonpost.com/wp-dyn/content/article/2005/08/25/AR2005082501892 .html.

35. For details on the role of Howard University law faculty in civil rights work, particularly the career of Charles Houston, vice dean of Howard University's School of Law (1929–35), see J. Williams, *Eyes on the Prize: America's Civil Rights Years, 1954–1965* (New York: Penguin Books, 1987).

36. "Slowly through the years while enriching the curriculum Lulu V. Childers also assembled an able and progressive faculty." Dyson, *Howard University*, 133.

37. Notably, *Marion Anderson vs. DC Board of Ed* (1939). See also, Louia Vaughn Jones, the first African American to play with the National Symphony Orchestra, Hazel Harrison, Todd Duncan, and others. Harrington, "The Classical Muse."

38. Duke played the Howard Social Club in 1916. Courtland Milloy, "What Good Are We? Turns out Not So Bad, Especially for a Black Social Club Turning 100," *Washington Post*, October 20, 2015, https://www.washingtonpost.com/local/what-good-are-we-turns-out-quite-a-bit -for-a-black-social-club-turning-100/2015/10/20/fafaea0e-775d-11e5-bc80-9091021aeb69_story .html.

39. Collis Davis Jr. "Jazz Greats Galore Coming, Club Offers Student Rates," *Hilltop*, October 27, 1961, p. 2.

40. "Washington; Les McCann; Nick Kirgo; Howard University; Phi Mu Alpha; Approximately." *Chicago Metro News*, December 9, 1978.

41. Howe, S. W., *Women Music Educators in the United States: A History* (Lanham, MD: Scarecrow Press, 2014), 183.

42. Peter Keepnews, "Billy Taylor, Jazz Pianist and Educator, Dies at 89," *New York Times*, December 29, 2010. www.nytimes.com/2010/12/30/arts/music/30taylor.html.

43. Fred Irby III, interview with author, December 12, 2016.

44. "Howard University Set to Reopen after Protest," *Washington Post and Times-Herald*, March 25, 1968.

45. "Byrd Makes Music to Recreate Heritage." *Milwaukee Star*, September 18, 1971. Killgo also studied piano with Roberta Flack, who was teaching at Howard. He went on to record "Killing

Me Softly" with her under contract with Atlantic Records. "The Blackbyrds," *Harbus*, June 2, 2003, www.harbus.org/2003/the-blackbyrds-2197/.

46. "Byrd Makes Music to Recreate Heritage."

47. Pete Lewis, "The Blackbyrds: Talking in Rhythm." *Blues and Soul*, no. 1083, accessed December 10, 2016, www.bluesandsoul.com/feature/288/the_blackbyrds_talking_in_rhythm/.

48. "Jazz Great Donald Byrd at George's," *Chicago Metro News*, December 31, 1983.

49. Steve Huey, "Donald Byrd: *Fancy Free*," All Music Review, n.d., accessed November 7, 2016, www.allmusic.com/album/fancy-free-mw0000103324.

50. See "Dr. Doris Evans McGinty," Howard University, n.d., http://coas.howard.edu/music/huje/McGinty.htm; and the Washington DC Jazz Network website, n.d., http://washingtondc jazznetwork.ning.com/profiles/blogs/washington-dc-jazz-network-4.

51. "Doris Evans McGinty Music Professor," *Washington Post*, April 8, 2005, http://www.washingtonpost.com/wp-dyn/articles/A35786-2005Apr7_2.html.

52. "Happy Birthday FRED IRBY III, Professor of Music & Director of Howard University Jazz Ensemble. One of America's Great Educators," Washington DC Jazz Network, November 30, 2010, http://washingtondcjazznetwork.ning.com/profiles/blogs/washington-dc-jazz-network-4.

53. See HU website for full list: "Jazz Greats Who Have Appeared in Concert with HUJE," http://coas.howard.edu/music/huje/jazzgreats.htm.

54. Benny Golson, *Benny Golson's Honorary Doctorate* [speech]. From: "Benny-Golson.pdf," October 3, 2014, http://coas.howard.edu/music/huje/benny-golson.pdf.

55. Michele Norris, "Student Jazz Singers of Howard University." *Morning Edition* (NPR), May 26, 2008, www.npr.org/templates/story/story.php?storyId=90832142.

56. "The Howard University Jazz Ensemble in a Tribute to Westminster, D.C. Presbyterian Church: Jazz Night in Southwest, D.C. featuring Afro Blue" (program), Andrew Rankin Memorial Chapel, March 12, 2015.

57. Ross Parmenter, "The World of Music: Cramton Hall at Howard University to House Inter-American Festival," *New York Times*, April 9, 1961.

58. Hollie I. West, "A Sad Occasion," *Washington Post and Times-Herald*, February 22, 1972.

59. West, Hollie I. "Left Bank Jazz," *Washington Post and Times-Herald*, May 15, 1972.

60. "Lionel Hampton to Be Honored at Howard." *Afro-American*, February 24, 1979; and "Howard University to Honor Ella Fitzgerald," *Washington Informer* 14, no. 53 (September 25, 1980): 15.

61. Brian M. Walton, "What's Going on in Arts & Entertainment." *Washington Informer*, January 22, 1997; "All That Jazz," *Washington Informer* 20, no. 28 (May 2, 1984): 24; and Karina Porcelli, "Weekend's Best," *Washington Post*, January 22, 1988.

62. "Obituary: Cronner Eckstine a Modern Jazz Pioneer," *Afro-American Gazette*. April 5, 1993.

63. Christopher Popa, "Billy Eckstine 'Mr. B. and His Band.'" *Big Band Library*, November 2008, www.bigbandlibrary.com/billyeckstine.html.

64. Fred Irby III is the principal trumpeter with the Kennedy Center Opera House Show Orchestra and has received multiple awards for his role in jazz education. See "HUJE Director—Fred Irby, III," HUJE website, accessed December 17, 2016. http://coas.howard.edu/music/huje/irby.htm.

65. See HUJE website for full list: "Tours," http://coas.howard.edu/music/huje/tours.htm.

66. W. R. Stokes, "Jazzing up the Curriculum: At Howard U., Thelonius Monk's Music." *Washington Post*, March 13, 1985.

67. Harrington, "John Malachi, the Professor of Jazz."

68. Rusty Hassan, "Jazz Radio in Washington: A Personal Retrospective," *Washington History* 26 (2014): 74–87.

69. Rusty Hassan, interview with author, December 23, 2016

70. Richard Paul, "Remembering Jazz Legend Frank Wess," *Voice of America News*, November 6, 2013, www.voanews.com/a/remembering-jazz-legend-frank-wess/1785121.html; and

Peter Vacher, "Frank Wess Obituary," *Guardian*, November 4, 2013, https://www.theguardian.com/music/2013/nov/04/frank-wess.

71. F. Irby III to L. Sinclair, July 9, 2017, personal correspondence.

72. Richard Harrington, "The Rising Scale of Geri Allen: Jazz Piano and the Composer's Art Jazzy Geri Allen," *Washington Post*, October 1, 1988.

73. M. Jackson to L. Sinclair, July 21, 2017, personal correspondence.

74. Ibid.

75. Harrington, "The Rising Scale of Geri Allen."

76. S. Mervis, "Fellow Musicians Pay Tribute to Geri Allen," *Pittsburgh Post-Gazette*, July 5, 2017, www.post-gazette.com/ae/music/2017/07/05/Tributes-pour-in-for-Geri-Allen-pianist-Pitt-jazz-studies-director-Dianne-Reeves-Esperanda-Spalding-Ahmad-Jamal-McCoy-Tyner/stories/201707050104.

77. Betts played with Fitzgerald beginning in 1965 and officially joined her band in 1971, playing with her until her final performance in 1993. See "Keter Betts: Biography," Kennedy Center, n.d., accessed December 24, 2016, www.kennedy-center.org/Artist/B9821.

78. "William 'Keter' Betts," Howard University, n.d., accessed December 24, 2016. http://coas.howard.edu/music/huje/Betts.htm.

79. P. Sullivan, "Calvin Jones Dies; Began Jazz Program at UDC." *Washington Post*, October 15, 2004, http://proxyau.wrlc.org/login?url=http://search.proquest.com/docview/409857772?accountid=8285.

80. "Wallace Roney," Howard University, n.d., accessed December 24, 2016. http://coas.howard.edu/music/huje/Roney.htm.

81. Fred Irby III, interview with author, December 12, 2016.

9 From Federal City College to UDC

A Retrospective on Washington's Jazz University

Judith A. Korey

It's probably the only art form that America has produced. It's representative of America's spirit of innovation, spirit of diversity. . . . You can't talk about America without jazz. . . . It's just very good to be here to see that the District of Columbia and the University value this very important art form.
—TONY GITTENS, interview, Felix E. Grant Jazz Archives, 2006[1]

"From its founding, University of the District of Columbia [UDC] has been a hot spot for jazz performance, education and history."[2] The journey to JAZZAlive that we enjoy today—a jazz studies program, citywide and regional events that culminate each year with the Calvin Jones BIG BAND Jazz Festival, education and outreach programs, and the acclaimed Felix E. Grant Jazz Archive, all at the only institution of public higher education in the nation's capital—reflects the vision and contributions of many dedicated individuals and reveals a story that continues to unfold.

The history of public higher education in Washington, DC, is "as rich and diverse as our city itself," and one that is documented in the 2011 commemorative publication, *Since 1851: 160 Years of Scholarship and Achievement in the Nation's Capital: University of the District of Columbia:*[3] "The University is who we were, are and can become. . . . With a commitment to research, scholarship and teaching, on the one hand, and service to the community, on the other, it embodies the aspirations and dreams of the people, the city, and the nation it serves."[4]

The history of jazz at UDC has been the story of "lives engaged in building a culture,"[5] and one that begins at the Federal City College, a predecessor institution that was a leader in urban higher education.

Federal City College (1968–76)

Formal jazz education in Washington, DC, was affected by choices made at the Federal City College (FCC), where progressive-thinking faculty were creating a bridge between the African American experience and the academic institution. A pianist and one of the leading scholars on the history of African American music, Hildred Roach, joined the faculty at the Federal City College at its inception in 1968. Her decision to recruit fellow

Fisk University alumni Robert N. Felder and William H. Moore as well as the addition of jazz historian Ernest Dyson to the music faculty in 1969 were determining factors for the inclusion of jazz and gospel music courses in the curriculum.[6]

In 1968 course offerings included The History of Afro-American Music, and by 1969 Stage Band and The Voices (Gospel Music Ensemble) were added. A course in jazz history was designed to provide insight into the role of jazz in the social, historical, economic, and literary development of a people's culture. The Sound of Soul discussed the history and development of gospel, rhythm and blues, and soul music and examined the musical influences and social impact surrounding the growth of each form. By 1970 the Department of Music had established a bachelor of music education degree and an associate in arts in music degree.[7] In addition to the traditional music curriculum required by national accrediting agencies, jazz and gospel music courses were offered for credit as part of the program of study.

The Department of Music at the Federal City College had a faculty of highly qualified artist-teachers with extensive experience in performance and pedagogy. The department was also fortunate that the faculty included seasoned performers in the areas of jazz and gospel music and experienced public school educators.

When Robert "Bobby" Felder joined the FCC faculty, he was an established performer in Washington, DC, and had shared the stage with some of DC's top jazz musicians. His signature group, Bobby Felder and His Blue Notes, provided jazz or rhythm and blues for private dances and events, and eventually became a household name in music and entertainment circles along the East Coast. A trombonist, organist, and composer-arranger, Felder earned a baccalaureate degree from Fisk University and a master of arts degree from the Catholic University of America. His performing background and experience as a composer-arranger, educator, and band director as well as his business acumen would serve the program and jazz studies in significant ways.

Pianist, composer, and choral director Dr. William H. Moore chaired the music department at Federal City College and established the gospel music ensemble The Voices and the FCC Chorale. His traditional classical training coupled with his gospel roots and background in music education provided a distinctive combination for steering the development of the music program. He received a baccalaureate degree from Fisk University, did graduate study at the Juilliard School, and earned a doctorate of education degree from Teachers College, Columbia University.

The music department's community-oriented reputation was enhanced by recruitment activities and performances by the instrumental and choral ensembles. As early as 1969, Felder organized musical presentations by FCC students at DC public schools and local government agencies. The Federal City College Entertainment Group On Stage 1970, proved an outstanding recruitment and public relations vehicle for the college and was supported by FCC president Dr. Harland Randolph.[8] The Office of Student Activities sponsored a program, Soul on Campus, for two performances that featured music students and jazz great Julian "Cannonball" Adderley, who was Felder's personal friend.[9] The presentation attracted the attention of the F. & M. Schaefer Brewing Company and a financial donation to the music department. In a letter to Dr. Randolph, Schaefer's director of urban affairs, Andrew Cooper, stated that "Federal City is rapidly becoming the mecca for young musicians in the Washington-Virginia area."[10]

In his position as director of instrumental music at the Federal City College, Felder recruited music educator and jazz saxophonist Arthur Dawkins from T. C. Williams High School in Alexandria, Virginia, in 1970. In a recent JAZZforum at UDC, Dr. Dawkins commented on his years at the Federal City College and teaching the "sound of blackness":

> I was tickled to death to come to Federal City because they were beginning a very progressive educational setting. For the first time in my life we could say we're going to teach jazz. Bobby [Robert Felder] and Bill Moore [William H. Moore]. It wasn't a jazz program yet, but it was a very good general music [education] program. Pearl Williams Jones was part of that. It was a very important part of the curriculum. That was something for me that really attracted my attention.
>
> Federal City was more progressive and open minded than Howard [University] was. Howard was not an open arms situation when I came there. Federal City was open. They opened the school. They said that we were going to have black music here and we're going to have a gospel choir, a jazz band and every one's going to get credit. That's not something you would find at DC Teachers College. Gil Scott Heron was there. We were part of a movement going on. Howard eventually joined in the 70s. But Federal City already had it going on. Many looked on it as being loose and out of control. But as you can see it's still thriving."[11]

When Ernest Dyson left Federal City College in 1974 to direct the Washington Community School and later to work at Voice of America as a radio production specialist, Dr. Moore engaged the internationally recognized gospel performing artist, scholar, and educator Pearl Williams-Jones to teach jazz history, direct the gospel music choir, and eventually develop the gospel music studies program.

> Gospel music was more than simply another musical form. It was, for Williams-Jones, the consummate expression of African American identity and Black Christian spirituality—"a crystallization of the Black aesthetic."[12]

> Moore [Dr. William H. Moore] said Jones "saw gospel music as a legitimate and recognizable art form unto itself. She did all of the scholarly research to put gospel in its rightful place."[13]

Although Dawkins would move to Howard University in 1975 to head the Jazz Studies program, his efforts, along with Felder's, greatly influenced the program and the recruitment of students. Davey Yarborough—performer, educator, director of Jazz Studies at the Duke Ellington School of the Arts and a University of the District of Columbia alumnus (1978)—credits both Felder and Dawkins for starting him on his musical path.[14]

With Dr. Dawkins's departure, Felder made the critical decision to recruit longtime colleague Calvin Jones to the department.[15] Jones's acceptance of the faculty appointment was a key factor in determining the direction of jazz at the university and, together with Dawkins and Felder, the direction of jazz studies in this city. Dr. William Moore wrote in his recommendation for the appointment of Calvin Jones:

> When Arthur Dawkins resigned from the FCC Music Department to assume the job as Director of Jazz Studies at Howard University, he left a tremendous void in the department. Under most conditions, this void would be impossible to fill; namely because Dr.

Dawkins was an expert in applied music, jazz studies and music education. However, the department has been fortunate in finding a person to take Dr. Dawkins' place.

The suggested person is Mr. Calvin Jones, who is at present an instructor at Cardozo High School in Washington, DC. Not only is Mr. Jones an expert in the areas of applied music, jazz studies and music education, but he also brings added specialties to the department, such as vocal coaching, jazz keyboard improvisation and above all, arranging. These specialties provide further depth to the offerings of the music program, which has heretofore been unable to fully realize its dual emphasis, i.e., traditional classical music and jazz studies.

Since he is highly respected by Washington musicians for his outstanding musicianship and professionalism, we feel that Mr. Jones' presence on the faculty of the Music Department would enhance the image of FCC and would attract highly talented students from area high schools and community.[16]

University of the District of Columbia

Although the University of the District of Columbia was established with the merger of the three predecessor institutions—Federal City College, District of Columbia Teachers College, and the Washington Technical Institute—the Department of Music maintained the programmatic direction and leadership established at the Federal City College. The curriculum design continued to integrate traditional content with a program of study that emphasized the cultural heritage of African Americans, and the department continued to expand its reach into the cultural life of the Washington, DC, metropolitan area community.

The Legacy of Calvin Jones

As the director of Jazz Studies from his appointment in 1976 until his death in 2004, Calvin Jones created a legacy that reflected his passion for jazz, his love of teaching America's music and its history, and his knowledge of the music's importance to American history and culture. His approach to teaching supported an understanding and appreciation of jazz well before it was considered mainstream and served as a model for generations of musicians and music educators.

Composer-conductor-author-educator and former director of the Smithsonian Jazz Masterworks Orchestra, David Baker (1931–2016) told *Washington Post* staff writer Richard Harrington, "You can't overestimate what Calvin Jones brought to the table because he was a visionary—he was doing a lot of these [jazz education] things before it was fashionable to do them."[17]

Calvin Jones was born in Chicago, Illinois, but was raised in Memphis, Tennessee. He graduated from Tennessee State University in Nashville (1953), where he was an original member of the celebrated Tennessee State Jazz Collegians. After serving in the U.S. Army as a member of the 75th Army Band, he decided to remain in the Washington, DC, area. He later continued graduate studies at Howard University, where he received a master of arts degree in music education (1970). Prior to coming to the university, Jones taught instrumental music in the District of Columbia Public Schools system for over ten years.

Photo 9.1 *Calvin Jones*
Calvin Jones, director of UDC Jazz Studies, 1976–2004.

A trombonist of national recognition, he performed at the Wolf Trap Jazz Festival and the Beale Street Jazz Festival and at events such as "Howard University Jazz Repertory Orchestra Performing the Music of the Legendary Billy Eckstine Orchestra," "A Jazz Salute to Lionel Hampton," "A Tribute to Eubie Blake," and "All-Star Celebration Honoring Martin Luther King, Jr." He was a member of the orchestras of the legendary Howard Theatre and the Ray Charles band and had performed with the Smithsonian Jazz Masterworks Orchestra. The Smithsonian Movement in Classic Jazz, led by Jones, appeared on programs produced by the Program in African American Culture at the Smithsonian National Museum of American History.

He performed with the orchestras of touring stage productions at all the major theaters in Washington, DC, and was the first African American to play in the orchestra at the National Theatre after the merger of the formerly segregated local offices of the American Federation of Musicians. Although the trombone was his signature instrument, he was also a distinguished pianist and an accomplished bassist.

Jones's reputation as a band director, composer-arranger, and educator had been established during his years at the District of Columbia Public Schools. His innovative teaching methods and original teaching materials earned him accolades, and his accomplishments ranged from developing an elementary school jazz string orchestra to the establishment of the Cardozo High School Stage Band, which was renowned throughout the metropolitan area.[18] He was a mentor and role model for students and many of his band members from Cardozo High School and the DC Youth Orchestra followed him to the University of the District of Columbia.

Jazz Studies, 1976–87

Calvin Jones's approach to teaching was based on his experiential understanding of the rich tradition of the music both as a practicing performer and as a composer-arranger. His gift as a creative educator was his ability to maintain the spirit of how jazz musicians traditionally learned their craft and adapt it to the academic environment.

Jones's skills as an applied music instructor, band director, jazz vocal coach, and composer-arranger were immediately put to use as the music department transitioned from the Federal City College to the University of the District of Columbia. As early as 1976, regularly scheduled concerts featured the jazz instrumental and vocal ensembles with compositions and arrangements penned by Jones for the specific instrumentation and performing level of the ensemble personnel. Students were guided by a musician who understood the history of the music and its performance practices, and by an enthusiastic teacher who was able to communicate by demonstration. His instructional approach would provide a model for the future teachers in his ensembles and classes.

In addition to the university-based concerts and programs during the period from 1977 to 1981, the ensembles routinely performed at area schools, government and civic organizations, community centers, and senior citizen organizations. The big-band ensemble, the Jazz Laboratory Band, performed for a variety of organizations and events throughout the city.[19]

One of the signature groups, the UDC Jazz Septet, rehearsed on Saturdays.[20] In addition to concerts, clinics, and workshops, the group performed at the Lorton Reformatory as part of the Cultural Arts Forum for the university's Lorton Prison College Program during 1979 and 1980.[21] LETTUMPLAY, a community-based arts organization founded and headed by jazz promoter and patron Tony Taylor, featured the septet led by Jones in two major projects: LETTUMPLAY presents "The History of Jazz" (December 1979) and "Jazz for the Sometimes Forgotten" (February 1980).[22] The two series were supported by a grant from the National Endowment for the Arts and brought the music to those unable to "get to the music." Performances took place at the Oakhill Detention Center, Veteran's Hospital at the Washington, DC Medical Center, Northern Virginia Juvenile Detention Center, the Lorton Reformatory, Forest Haven, the DC Jail for Women, and St. Mary's Court senior citizen facility.

During the summer months Jones would hold informal workshops. In a recent Facebook post, Eric M. Summers, the assistant principal at Charles H. Flowers High School in Prince George's County and a UDC music education graduate and former bassist with the UDC Jazz Ensemble, describes how the workshops began:

> This man would give you his all if you showed him you wanted to learn and I became a questioning machine. Every question was answered with stories of how he got the answers. He was teaching a summer jazz appreciation class and I asked him how do I learn tunes and changes. . . . I came back the next day and he called me into his office and told me "Look man I can do an hour after I take a break and workout with you." So John Bell,

Photo 9.2 *UDC Jazz Ensemble, 1980*
Calvin Jones conducting the UDC Jazz Ensemble, 1980.

drummer, Calvin playing piano, and me on bass, started the summer Jazz Workshop that ballooned into a regular place for . . . about 10–15 cats playing tunes and changes in the summer. Undercover, I was mad as hell because I was getting free private sort of lessons and then everybody started coming and it spread. But that was great for all who came and I learned to share with my students in my educational career that the more the merrier. This is one in TOO many Calvin Jones stories that I have in my memory bank of life.[23]

The Department of Music's move from its location at the Mount Vernon Campus to the University's Van Ness Campus for the fall 1981 semester provided an upgraded facility with soundproof teaching studios and practice modules, classrooms, ensemble rehearsal rooms, and access to a state-of-the art auditorium.[24] The opening of the Van Ness–UDC Metro station on December 5, 1981, offered convenient access to the campus for the university community and general public.

By 1984, a bachelor of music degree was offered in both Jazz Studies (directed by Calvin Jones) and Gospel Music Studies (directed by Pearl Williams-Jones). The University of the District of Columbia was notably the first in the nation and remains the only university in the DC area to offer a degree in gospel music. In addition to the baccalaureate programs, jazz and gospel music studies continue to be important components of all other music degree, nondegree, and professional programs. This curriculum design offers prospective music educators a background that better prepares them as teachers in an urban setting and, consequently, better serves the needs of the District of Columbia Public Schools.

Calvin Jones continued to produce premier jazz ensembles that performed regularly throughout the Washington, DC community. Over twenty-five university-based concerts and eighty concerts in the community took place between 1982 and 1987.[25]

WDCU-FM Jazz90 and Jazz Studies

The Jazz Studies program was thriving in an environment enhanced by the presence of the university's public radio station, WDCU-FM Jazz90 (1982–97), which was recognized citywide as one of the finest showcases of jazz in the area. Rusty Hassan's chapter in this work, "Jazz Radio in Washington, DC," provides insight into WDCU's significant role in the community.[26]

The jazz program's interaction with the station led to many collaborative projects that complemented UDC's program offerings and outreach. In addition to concerts that were scheduled as part of a series or as regular programming, WDCU brought artists to the campus for seminars, workshops, and interviews. However, one project set in motion a series of events and relationships that would influence the development of jazz at the university and in the city.

In 1987 the legendary radio broadcaster Felix Grant, along with executive director of the DC Commission on the Arts and Humanities, Barbara Nicholson, cochaired the Duke Ellington Commemorative Committee that came together to plan a month-long festival celebrating Washington DC's native son Edward Kennedy "Duke" Ellington and his contributions to America's music.[27] The idea for a festival grew out of Grant's proposal to place a historic marker at Ellington's birth site at 2129 Ward Place, NW.[28] (The dedication ceremony would eventually take place in 1989.[29]) More than twenty organizations were involved in the series of concerts, film screenings, symposiums, and lectures. The festival was honored with a proclamation from the mayor of the District of Columbia, Marion S. Barry Jr., designating April 1987 as "Duke Ellington Month" in Washington, DC.[30]

One of the highlights of the month was a collegiate big-band festival proposed by Robert Felder,[31] featuring jazz ensembles from the University of the District of Columbia (led by Calvin Jones), Howard University (led by Fred Irby III), and University of Maryland (led by George Ross). The first University Big Band Jazz Festival, "A Tribute to Duke Ellington," took place on April 27, 1987, at the University of the District of Columbia. The sold-out concert was hosted by WDCU-FM Jazz90 and sponsored by the University of the District of Columbia, the Undergraduate Student Government Association, the Department of Music, and Lottery Technology Enterprises. Mass Media professor Joseph "Tex" Gathings reviewed the concert in the University's news laboratory publication, the *Free Voice*:

> Standing ovations were the style of the evening on Monday night, April 27 when the first annual University Big Band Jazz Festival played to a packed house in the UDC auditorium. . . . The show was the first time all three university jazz groups have appeared

together, the first sellout of the auditorium for a UDC sponsored event and the first of a series that may become an annual event. . . . The UDC group, directed by Calvin Jones, broke up the house with a multi tempo rendition of the beautiful Ellington standard "In a Sentimental Mood." Professor Jones was the only faculty director to do a solo and his trombone work on "In My Solitude" earned one of the evening's many prolonged ovations.[32]

However, the joy was short-lived. The university was in a state of financial exigency, and during July 1987 the Board of Trustees adopted a resolution authorizing a faculty reduction in force.[33] The reduction would have effectively wiped out the Jazz Studies and Gospel Music Studies program faculty. Students protested, led by music students Tracey Cutler, Kenny Dickerson, Vesper Osborne, and Katea Stitt, and many supporters throughout the city, including alumnus Davey Yarborough, demonstrated at the District Building on July 24, 1987.[34] Calvin Jones was interviewed by *Washington Post* staff writer Richard Harrington, and several articles appeared in the *Washington Post*.

[Jones said] "I don't see how you can turn your back on your own culture. Jazz is one of the greatest art forms this country has produced, one that's recognized all over the world. All around the country, the big white universities are all really moving up with jazz programs and with jazz artists in residence. That this should occur in the city university of the nation's capital . . . is inexcusable."

Jones has been in the music department for 11 years, bringing the jazz studies program up to degree status in the last four years. . . . The UDC Jazz Ensemble has earned accolades not only for its performances but for its involvement in the community.[35]

Upon further review of programmatic needs and in an effort to minimize the impact of the reduction in force, the university ultimately rescinded the separation notices to the faculty in those areas, and they were directed to report to the university, effective August 17, 1987.[36]

Felix E. Grant Jazz Archives (1987–97)

Another consequential connection was made when WDCU-FM general manager Edith Smith invited Felix Grant to host his *World of Jazz* show after WWRC-AM, where Grant had been broadcasting, decided to change to an all-talk format. On Saturday, August 8, 1987, the renowned jazz authority moved to WDCU-FM Jazz90, where he introduced jazz, blues, and international music to another generation of listeners.[37]

In 1988 Robert Felder initiated the efforts to establish a jazz archives at the university to house, promote, and disseminate information about this invaluable part of our American heritage. Felix Grant had offered to donate to the university's music department his collection of sound recordings, books, and interviews of jazz artists and personalities recorded by him during his years as a radio broadcaster. Grant's wife, June Deeds Grant, remembered that Grant wanted the students to have access to his vast collection, especially the recordings of his priceless interviews with jazz greats. Felder's initial proposal to create a national archives for black jazz artists was supported by a grant from the UDC Center for Applied Research and Urban Policy.[38] The archives began with Robert Felder's vision to create an archive at the university and Felix Grant's decision to donate his collection. A ceremony and reception honoring Felix Grant for his contributions toward the establishment of the jazz archives took place on November 9, 1988.[39]

The dedication and unveiling of the plaque at the birth site of Edward Kennedy "Duke" Ellington at 2120 Ward Place, NW, was celebrated on April 29, 1989.[40] Although the original home had been demolished, Ulysses "Blackie" Auger, owner of the building standing in its place, agreed not only to mount the commemorative plaque but also to name the building the "Duke Ellington Building."[41] The program included Duke's son, Mercer Ellington, WDCU's Faunee Williams, Ulysses "Blackie" Auger, Del. Walter Fauntroy, Calvin Jones and the UDC Jazz Ensemble, Ann Ledgister of the Duke Ellington Society, and June Grant. Felix Grant, who had devoted over fifteen years to this project, was hospitalized and unable to attend the memorable event.[42]

On January 22, 1990, the University of the District of Columbia, along with Blues Alley, CBS Records, and the Committee to Salute Felix Grant, presented "A Musical Tribute to Felix Grant," hosted by WDCU-FM Jazz90 at the UDC Auditorium.[43] The program featured stellar performances by Sir Roland Hanna, Shirley Horn, Calvin Jones, Charlie Young, Kent Jordan, Reuben Brown, Steve Novosel, Ellsworth Gibson, Christopher Hollyday, Marshall Keyes, Tim Eyermann, and the Blues Alley Big Band. Proceeds from the tribute concert were used to establish the Felix E. Grant Scholarship Fund at the University of the District of Columbia Foundation.

An editorial in the *Washington Post*, "The Richness of Jazz at UDC," recognized that

gradually but impressively, the capital city's own university is on its way to becoming an internationally known sanctuary, archive and living work center for the study and appreciation of jazz. Already the home of a first-rate, 24-hour-a-day radio showcase of jazz—WDCU-Jazz 90—the University of the District of Columbia also fields one of the premier collegiate jazz ensembles in the country, under the direction of trombonist and popular professor Calvin Jones. Last Monday, as it does each year at this time, UDC hosted its annual automatic sellout: the University Big Band Jazz Festival, a romping array of young talent featuring the UDC ensemble and those of Howard University and the University of Maryland—each a varsity team of special note.

Felix Grant, the mellow-voiced jazz scholar of Washington radio for more than 40 years, has been a key force in the project. Last year, the WDCU "World of Jazz" host made arrangements to turn over his extensive, unmatched music collection to UDC, as a first step in creating a library there.[44]

In 1992 UDC president Tilden J. LeMelle (1991–96) allocated space, and the archives found its first home in a suite of rooms located in Building 48, 4250 Connecticut Avenue, NW. Music department technician Willie Gardner worked to prepare the facility and transport the collection from Grant's home. Although Felder retired from the university in 1992, he continued to coordinate activities related to the archives through May 1993. In a May 15, 1993 program proposal and status report for the now-named University of the District of Columbia Felix Grant Jazz Archives, Felder indicated the need for funding to support staffing and equipment.[45]

Felix Grant died on October 12, 1993, after a long battle with cancer. Rusty Hassan writes that his legacy is preserved at the University of the District of Columbia, and his donation was "the first step in creating a jazz archives at the University."[46] June Deeds Grant remained an avid supporter of the archives and continued to donate a personal collection of Felix Grant memorabilia and archival materials that included correspondence, radio program logs, lectures, reviews, concert programs, magazine and newspaper articles, awards, commendations, and a unique collection of photographs.

During this period, the university requested that the Jazz Studies program guide the development and operation of the archives, and I stepped in to assist in its administration. We had the distinct advantage of having access to individuals at the Smithsonian Institution and Library of Congress who provided professional guidance in our organizational efforts. Smithsonian archivist and jazz specialist Reuben Jackson made recommendations and has remained an active advisor, consultant, and collaborator over the years.[47] His suggestion to involve Library of Congress senior engineer and jazz music specialist Larry Appelbaum had significant results. Appelbaum told us he was reluctant to take on such a commitment because of his extremely busy schedule. However, because he liked the idea of the archives and had great respect for Felix Grant, he decided to donate all the information that he would have submitted as a paid consultant.[48]

Based on Appelbaum's recommendations, we began to work on a strategy for organizing the archives as a serious resource. The Felix Grant radio interviews and shows were a top preservation priority, and recording engineer and consultant Michael Turpin began the audiotape transfers of this unique part of the collection.[49] Although the archives did not have an official acquisition policy, donations from private collectors and friends of Grant were added to the inventory of sound recordings. Early usage of the archives' resources focused primarily on music students at the university, and staffing needs were initially met by student technicians and volunteers.

A dedication and open house of the Felix E. Grant Jazz Archives was held Wednesday, October 11, 1995.[50] The event successfully introduced the facility and this impressive collection to the university and the Washington, DC, community and provided an opportunity to thank individuals who had contributed to its development.

In 1995 Jazz Studies major Rachel Elwell was assigned to the archives as a student educational technician, and in 1997 both Elwell and Music Education major Jamal Brown were competitively chosen to participate in the Historically Black Colleges and Universities Pilot Internship Program funded by the National Endowment for the Arts and Norfolk State University.[51] The goal of the twelve-week supervised internship experience is to enhance the students' knowledge and skills in several areas: preservation of archival materials, cataloging, grant research, and developing outreach projects that would coordinate the resources of the archives with the community.

After the opening of the 1996–97 school year, the District of Columbia Financial Responsibility and Management Assistance Authority, known as the Control Board, "demanded that the University immediately cut $16.2 million from its operating budget. That reduction required the dismissal of 125 instructors and the reduction of degree programs from 132 to 76."[52] During the summer of 1997, the university was forced to put one of its greatest assets on the selling block. WDCU's license was sold to C-SPAN to close the budget gap, and the station went off the air at midnight, September 27, 1997.[53] The loss of WDCU was a heartbreaking moment in the university's history and one that greatly diminished the cultural life of the city. There was confusion related to the sale, and we received inquiries concerning the continued existence of the Jazz Studies program. Many individuals wrongly assumed that the sale included the collections at the Felix E. Grant Jazz Archives and WDCU-FM. This misperception confirmed the closeness with which these components had operated and collaborated over the years. Calvin Jones and I immediately contacted Acting President Julius F. Nimmons Jr. and requested and received verification that the entire WDCU collection would remain at the university as part of the Felix E. Grant Jazz Archives.[54] Faculty, students, and staff from the music program transported the collection to the archives facility in Building 48.

Jazz Studies, 1987–97

Jazz Studies began to enroll majors into the degree program, and jazz courses and ensembles remained an integral component of the music education program. The preparation of future generations to pass on the traditions of the art form and move the music forward has always been a fundamental goal of the program. The musicians and educators who have passed through our programs provide testimony to the profound effect that UDC has had on music education at every level.[55]

Pianist Allyn Johnson entered the jazz program in 1992 after attending George Washington University for one semester as a premedical student. Johnson had been playing the piano since the age of five and had honed his musical gifts in the church. After meeting and hearing pianist Dwayne Adell, he was encouraged by Adell to come to UDC and study with Calvin Jones. An exceptional talent, Johnson was the first recipient of the Felix E. Grant Scholarship in jazz performance and completed the bachelor of music degree in Jazz Studies in 1997. The program's reputation began to spread beyond DC.

From its inception, the jazz program provided a stimulating environment that attracted gifted musicians from all ages and backgrounds to study at UDC and perform with the jazz ensembles before starting out or continuing with their professional careers.[56] The UDC jazz ensembles were recognized throughout the community, and over 125 concerts and programs took place between 1987 and 1997.[57] In addition to concert appearances at the John F. Kennedy Center for the Performing Arts, the UDC Jazz Ensemble performed to appreciative audiences outside the District of Columbia.[58]

Jones continued to rehearse the septet group on Saturdays, and during the summer the jazz workshop became a gathering place for musicians. The annual workshops provided continuity for UDC students, a recruitment vehicle for the program, and a jazz community center for local and visiting musicians.

The University Big Band Jazz Festival developed into an annual event produced by the Department of Music's Jazz Studies program and cohosted by WDCU-FM.[59] The festival continued to feature performances by the local jazz ensembles from UDC directed by Calvin Jones, from Howard University directed by Fred Irby III, and from the University of Maryland directed by Dr. George Ross. The Capital Jazz Quintet with Calvin Jones (trombone), Arthur Dawkins (saxophone), Reuben Brown (piano) James King (bass) and Nasar Abadey (drums) was featured in the 1993 concert in a special tribute to Ross, who had died that year. In 1994 Chris Vadala made his debut as director of the University of Maryland Jazz Ensemble at the festival's "A Tribute to Felix Grant." UDC-TV recorded the 1996 tenth anniversary of the concert for the first video broadcast of the festival.[60]

Photo 9.3 *UDC Jazz Ensemble and Allyn Johnson*
UDC Jazz Ensemble, Allyn Johnson, director at the Calvin Jones BIG BAND Jazz Festival, April 30, 2007.

The program was fortunate in recruiting talented musicians and educators to its list of adjunct faculty. Davey Yarborough taught at his alma mater before moving on to the position in jazz studies at the Duke Ellington School of the Arts. Carroll V. Dashiell Jr. shared his expertise with bass students before leaving Washington, DC, to head the jazz program and ensembles at East Carolina University. Former US Army blues director and tenor saxophonist Jacques Johnson Sr. instructed for two years. The legendary bassist Steve Novosel joined the adjunct faculty in 1989, followed by world percussionist Tom Teasley in 1990. Music educator and administrator Dr. Leroy Barton Jr. joined the adjunct faculty as a woodwind specialist and was eventually recommended for a full-time position as instrumental music and music education coordinator in 2001.

The music department lost key full-time faculty with the passing of gospel music coordinator Pearl Williams-Jones (1931–91), pianist Percy L. Gregory (1937–93), and longtime chair Dr. William H. Moore (1934–94). After an administrative consolidation in 1994, the music department was placed within the Department of Mass Media, Visual and Performing Arts under the leadership of Joseph "Tex" Gathings (1994–95) followed by Yvonne Pickering Carter (1995–2003), who consistently provided outstanding support for jazz studies and the archives. In 1997 two additional positions were eliminated due to the faculty reduction demanded by the Control Board, and I was asked to step in as coordinator of the music program.

The administrative consolidation led to closer relationships among the department programs and faculty. Jazz Studies collaboration with artist and graphic designer Rufus Wells III and art student Serdar Sirtanadolu produced impressive publicity and promotional design materials for the program. After receiving degrees in art and design in 1995,

Sirtanadolu went on to a successful professional career and was to later play a major role in the program and the archives' activities and projects.

Felix E. Grant Jazz Archives (1997–2004)

With the addition of the WDCU collection, the archives had outgrown its allocated space in Building 48, and we were notified that the university would be vacating this rental property no later than September 1998. Albert J. Casciero, dean of the Learning Resources Division (LRD) recognized the significance of the archives' holdings and offered a solution that provided the support of the library's resources and relocation to a prominently positioned facility in the LRD that was redesigned to accommodate the archives' collections.[61] Intense preparations began during summer 1998, and on September 11, 1998, the archives began moving into larger quarters within the library.

The new location provided ease of access to users, space for displays, proximity to the multimedia laboratory, and security as well as an extended schedule of access that facilitated the use of the collections. An open house was held Wednesday, October 27, 1999, to introduce the new facility to the university and the Washington, DC, community and to acknowledge the contributions of June Deeds Grant and Robert Felder.[62]

The LRD offered support not only in housing the collections and sharing the collective expertise of LRD faculty and staff but also for future projects in cooperation with the Washington Research Library Consortium, which was established in 1987 to support and enhance the library and information services of universities in the Washington, DC, metropolitan area.[63] This collaboration has been vital to the archives, particularly in establishing digital collections and online presence. In 2000 the LRD made another investment in the archives by hiring Jazz Studies graduate Rachel Elwell as media technician and full-time staff member for the Felix E. Grant Jazz Archives. Having previously served as an educational technician and archives' project assistant, Elwell was well acquainted with the collections and had the subject knowledge, training, and technical skills essential to the archives' operation and development.

In 2000 the Felix E. Grant Jazz Archives website was created, which allowed researchers to learn about its collections, policies, and history, and a pilot project aimed at providing online access to the Felix Grant radio interviews was initiated in collaboration with the LRD, the Washington Research Library Consortium, and the College of Arts and Sciences.[64] After implementing access to the radio interviews, the archives continued with the second phase of the Felix E. Grant [Digital] Collection, which added a selection of photographs and associated resources that not only document the career of this jazz authority and media personality but also serve as a rich source for the study of broadcast radio and jazz in Washington, DC, during Grant's forty-eight-year career.[65] The collection also highlights many jazz artists and events, and it documents Grant's fascination with Duke Ellington and the music of Brazil as well as Grant's commitment to community service. On January 21, 2003, the Felix E. Grant [Digital] Collection went public as the first digital collection at the University of the District of Columbia, and researchers around the world had online access to the materials.

In 2001 the archives was invited to participate as an exhibitor at the Archives Fair hosted by the DC Caucus of Mid-Atlantic Regional Archives Conference; the archives has continued to showcase its collections, research services, and outreach programs at the annual event.[66] The archives began to attract public attention that resulted in gifts of many important collections and became the repository for materials that support the curriculum and document the history of the UDC Jazz Studies program. The Felix E. Grant Jazz Archives and UDC Jazz Studies program began to cosponsor performance programming and outreach activities designed to bring the archives' resources to the local community and wider public, and they continued to collaborate with UDC-TV and the Mass Media-TV academic program on a variety of projects.

The expansion of services and continued growth of the archives' collections necessitated a request for a renovation of the facility that was recognized and supported by university president Dr. William L. Pollard (2002–7). Planning for its implementation, along with the renovation of the LRD, began in 2004 under the direction of LRD's dean, Albert Casciero, and Capital Construction in consultation with archives' staff.

Jazz Studies, 1997–2004

Calvin Jones recruited Allyn Johnson to the jazz program's adjunct faculty as his assistant director in the fall of 1997. Johnson was already establishing himself as one of the most sought-after pianists by the revered musical giants as well as a "young lion" of his generation. Following in the footsteps of his mentor, Allyn began composing and arranging music for the ensembles. He was chosen for the highly competitive Betty Carter Jazz Ahead residency program in 2001 and returned to teach in that program in 2002.

The jazz program continued to attract and graduate talented musicians, and the numerous university- and community-based performances and outreach programs served as a rich resource for the community.[67] In a special to the *Washington Times*, Raymond M. Lane commented on jazz at UDC:

> Possibly the most ambitious is the jazz studies program at the University of the District of Columbia, Van Ness campus on Connecticut Avenue, NW. UDC's calendar of recitals and public performances by student and faculty jazz performers is one of the most ambitious of those presented by area universities' music departments. UDC boasts the world-famous Felix Grant Jazz Archives and a faculty of jazz performers including director Calvin Jones, who played under Ray Charles and many other jazz ensembles in the glory days of jazz.[68]

In 1998 the Jazz Studies program and the Felix E. Grant Jazz Archives began producing the University Big Band Jazz Festival, and former WDCU programmers Candy Shannon and Faunee Williams, who had moved to WPFW, continued to serve as hosts for the concert, along with retired music professor Robert Felder. BET on Jazz taped the 1998 festival for broadcast on BET on Jazz's *Jazz Scene*, and Washington DC's *Jazz Messenger* on WPFW 89.3 FM aired the concert live.[69] In 2002 the festival began celebrating Jazz Appreciation Month—an initiative launched by the Smithsonian Institution that serves as an annual affirmation of jazz.[70]

Jones's compositions and arrangements continued to showcase the ensemble and UDC's outstanding soloists. He composed a "Sonata for Steel Drum and Orchestra" and the "Steel Drum Sonata No. 2" for Trinidadian music student Francis Richards, who premiered the compositions at the 2001 and 2003 festivals, respectively. In a special to the *Washington Post*, "College Jazz to the Nth Degree," Mike Joyce wrote:

> The UDC Jazz Ensemble drew the most cheers and applause from the packed house, not merely because it was playing on its home turf. Director Calvin Jones used the occasion to premiere his "Sonata for Steel Drum and Orchestra," a delightfully sunny and swinging piece designed to highlight the virtuosity of steel drummer Francis Richards. . . . The audience was also quick to embrace singer Angela Gray, who soulfully offered "I'm Glad There Is You," and the ensemble's purring swing on "Shiny Stockings" proved similarly hard to resist. For lagniappe, Jones offered his own "Leavin' the Cookout," a brash and swaggering jump blues that left nearly everyone in the auditorium standing and cheering.[71]

During the 2004 concert, Allyn Johnson was featured as conductor and arranger on "Have You Met Ms. Jones," and, in a reversal of roles, Calvin Jones sat at the piano, to the delight of the audience.

After the annual summer workshop, the fall 2004 semester began with classes, rehearsals, and a full schedule of performances. On September 28, 2004, tenor saxophonist and Jazz Studies major Anthony Nelson performed at UDC's Opening Convocation accompanied by Calvin Jones on the piano. During the convocation ceremonies, university president Dr. William L. Pollard recognized Calvin Jones as the "2004 Faculty Member of the Year" for his outstanding academic leadership, instruction, and dedication. Dr. Pollard succeeded in surprising Jones, who accepted the award with the following comments: "I got caught off-guard today. This is really soul-stirring. . . . It looks like my hard work hasn't gone in vain. So I'll continue to do the same and be a credit to this institution and have these students to go out and represent this University the way that they should."[72]

Calvin Jones contacted me and Allyn Johnson on the morning of October 5, 2004, to tell us that he was being admitted into the hospital, and he asked Allyn to take over the Small Jazz Ensemble concert that was scheduled for that afternoon. Calvin Jones died on Sunday, October 10, 2004, following unforeseen medical complications. There was an immediate outpouring of support for the Jones family and his UDC family from former students, colleagues, friends, and the close-knit jazz community. "Words cannot express the shock we all feel in association with the passing of a man not only dedicated to the University, but also to his art form," said Charles J. Ogletree, chairman of the UDC Board of Trustees. "His passing will leave an incredible void not only in our music program, but also in the lives of all those he touched. Calvin's impact on the University of the District of Columbia was rich and unmistakable."[73]

A memorial service was held in the University Auditorium on Saturday, October 16, at 11:00 a.m. following a two-hour jazz jam session. Allyn Johnson led the UDC Jazz Ensemble and an overwhelming number of musicians arrived to pay tribute to this "Pillar of Jazz."[74]

A *Washington Post* editorial, "Calvin Jones," spoke about Jones's career and his impact on jazz education:

> Calvin Jones—versatile trombonist, pianist, bassist, composer and arranger—was one who extended his talents to the classrooms of Washington, from elementary schools

to college, sharing a keen insider's knowledge of the music's importance to American history. Mr. Jones, who died this month at the age of 75, also founded a nationally recognized jazz studies program at the University of the District of Columbia that is fielding top-notch musicians all over the world.

"This precious art of jazz, which is so close to America's heart and from the heart of black America's experience of triumph and rising, is never going to take over TV or anything like that," Mr. Jones said to a *Washington Times* writer three years ago. "But it lives when people come and listen to it." Because of Calvin Jones, countless well-schooled musicians will be seeing to that.[75]

The Legacy Continues

During the period following Jones's passing, there was a source of hope that provided us with a sense of continuity. When you entered the campus, you still heard the sounds of the UDC Jazz Ensembles—just the way Jones would have wanted it, *without missing a beat*. When Calvin Jones chose Allyn Johnson as his assistant director, he provided a seamless transition for the program. Johnson accomplished what many thought would be impossible. He was able to cover an intensive workload of teaching responsibilities and continued to implement the established calendar of performances that the university and DC community had come to expect. In an interview with UDC-TV's Cheryl Hawkins, Allyn Johnson remarked:

> It's definitely an honor and privilege to be chosen by Calvin Jones to carry on his legacy and the legacy of his music. Hopefully, when you see me, you'll see the spirit of Calvin Jones and when you hear me you'll hear the spirit of Calvin Jones and you'll get a sense of his character and spirit and how he was as a person and musician. And in that way, if you didn't know him, you'll get to know him.[76]

On October 21, 2004, the University Big Band Jazz Festival was renamed the Calvin Jones BIG BAND Jazz Festival by a UDC Board of Trustees resolution in memory of Calvin Jones. "A Tribute to Calvin Jones" on April 25, 2005, was a special evening when Allyn Johnson made his big-band festival debut as director of the UDC Jazz Ensemble, and Calvin Jones Jr. presented his father's trombone to the Jazz Studies program, which is now on permanent display at the Felix E. Grant Jazz Archives.[77] During that week, the UDC Foundation's "Annual Gala" headlined tenor saxophonist and twelve-year member of the Ray Charles Band, David "Fathead" Newman, in a tribute to Calvin Jones, and featured a screening of Cheryl Hawkins's homage, "In His Own Words."[78]

JAZZAlive

Jazz Alive at UDC became JAZZAlive—University of the District of Columbia, and on October 17, 2005, the Jazz Studies program and Felix. E. Grant Jazz Archives launched JAZZAlive and a scholarship benefit series with a concert highlighting the musicians and ensembles from the UDC Jazz Studies program—"The House That Jones Built."[79] In a special contribution to the *Washington Afro-American*, Nasar Abadey wrote: "Though he never seemed to tire of his teaching and performance schedule, Jones still devoted time

Photo 9.4 *BIG BAND Jazz Festival*
Allyn Johnson conducts the UDC Jazz Ensemble's saxophone section at
the Calvin Jones BIG BAND Jazz Festival, April 29, 2013.

to mentoring someone to step in for him when needed. Pianist, composer and arranger Allyn Johnson, one of Jones' protégés and director of the UDC Jazz Ensemble, was that someone. Johnson, a graduate of the Jazz Studies department under Jones, has continued what Jones started, and during the event, it was apparent to all that the band was in good hands."[80]

On September 19, 2006, the University of the District of Columbia celebrated the renovation of the Learning Resources Division and the expansion of the Felix E. Grant Jazz Archives with an open house and reception that also featured the unveiling of an exhibit showcasing the trombone of Calvin Jones.[81] In attendance were university administrators, faculty, staff, students; archives donors that included June Grant and radio broadcaster Paul Anthony; and the Washington, DC, jazz community.[82] The Jazz Studies program joined the open house festivities with a performance by the UDC JAZZtet, led by Allyn Johnson, and UDC-TV's Cheryl Hawkins conducted interviews and recorded the evening's remarks and presentations that she later included in a commemorative video.[83]

JAZZAlive—The Legacy Continues was produced annually as a showcase of the UDC Jazz Studies program with performances by the UDC Jazz Ensembles and the Calvin Jones Legacy Ensemble led by Allyn Johnson.[84] For the fifth anniversary in 2009, DC jazz great saxophonist Roger "Buck" Hill (d. 2017) was honored for his contributions to jazz and to the musical life of Washington, DC.

In addition to the university- and community-based performances, JAZZAlive capped off the year and Jazz Appreciation Month with the Calvin Jones BIG BAND Jazz Festival.

UDC-TV, in cooperation with the District of Columbia Office of Cable Television, began recording the festival for broadcast throughout the year on UDC-TV.[85]

On April 25, 2011, the Calvin Jones BIG BAND Jazz Festival marked a milestone twenty-fifth anniversary with a proclamation by the Honorable Vincent C. Gray, mayor of the District of Columbia.[86] The longtime distinguished advocate for jazz, Rep. John Conyers Jr. served as honorary chair for the festival. During the program Cedric Hendricks, the executive producer of the Congressional Black Caucus Foundation's Annual Legislative Conference "Jazz Issue Forum and Concert," announced Representative Conyers's proposal for a National Jazz Preservation and Education Initiative. (The legislation was formally introduced on March 21, 2014, as H.R. 4280, the National Jazz Preservation, Education, and Promulgation Act, and on March 26, 2015, as H.R. 1682.[87])

The Felix E. Grant Jazz Archives was building a solid reputation in the research world and in the local community.[88] In 2008 author, musician, and jazz discographer Michael Fitzgerald chose the Felix E. Grant Jazz Archives as one of the five case studies for his master's thesis, "Jazz Archives in the United States."[89] He commented very positively on the archives' accessibility to researchers and interaction with the community:

> Although decades younger than some of the other archives considered in this study, the Felix E. Grant Jazz Archives, part of the University of the District of Columbia (UDC) in Washington, DC, has made significant impact on the world of jazz research in a relatively short time. It brings a different perspective, both because of its institutional history and because of its close affiliation with an active jazz performance program. Its youth has also allowed it to learn from the earlier groundbreaking efforts of others, following established best practices rather than being forced to invent them. Despite the fact that its holdings are nowhere near the size of those at the Rutgers Institute of Jazz Studies or the Chicago Jazz Archive at the University of Chicago, the Jazz Archives at UDC has worked with a number of partners, in consortia and through consultancies, to provide access to a large number of its important archival collections. In doing so, it has helped to raise the bar for how jazz materials can be presented on the Internet as well as how a jazz archive can interact with its local community.[90]

Fitzgerald later joined the faculty at the Learning Resources Division in 2009 as the electronic services librarian and has remained closely involved with the archives. One of the significant collaborations is the JAZZforum research and outreach initiative that began in 2009.[91]

In addition to having presented at conferences, forums, and festivals, the archives participated in the critically acclaimed Jazz Samba Project at Strathmore with the exhibition *Bringing Bossa Nova to the United States.*[92] The exhibition, which includes photographs, concert programs, correspondence, awards, unique interviews of prominent artists, and a digital collection—Bossa Nova Project—returned to the university after the debut at Strathmore and is now on display at the archives.[93]

Under Allyn Johnson, the jazz program has continued to prepare musicians for careers as performers, bandleaders, educators, and composers-arrangers as well as for entrance into prestigious graduate programs. Jazz Studies and ensemble alumni and students figure prominently in jazz performance, composition/arranging, and education in our community.[94]

Allyn Johnson continues to evolve as an artist and educator and remains a highly sought-after pianist, composer-arranger, and producer with a trademark sound in the world of jazz. He performs and records with a "who's who" of jazz musicians at major jazz venues, festivals, and events and has a growing library of works for ensembles of various formats. He is the founder and director of Divine Order, an ensemble combining gospel, jazz, and classical music, and Sonic Sanctuary, a small group whose repertoire ranges from acoustic straight-ahead jazz to jazz-fusion and funk. Johnson has served as musical director, conductor, and pianist for the inaugural performance of the Washington Jazz Orchestra at the People's Inaugural Jazz Concert (2009) at the Lincoln Theatre and with Nasar Abadey's Washington Renaissance Orchestra.

Described by Luke Stewart in the DC jazz guide, *Capital Bop*, as the "Dean of DC Jazz," Allyn Johnson "is known as both a performer who can draw capacity crowds to venues around the city and an educator whose position as the director of Jazz Studies at the University of the District of Columbia makes him a key player in the cultivation of DC's next generation of torch carriers."[95]

The University of the District of Columbia's impact on jazz performance, education, and research is "rich and unmistakable." As Faunee Williams expressed in an interview, "This says that jazz lives. That it really lives at UDC. That we are doing something important, we're making a difference in jazz music. We're preserving it so that young people will have something to listen to, to know what went on and to know the legacy that has been given to them, and that they have to perpetuate and carry on."[96]

The music moves forward at the University of the District of Columbia in the rich tradition and spirit of the ancestors. In the words of Calvin Jones, "There's so much to get from jazz . . . it's our culture."[97]

Notes

For their support in this project, I thank Dr. Christopher Anglim, Rachel Elwell, Allyn Johnson, Michael Fitzgerald, Serdar Sirtanadolu, and Cheryl L. Hawkins.

1. Tony Gittens, interview by Cheryl L. Hawkins, September 2006, in Cheryl L. Hawkins, ed., *Open House: Felix E. Grant Jazz Archives*, Video, Jazz Archives Collection, Felix E. Grant Jazz Archives, University of the District of Columbia. Tony Gittens is executive director of the Washington, DC, international film festival, FilmfestDC (1986–Present) and former executive director of DC Commission on the Arts and Humanities (1996–2009).

2. Marjorie Lightman and William Zeisel, *Since 1981: 160 Years of Scholarship and Achievement in the Nation's Capital: University of the District of Columbia* (Washington, DC: University of the District of Columbia, 2011), 176.

3. Ibid.

4. Allen L. Sessoms, "President's Welcome," in *ibid.*, 5.

5. William A. Brower in discussion with Robert N. Felder, "JAZZforum: Robert 'Bobby' Felder (Part 2)," October 21, 2015, Video, JAZZforum Collection, Felix E. Grant Jazz Archives, University of the District of Columbia.

6. Report, Department of Music Chronological Chart of Faculty Progress and Music Curriculum Development, September 1968–January 1972, Federal City College Collection [hereafter, FCCC], University Archives, University of the District of Columbia. (In 2003 the Felix E. Grant Jazz Archives acquired the "Ernest Dyson Collection" as a donation from his family. For information on the collection, see www.jazzarchives.info/includes/collections/dyson.php.)

7. Ibid., 6.

8. Memorandum, Robert N. Felder to Faculty Members and Staff, April 16, 1970, "Federal City College Entertainment Group: On Stage 1970," FCCC.

9. Memorandum, Kenneth C. Kennedy for President, FCC, March 19, 1970, "*Soul on Campus* Musical Affair, March 18," FCCC.

10. Letter, Andrew W. Cooper, Director of Urban Affairs, F & M Schaeffer Brewing Co. to Dr. Harland Randolph, President, April 1, 1971, FCCC.

11. Arthur C. Dawkins, PhD, interview by William A. Brower, "JAZZforum: Arthur C. Dawkins, Ph.D.," March 24, 2014, Video, JAZZforum Collection.

12. Yvonne Jones Pettis, "Pearl Williams-Jones: Gospel Music Pedagogue, Performer, and Preacher of Sermon in Song," in *We'll Understand It Better By and By*, A National Conference on African American Gospel Music Scholarship—In Tribute to Pearl Williams Jones, ed. Bernice Johnson Reagon and Niani Kilkenny (Washington, DC: National Museum of American History, Smithsonian Institution, 1993), 15.

13. Quoted in H. R. Harris, "Gospel Community Loses a Pivotal Voice," *Washington Post*, February 9, 1991.

14. Steve Monroe, "Davey Yarborough: A DC Jazz Icon," *Capital Community News*, February 2012, www.capitalcommunitynews.com/PDF/20-23_EOR_0212.pdf.

15. Robert N. Felder, "JAZZforum: Robert 'Bobby' Felder (Part 2)," JAZZforum Collection.

16. Letter, William H. Moore, PhD, for Calvin Jones, September 1976, Jazz Studies Collection, Felix E. Grant Jazz Archives, University of the District of Columbia.

17. Richard Harrington, "This Week, Jazz Gets a Big Boost," *Washington Post*, April 22, 2005.

18. Letter, Frank H. Maxwell for Calvin Jones, September 9, 1976, Jazz Studies Collection; and Letter, Carolyn R. Wilson for Calvin Jones, September 8, 1976, Jazz Studies Collection.

19. Concerts included performances at the National 4-H Conference, US Department of Agriculture (1978); International Senior Citizen's Day, Departmental Auditorium (1979); US Savings Bond Campaign, Federal Aviation Administration, US Department of Transportation (1981); National Urban League Conference, Sheraton Washington Hotel (1981); Concerts on the Waterfront, DC Department of Recreation (1981); Concerts on the Canal, The Foundry Mall, sponsored by Mobil Oil (1981); and the NAACP Freedom Fund Dinner, Washington Hilton Hotel (1981). Programs and Publicity: UDC Jazz Ensembles, Jazz Studies Collection.

20. UDC Septet performed original composition and arrangements by Calvin Jones. Original members included Ralph Peters (saxophones), Keith Holmes (trumpet), Clint Hyson (trombone), Ernest Mitchell (guitar), Kenny DeFinis (guitar), Calvin Jones (piano, trombone, and bass), James King (bass), Erik Johnson (drums), and Nasar Abadey (drums).

21. Letters, Gloria O. Stokes, Coordinator of the Cultural Arts Forum, Lorton College Prison Program to Calvin Jones, October 19, 1979, and November 18, 1980, Jazz Studies Collection.

22. Press Release, "LETTUMPLAY presents *The History of Jazz*," November 1979, Jazz Studies Collection; and Press Release, "LETTUMPLAY presents *Jazz for the Sometimes Forgotten*," January 23, 1980, Jazz Studies Collection.

23. Comment by Eric Summers on Howard "Kingphish" Franklin Jr.'s Facebook page, September 28, 2016 (5:34 a.m.), accessed September 29, 2016, https://www.facebook.com/howard.k.franklin?hc_location=ufi.

24. Lightman and Zeisel, *Since 1981*, 143–45. See chapter 11 for additional information on "The Master Consolidation Plan" that supported two campuses—Mount Vernon Square and the Van Ness Campus, but was rejected by Congress.

25. Performance highlights during this period included "Black Composers Salute the Black Colleges and Universities," John F. Kennedy Center for the Performing Arts (1982); the National Urban Coalition's "Salute to the Cities Awards Dinner," Washington Hilton Hotel (1982); the United Black Fund of Greater Washington, DC's "Annual Victory Luncheon," Sheraton Washington

Hotel (1982); *Jazz Spotlight*, Blues Alley (1983 and 1984); "A Banquet Welcoming Premier Zhao Ziyang from the People's Republic of China," Washington Hilton Hotel (1984); "Musical Celebration of Black History Month," Government Printing Office (1984); "Concert in Honor of Black History Month," Department of Interior (1985); the "Black President's Roundtable Association Awards Banquet," L'Enfant Plaza Hotel (1985 and 1986); and "College Band Night," Jazz Heritage Foundation of Baltimore, Coppin State College, Baltimore, Maryland (1987). Programs and Publicity: UDC Jazz Ensembles, Jazz Studies Collection.

26. First published as Rusty Hassan, "Jazz Radio in Washington: A Personal Retrospective," *Washington History* 26 (Spring 2014): 75–87.

27. Committee members included UDC's Robert (Bobby) Felder; Edith Smith (Billups), general manager, WDCU-FM Jazz 90; Scheherazade Martin, WRC-AM; Charles Cassell and Linda Wernick, Charlin Jazz Society; W. A. Brower, Capital City Jazz; Bob Israel and Tony Wheelock, Blues Alley; Theodore Hudson, Duke Ellington Society, Washington, DC; and several other participants. Minutes, Duke Ellington Commemorative Committee Meeting, December 10, 1986, Felix E. Grant Collection, Felix E. Grant Jazz Archives, University of the District of Columbia.

28. Letter from Felix Grant to Gary Blond, March 31, 1989, Felix E. Grant Collection. http://hdl.handle.net/1961/2041-7546.

29. Program and Invitation entitled "the Dedication of the Birth Site of Edward Kennedy 'Duke' Ellington" at 2129 Ward Place, N.W.," Washington, DC, April 29,1989. Felix E. Grant Collection. http://hdl.handle.net/1961/2041-7588; and Proclamation, Mayor of the District of Columbia Marion S. Barry Jr. entitled "Duke Ellington Month, April 1987," Washington, DC, Felix E. Grant Collection. http://hdl.handle.net/1961/2041-7603.

30. Minutes, Duke Ellington Commemorative Committee Meeting.

31. Program, "University Big Band Jazz Festival: In Tribute to Duke Ellington," University of the District of Columbia Auditorium, Washington, DC, April 27, 1987, Felix E. Grant Collection. http://hdl.handle.net/1961/2041-7585.

32. Joseph "Tex" Gathings, "University Big Bands Jam for Duke at UDC," *Free Voice* 8, no. 1 (May 1987).

33. Lawrence Feinberg, "Layoffs Asked by UDC Head," *Washington Post*, July 11, 1987, D2-3. For additional information on faculty reduction, see correspondence from Acting President Claude A. Ford to faculty, July 14, 1987, Jazz Studies Collection.

34. Gwen Ifill, "UDC Students Protest 10 Percent Faculty Cut," *Washington Post*, July 25, 1987, C3.

35. Quoted in Richard Harrington, "At UDC, the Jazz-Gospel Blues," *Washington Post*, July 22, 1987, C7.

36. Lawrence Feinberg, "UDC to Save Programs in Jazz, Gospel," *Washington Post*, August 17, 1987. For additional information on faculty reduction, see correspondence from Acting President Claude A. Ford to faculty, August 12, 1987, Jazz Studies Collection.

37. Jeffrey Yorke, "Airwaves," *Washington Post*, July 31, 1987.

38. Robert N. Felder, "National Archives for Black Jazz Artists," Application for Faculty Fellowship, April 11, 1988, Jazz Archives Collection.

39. Program, "Ceremony in Honor of Felix Grant," Music Department Recital Hall, November 9, 1988, Jazz Archives Collection.

40. Program and Invitation entitled "the Dedication of the Birth Site of Edward Kennedy 'Duke' Ellington."

41. Ibid.

42. Letter from Mrs. June Grant to Ulysses G. Auger, May 2, 1989, Felix E. Grant Collection. http://hdl.handle.net/1961/2041-7551.

43. Program, "A Musical Tribute to Felix Grant," University of the District of Columbia Auditorium, Washington, DC, January 22, 1990, Felix E. Grant Collection. http://hdl.handle.net /1961/2041-7592.

44. "The Richness of Jazz at UDC," *Washington Post*, May 5, 1990, A20.

45. Robert N. Felder, "University of the District of Columbia Felix Grant Jazz Archives," May 15, 1993, Jazz Archives Collection.

46. Hassan, "Jazz Radio in Washington," 86.

47. Archivist, writer, music critic, poet, and jazz music historian Reuben Jackson served as archivist at the Smithsonian Institution's Archives Center from 1989 to 2010 and was a featured music critic with the *Washington Post*. He is currently the host of Vermont Public Radio's *Friday Night Jazz*. He has worked with the archives as a consultant on many archival projects and continues participate in our outreach programs.

48. Report, Larry Appelbaum, "Felix E. Grant Jazz Archives—Consultant Report," August 15, 1994, Jazz Archives Collection.

49. Audio engineer Michael Turpin has worked with the archives as a consultant on several sound-preservation and digitizing assignments, including the Felix E. Grant radio interview pilot project, and remains an active advisor. He was instrumental in the archives acquiring two collections: the Albert and Elaine Burgess donation and the extensive collection of noted researcher and discographer George Hall.

50. Program, "Felix E. Grant Jazz Archives: Open House and Dedication," Felix E. Grant Jazz Archives, October 11, 1995, Jazz Archives Collection.

51. Report, HBCU Pilot Internship Program, Summer, 1997, Jazz Archives Collection.

52. Lightman and Zeisel, *Since 1981*, 155–57.

53. Marc Fisher, "From Jazz to Blues; Notes on WDCU's Last Night on the Air," *Washington Post*, September 27, 1997.

54. For information on the WDCU-FM Jazz90 Collection, see www.jazzarchives.info/includes /collections/wdcu.php.

55. Trumpeter Keith A. Mathis received the first bachelor of music degree in Jazz Studies in 1991, followed by vocalist Constance Dean Qualls in 1992 and bassist Errica Poindexter in 1996. In addition to three of the early music education alumni, Davey Yarborough (1978), Tariq Johnson (1981), and Eric Summers (1982), the following selection of music education graduates also benefited from a firm background in jazz studies, which proved to be an invaluable asset to their teaching and performing careers: Yusef Chisholm (1988); David Cole (1989); Clinton Hyson (1989); Tracey Cutler (1990); Nathaniel Brown (1991); Ronald Compton (1991); Gerry Gillespie (1992); Kenneth Dickerson (1993); Yarbrough Laws Jr. (1993); Darrell Watson (1995); Antonio Parker (1997); and Jamal Brown (1998).

56. The following performers, composers, bandleaders, recording artists, and educators are a selection of musicians that have been part of the musical family at the University: Nasar Abadey (percussion); Dwayne Adell (piano); Kiyem Ade Ali (Keith Ailer) (vocalist); Frankie Addison (saxophones); Tony Addison (percussion); Michael Bowie (bass); Marc Cary (piano-keyboards); Dupor Georges (trombone); Aaron Graves (piano); Keith Holmes (trumpet); James King (bass); Heidi Martin (vocalist); Kelvin Montgomery (trombone); Eric Valentine (percussion); and Bruce Williams (saxophones).

57. Programs and Publicity: UDC Jazz Ensembles, Jazz Studies Collection.

58. Programs at the Kennedy Center include "A Showcase of the University of the District of Columbia Jazz Studies Program," Terrace Theater, John F. Kennedy Center for the Performing Arts, November 4, 1990, and "A Musical Showcase of the Diversity of Talent at the Historically African-American Colleges and Universities," Terrace Theater, John F. Kennedy Center for the Performing Arts, February 11, 1991, Jazz Studies Collection. The ensemble was featured in

concerts at the East Carolina University Jazz Festival in Greenville, North Carolina (1991), Martin Luther King Jr. Performing & Cultural Arts Complex in Columbus, Ohio (1993), and the East Coast Jazz Festival in Potomac, Maryland (1994), Jazz Studies Collection.

59. For additional information on the festival, see http://lrdudc.wrlc.org/jazz/festivalhistory.php.

60. University BIG BAND Jazz Festival, April 29, 1996, UDC Cable Television, Jazz Studies Program and Felix E. Grant Jazz Archives, University of the District of Columbia, VHS and DVD, Jazz Studies Collection.

61. Albert Casciero's support and participation has been critical at every stage in the archives' development, and he continues to serve on the Advisory Board.

62. Program, "Felix E. Grant Jazz Archives: Open House," October 27, 1999, Jazz Archives Collection.

63. Washington Research Library Consortium, https://www.wrlc.org.

64. Felix Grant Radio Interviews: Felix Grant inaugurated *The Album Sound* in September 1954 on WMAL Radio 630 in Washington, DC. He spent thirty years as its host and producer. The program featured the full spectrum of jazz and blues and had one of the widest listening audiences in the Washington metropolitan area. Most of the interviews in this collection were conducted live during the program or were produced in the studio for broadcast on the show during the period from 1965 to 1984. Felix E. Grant Collection. http://lrdudc.wrlc.org/jazz/interviews.php or http://dcislandora.wrlc.org/islandora/object/dcislandora%3Agrant_radio.

65. Felix E. Grant Digital Collection, Felix E. Grant Collection. http://dcislandora.wrlc.org/islandora/object/dcislandora%3A16.

66. For information on the Mid-Atlantic Regional Archives Conference, see "District of Columbia Caucus, www.marac.info/index.php?option=com_content&view=article&id=55.

67. Trumpeter and composer-arranger Douglas Pierce (1999); saxophonists Richard Noble (1999) and Rachel Elwell (2000); trombonist and composer-arranger Amadis Dunkel (2002); and trumpeter and composer-arranger DeAndré Shaifer (2004) have gone on to graduate school or successful professional careers. Both Pierce and Shaifer were also selected to participate in the "Jazz Ahead" program at the Kennedy Center.

68. Raymond M. Lane, "Appealing Venues Host Jazz Shows," *Washington Times*, August 16, 2001, M17.

69. BET on Jazz, *Jazz Scene, University Big Band Jazz Festival*, April 27, 1998, VHS and DVD, Jazz Studies Collection.

70. "Jazz Appreciation Month," National Museum of American History, http://americanhistory.si.edu/smithsonian-jazz/jazz-appreciation-month.

71. Mike Joyce, "College Jazz to the Nth Degree," *Washington Post*, May 2, 2001, C-04.

72. Calvin Jones, quoted in *A Tribute to Calvin Jones*, Cheryl L. Hawkins, producer and editor, 2004, VHS and DVD, Jazz Studies Collection.

73. Charles J. Ogletree, quoted in Press Release, Mike Andrews, "UDC Mourns the Loss of Jazz Legend," October 12, 2004, Jazz Studies Collection.

74. Nicole Fuller, "In Unison, Pillar of Jazz Recalled Fondly," *Washington Post*, October 17, 2004, C-03.

75. "Calvin Jones," *Washington Post*, October 23, 2004, A22.

76. Allyn Johnson, interview by Cheryl L. Hawkins, November 2004, Video, Jazz Studies Collection.

77. Program, "Calvin Jones BIG BAND Jazz Festival: A Tribute to Calvin Jones," April 25, 2005, Jazz Studies Collection.

78. Press Release, "David 'Fathead' Newman to Headline University of the District of Columbia Foundation's Annual Gala," April 6, 2005. Jazz Studies Collection; and Cheryl L. Hawkins, ed., *In His Own Words*, 2005, Video, Jazz Studies Collection.

79. Programs and Publicity, "A Showcase of the University of the District of Columbia Jazz Studies Program—The House That Jones Built," October 17, 2005, Jazz Studies Collection.

80. Nasar Abadey, "The House That Jones Built," *Washington Afro-American*, November 2, 2005.

81. Program, "Learning Resources Division and Felix E. Grant Jazz Archives Open House and Reception," September 19, 2006, Jazz Archives Collection.

82. June Deeds Grant (d. May 11, 2009) was a great supporter of the archives and the Jazz Studies program. After Felix Grant's death, she continued to donate archival materials to the collection. She was a rich source of information on the professional career of her husband and was a partner in his commitment to and involvement in community service. In 2006 jazz music specialist and veteran radio broadcaster Paul Anthony donated over 5,100 LP records, almost entirely of American jazz artists of the mid- to late twentieth century. The recordings were acquired throughout his extended career as a radio broadcaster. In 2011 the archives acquired his collection of over 100 radio interviews of jazz artists.

83. Hawkins, *Open House*.

84. Programs and Publicity, *JAZZAlive—The Legacy Continues*," 2006–2011, Jazz Studies Collection.

85. UDC-TV has worked collaboratively with the Jazz Studies program and the Felix E. Grant Jazz Archives to produce programming selected from the JAZZAlive calendar. All of these productions are part of the UDC Jazz Studies collection at the archives. The Office of Cable Television (OCT), now the Office of Cable Television, Film, Music & Entertainment (OCTFME), has worked with UDC-TV and the Calvin Jones BIG BAND Jazz Festival in providing video production and post-production services. For additional information on OCTFME, see http://oct.dc.gov/page/about-octfme.

86. Proclamation, Mayor of the District of Columbia Vincent C. Gray, "Congratulations, Calvin Jones Big Band Jazz Festival," April 25, 2011, Washington, D.C., Jazz Studies Collection.

87. For information on the National Jazz Preservation, Education, and Promulgation Act, see https://www.congress.gov/bill/114th-congress/house-bill/1682/text.

88. For information on the collections, see Felix E. Grant Archives, About the Collections, http://lrdudc.wrlc.org/jazz/collections.php.

89. Michael Fitzgerald, "Jazz Archives in the United States" (Master's thesis, University of North Carolina at Chapel Hill, 2008), https://cdr.lib.unc.edu/record/uuid:a1d6d2d2-7787-492f-9360-b5536ec7315b.

90. Ibid., 109.

91. The JAZZforum series features lively presentations on diverse aspects of jazz from writers, musicians, filmmakers, educators, and a wide range of scholars. Presentations are videotaped for broadcast on UDC-TV and for access on the website of the jazz archives. For more information, see http://lrdudc.wrlc.org/jazz/jazzforum.php.

92. A selection of conferences, forums, and festivals includes "Jazz in DC, On the Air: A Tribute to Felix Grant," May 30, 2009, (Panel, 43rd Annual ARSC Conference, Washington, DC, May 27–30, 2009); "A New Bill for Jazz: The National Jazz Preservation and Education and Promulgation Act," September 25, 2014, (Panel: Jazz Issue Forum, CBCF-Annual Legislative Conference, Washington, DC, September 24–27, 2014); and "Presenting . . . the D.C. Sound!" November 14, 2015, (Panel, 42nd Annual Conference on DC Historical Studies, Washington, DC, November 12–15, 2015). *Bringing Bossa Nova to the United States*, Exhibition, Jazz Samba Project at Strathmore, Strathmore Arts Center, North Bethesda, MD, May 30–June 15, 2014.

93. Bossa Nova Project, http://bossanovaproject.us/dc/streetprint300/index.php, and Mini-Exhibits, http://bossanovaproject.us/Mini-Exhibits/mini-exhibits/examples/index-mini-exhibit.html.

94. Alumni include bassist Dylan Stoddard (2006); percussionist Howard Franklin Jr. (2008); saxophonist and clarinetist Robert Landham (2008); guitarist Pete Muldoon (2010);

pianist-percussionist Samuel Prather (2010); trombonist Leon Rawlings (2013); trombonist Reginald Cyntje (2013); pianist Rico Huff (2013); saxophonist Russell Carter Sr. (2014); vocalist Krislynn Perry (2014); percussionist Jonathan Lewis (2015); percussionist Chantina Crawford (2016); and saxophonist Jordon Dixon (2016).

95. Luke Stewart, "Musician Profile—Allyn Johnson: Dean of D.C. Jazz," *Capital Bop*, www .capitalbop.com/musician-profile-allyn-johnson-dean-of-d-c-jazz/.

96. Faunee Williams, interview by Cheryl L. Hawkins, in Hawkins, *Open House*.

97. Calvin Jones, interview by Lloyd "Raki" Jones, Jazz Studies Collection.

10 Researching Jazz History in Washington, DC

Michael Fitzgerald

What is there to study about jazz in Washington, DC? As other essays in this book show, for nearly a century Washingtonians have played important roles in the development of jazz from its earliest roots through the swing, bebop, and avant-garde periods, and the city continues to attract performers and students to the area's clubs, concert halls, and universities. The DC jazz community consists of not only performers and composers but also promoters, teachers, and a wide variety of audience members and jazz fans. The journalists, folklorists, and photographers who document the jazz scene and the collectors of recordings and ephemera are an important part of the jazz scene. Thanks to them, there is abundant material to explore in the local repositories.

Those interested in the history of jazz in Washington will find themselves immersed in the history of the District's African American communities as well as institutions and traditions that predate the arrival of jazz. Gaining a better understanding of Washington's jazz past involves investigating people, places, and events; identifying networks of interactions and teasing out details in various ways; and placing all of this in the appropriate context. Triangulation using multiple sources is an essential technique because it is rare that one source will provide all the desired information.

Within the numerous libraries and archives in the Washington area, researchers will find extensive documentation of jazz in the nation's capital, though generally they will not find discrete collections on the subject in general. Because of the relatively late acceptance of the genre as an art form worthy of serious study, jazz history up to this point has largely been preserved through the memories and collections held by individuals. As some of these individuals have donated their collections to institutions, their passion has benefited the jazz community as a whole, forming the backbone of many of the resources described in this essay. This survey highlights the most significant public resources available for the study of DC jazz in a wide range of repositories. Website and telephone information is provided, and all researchers are strongly encouraged to contact staff at these institutions. They are the experts on their collections and may well be able to help uncover an item that might otherwise remain hidden.[1]

Found at Multiple Locations

One of the most important aspects of jazz history is the body of recordings created by its artists. Commercially issued records, in addition to their audio content, frequently provide crucial details of biography and history in their accompanying liner notes. One could scour the internet and used record stores, but first checking with the Felix E. Grant Jazz Archives and the Library of Congress might save some time and money.

Historical newspapers are primary sources that are now easier than ever to access with the shift from microfilm to digitization. Performance reviews, advertisements, and entertainment gossip columns can be vital in pinning down exactly when and where events occurred as well as who was involved. Two of the most important papers for the Washington, DC, area, the *Washington Post* (1877–1996) and the *Baltimore Afro-American* (1893–1988), have been digitized and are available online through ProQuest. Unfortunately, the national (not local) edition of the *Afro-American* was chosen for digitization, and many advertisements for area clubs and concerts do not appear. The *Washington Evening Star* (1852–1950) was recently scanned and, like the *Post* and *Afro-American*, is accessible at public and academic libraries that subscribe to these digital resources. The Library of Congress, through its Chronicling America project, has digitized many local newspapers up to 1922 (the current end of copyright protection), and researchers interested in early jazz and the period leading up to it will find this helpful. Washington titles include the *Times*, *Herald*, and *Star*. Microfilm is also available at the DC Public Library and at the Library of Congress. Printed indices exist for the *Post* (1971 on) and *Times* (1986 on), but these overlook many smaller items that may be of great jazz interest.

Specialized publications are especially useful to researchers. There are several regularly issued publications with strong reporting that focus on jazz in the Washington region. *Tailgate Ramblings*, the newsletter of the Potomac River Jazz Club, first published in 1971, focuses on traditional jazz activities and musicians with excellent coverage of local happenings. It has occasionally included historical articles that document Washington's thriving traditional jazz scene. Several of the institutions listed below have holdings of this publication.

National periodicals such as *DownBeat* magazine have at times included local correspondents in Washington who supply tidbits that can turn out to be treasures. Another national jazz magazine, *JazzTimes*, actually began as a local publication, *Radio Free Jazz*, in 1970. Created by Ira Sabin, owner of Sabin's Discount Records (then located at 3202 Pennsylvania Avenue, SE), the publication changed its name in 1980, broadening its scope well beyond the region. During its first decade, reports and photographs enriched its coverage of the Washington jazz scene. Neither *DownBeat* nor *JazzTimes* has been digitized, but print or microfilm copies are available in libraries. While the wide-ranging music periodical index *Music Index* purports to cover both titles, experience has proven that some of the best information can be found only by going through issues page by page. Even music-specific reference resources will not provide the fine level of detail on obscure figures and events often required by those studying jazz history. The added benefit of this approach is that serendipity may provide unexpected rewards.

University of the District of Columbia, Felix E. Grant Jazz Archives

The only jazz-specific archive in the DC area is found at the University of the District of Columbia. Its clear mission and focus have created an excellent starting place for jazz research. At the heart of the archives is the Felix E. Grant Collection, which includes sound recordings, audio interviews, photographs, books, and manuscript materials. These relate to Grant's fifty-year career as a jazz radio broadcaster in Washington. As the best-known spokesman for the music in the Washington area, Grant's name is ubiquitous in materials about jazz, and virtually all collections described here have some connection with him. Although internationally known, particularly for his involvement in promoting Brazilian music, Grant also had a keen interest in local history, evidenced by his research of Duke Ellington's life in the city. He also participated in events such as the Lorton Jazz Festival, an annual concert for the inmates of the Lorton Reformatory that drew some of the biggest names in jazz in the 1950s and 1960s. Felix Grant's final outlet as a broadcaster was on the UDC radio station, WDCU, and he discovered a kinship with the university, which has a strong jazz studies program. Following a 1987 symposium on Duke Ellington that placed him on a panel alongside UDC jazz studies professors, Grant decided to donate the materials that formed the core of the archives.

In subsequent years, the Grant Archives has acquired other materials of local significance, including the Ron Elliston Collection, which focuses on the East Coast Jazz Festival (now the Mid-Atlantic Jazz Festival) that Elliston coproduced with his wife, vocalist Ronnie Wells, between 1992 and 2007. The now-defunct university radio station WDCU was an important jazz resource, and its holdings and history are preserved in

Photo 10.1 *Felix Grant*
Felix Grant poses with some of the records he played on his WMAL radio show, *The Album Sound*.

the WDCU-FM Jazz90 Collection. Collections of other Washington-area broadcasters such as Paul Anthony include thousands of sound recordings and over two hundred digitized audio interviews. Created by the author and longtime Washington resident, the extensive W. Royal Stokes Collection contains books as well as compact discs, including numerous recordings by DC artists. Recently the Grant Archives acquired the collection of another local researcher, noted discographer George Hall. A diligent discographer, author, and publisher with a special interest in big-band music, Hall amassed a large number of pristine 78 rpm discs as well as LPs and CDs to support his work. Researchers can learn more about jazz artists from Washington and beyond in the Herb and Will Friedwald collection of LPs. Herb Friedwald was an early jazz scholar, involved in the creation of Preservation Hall in New Orleans. His son, award-winning jazz author Will Friedwald, shared his father's passion. Over the course of decades, the two of them created a collection that covers almost every development in the history of jazz, from traditional 1920s New Orleans style to avant-garde experimentalism of the 1960s, 1970s, and beyond. Also included in the Felix E. Grant Jazz Archives is the UDC Jazz Studies Program Collection, which has textual records and audio recordings related to the university's jazz program, founded in 1976 by Calvin Jones. A significant portion of the Felix E. Grant Collection, including nearly two hundred radio interviews as well as photographs and paper materials, has been digitized and is currently available.

The JAZZforum series is a research and outreach initiative started in 2009. These regular events feature lively presentations on diverse aspects of jazz from writers, musicians, filmmakers, educators, and a wide range of scholars. Presentations are videotaped for broadcast on UDC-TV and for access on the website of the Grant Archives.

Repository

Felix E. Grant Jazz Archives
4200 Connecticut Avenue, NW, Building 41, Washington, DC 20008
www.jazzarchives.org
(202) 274-5265

Research appointments are strongly encouraged. Many of the collection inventories are online at the above website, but researchers should contact the archives as well. Some materials are housed off-site. A significant portion of the Felix Grant Collection has been digitized and is available online for remote access.

National Museum of American History, Archives Center

The Archives Center of the National Museum of American History, part of the Smithsonian Institution, holds much related to jazz, and some of these materials have DC connections. The largest such collection is the Duke Ellington Collection (1928–88), approximately four hundred cubic feet of scrapbooks, musical scores, and other materials related to the District's native son. Other Ellington collections created by fans and scholars have been acquired by the Smithsonian. These include the Dr. Theodore Shell Collection of Duke Ellington Ephemera (1933–90), the Earl Okin Collection of Duke Ellington Ephemera (1933–87), the Frank Driggs Collection of Duke Ellington Photographic Reference Prints (1923–72), and the Carter Harman Collection of Interviews with Duke Ellington (1956–64). Several collections document the activities of the Ellington circle: the Billy Strayhorn Ephemera Collection (collected by Gregory Morris, 1965–69), the Rex Stewart Papers (ca. 1875–90s, 1924–88), the Willie Smith Collection (1945–87), the Al Celley Collection of Duke Ellington Materials (1933–62), and the Ruth Ellington Collection (1940–91).

The W. Royal Stokes Collection of Music Publicity Photoprints, Interviews and Posters (ca. 1970–2003) contains unique audio interviews by the noted Washington jazz writer, many of which relate to his books on jazz history and include local artists who have not been interviewed elsewhere. The Archives Center also holds the Jazz Oral History Program Collection (Smithsonian Jazz Masterworks Orchestra, 1992–2009), which features in-depth interviews with major artists, including some with Washington connections such as Jimmy Cobb, Frank Wess, and Billy Taylor. Transcriptions of a number of these are available online.

The Scurlock Studio Records (ca. 1905–1994) has a quarter of a million items from the Scurlock photography business. Addison Scurlock and his sons documented the rich culture of Washington's African American community, including jazz materials such as 1932 photographs of the Crystal Caverns club (later known as Bohemian Caverns). The 1980s jazz scene is covered in the Pat and Chuck Bress Jazz Portrait Photographs (ca. 1984–90), created by a husband-and-wife team of photographers and jazz fans. A generous helping of Duke Ellington records collected by the prolific Felix Grant (donated well before the existence of the UDC jazz archive that bears his name) resides at the Smithsonian as well (Felix Grant Collection, 1935–85). Finally, as the Smithsonian itself has been responsible for such projects as the Smithsonian Jazz Masterworks Orchestra and various exhibitions, the Archives Center also holds extensive documentation of these in their Productions collections.

Repository

National Museum of American History Archives Center

14th Street and Constitution Avenue, NW, Washington, DC 20560-0601

http://amhistory.si.edu/archives/

(202) 633-3270

Information on all collections at the Archives Center can be found in the shared Smithsonian Institution Research Information System (SIRIS) online catalog. Researchers should contact the Archives Center to discuss their research needs before making the required appointment to use the collections. Appointments must be scheduled two weeks in advance of visits. Details of policies and procedures are found on the Archives Center website. A registration form must be completed and first-time researchers must view a short presentation.

Library of Congress

The largest library in the world, the Library of Congress, is a "must stop" for anyone interested in researching the history of jazz. The holdings located in its Performing Arts Reading Room, American Folklife Center, Recorded Sound Division, and Prints and Photographs Division hold especially pertinent collections. Beyond these divisions, there

Photo 10.2 *Bessie Smith*
Blues singer Bessie Smith, photographed
by Carl Van Vachten in 1936.

are other collections and centers at the Library of Congress that might be relevant to jazz-related research, including the Newspaper and Current Periodical Reading Room and the Manuscripts Division. It is essential that researchers consult with the Library's reference experts to get the most out of its immense collections.

Repository

Library of Congress
American Folklife Center
10 First Street, SE, Room G53, Washington, DC 20540
www.loc.gov/folklife/
(202) 707-5510

Performing Arts Reading Room

Among the treasures held by the Library of Congress are a number of collections of textual records related to jazz in the Washington area. The multifaceted Dr. Billy Taylor was not only born and raised in Washington but also contributed significantly to jazz efforts at the Kennedy Center. The Billy Taylor Papers (1942–2004) consist of around 150,000 items related to the pianist/educator/broadcaster. Collections connected to other DC residents, such as the singer Pearl Bailey, are also held by the division. The Jerry Valburn collection of Duke Ellington materials (Valburn/Ellington Collection) includes clippings, memorabilia, and hundreds of photographs as well as a vast quantity of sound recordings.

American Folklife Center

Those interested in studying the musical and cultural origins of jazz will find much in this division of the Library of Congress. The Folklife Center dates back to 1928 and among its earliest directors were pioneering folklorist John A. Lomax and his son, Alan, who continued his father's work. Alan Lomax recorded a lengthy oral history by jazz pioneer Jelly Roll Morton in 1938, when Morton was a Washington resident. Some items from the vast Alan Lomax Collection (AFC 2004/004) are available online, but the entire collection has been processed and is available for research on-site. The collection created by jazz writer George W. Kay includes audio relating to Washington, DC, jazz researcher Roy Carew, who knew Morton in the 1930s. A 1964 Felix Grant radio broadcast is also in the Kay Collection.

Some recordings, including *The Complete Library of Congress Recordings* by Jelly Roll Morton, have been commercially issued through a partnership with Rounder Records. Some early recordings in the center's collection are available online through the National Jukebox, a streaming audio service available through the Library website.

Recorded Sound Division

The Recorded Sound Division of the Library of Congress acquires and preserves massive quantities of commercially issued recordings, but it also holds thousands of one-of-a-kind items. In this second category is a nearly complete set of recordings of the 1962 DC International Jazz Festival. Other recordings from Washington-area jazz festivals include some made at the Kennedy Center in the early 1980s. The division also holds the audio portion of the Jerry Valburn / Duke Ellington Collection, including test pressings and other rarities as well as nearly every commercially issued recording by Ellington. Some early recordings are available online through the National Jukebox. The SONIC catalog, which covers much of the Library's collection of sound recordings, can be searched online, but even between SONIC and the Library's main catalog, a significant portion of the collection is not included (nearly 50 percent of the pre-1948 commercial recordings, for example).

Recorded Sound Reference Center

101 Independence Avenue, SE, Room LM 113, Washington, DC 20540-4690

www.loc.gov/rr/record/

(202) 707-7833

Karen Fishman, reference librarian/archivist

A variety of online databases and catalogs give some idea of the holdings of the Library, but these are not complete. Similarly, the website displays but a tiny portion of the collections (although all of the William P. Gottlieb photos are online). A visit is necessary for comprehensive research, and researchers should contact the Library first so that their visits will be productive. Most materials must be requested for on-site use, and some items are housed at remote storage facilities (generally available within twenty-four hours). While the physical holdings of the Recorded Sound Division are now housed in Culpeper, Virginia, researchers can listen on-site in the Performing Arts Reading Room. Researchers should request audio materials ahead of time (two weeks minimum) to permit processing. Access to the Library of Congress reading rooms requires a free Reader Identification Card, valid for two years. The Library of Congress website provides detailed information on policies and procedures.

Prints and Photographs Division

The Prints and Photographs Online Catalog focuses on visual material and provides information on about 95 percent of the division's collection. Many of these have been digitized and can be viewed online. Jazz-related items include photographs of Washington theaters and musicians. The William P. Gottlieb Collection (1938–48) consists of photographs taken by a journalist who wrote about jazz for the *Washington Post* and *DownBeat* in the 1930s and 1940s. As a privileged insider, Gottlieb attended parties at the Turkish Embassy hosted by the Ertegun brothers, Ahmet and Nesuhi, which featured stars such as Duke Ellington, Teddy Wilson, and Zutty Singleton. This collection of over sixteen hundred photographs, which entered the public domain in 2010 and is available online, also includes shots from the Howard Theatre (both onstage and backstage).

Repository

Prints and Photographs Reading Room

101 Independence Avenue, SE, Room LM 337, Washington, DC 20540-4730

www.loc.gov/rr/print/

(202) 707-6394

DC Public Library, Washingtoniana Division

The public library system in Washington includes nearly two dozen neighborhood libraries, but for DC jazz research, the central Martin Luther King Jr. Library is the place to be.[2] Its Washingtoniana special collection (established in 1905) is the primary resource for local historical research. The vertical files are organized by subject and include clippings from local newspapers and magazines. The files of the defunct *Washington Star* newspaper, including most of its news photographs, are a major part of the collection. The entire run of the *Star* is available on microfilm on-site, and there is also a rudimentary legacy index created by the newspaper staff. Those seeking information on the history of buildings and neighborhoods will also find a wealth of resources. Researchers interested in photographs of musicians or venues should consult with the photographs librarian.

Repository

DC Public Library, Martin Luther King Jr. Library
Washingtoniana Special Collection
901 G Street, NW, Washington, DC 20001
www.dclibrary.org/research/collections
(202) 727-1213

The Washingtoniana collection is only accessible by visiting the library, although more online exhibits are being planned. Contacting a librarian ahead of time is encouraged but not required, except for photo research. A separate on-site card catalog contains information on items not listed in the online catalog. The library provides remote access to digitized newspaper databases such as ProQuest to library card holders.

Anacostia Community Museum

The Anacostia Community Museum, part of the Smithsonian Institution, has as one of its goals "to provide visitors with material evidence of the African American experience from a community perspective," and in addition to documenting the Anacostia neighborhood, it includes items from the broader DC metropolitan region. Of particular interest is the Henry P. Whitehead Collection (1922–97), created by a local historian who conducted significant research on the U Street neighborhood, especially the Howard and Lincoln theaters. Information on collections at the Anacostia Community Museum Archives can be found in the shared Smithsonian Institution Research Information System (SIRIS) online catalog.

Repository

Anacostia Community Museum Archives
1901 Fort Place SE, Washington, DC 20020
http://anacostia.si.edu/
(202) 633-4820

The Anacostia Community Museum Archives are open by appointment only. Contact archivist to schedule an appointment. Some materials are housed off-site, requiring prior request.

National Archives and Records Administration

It might seem unlikely that researchers would find jazz-related material among the federal records held by the National Archives and Records Administration, but the Records of the US Information Agency, 1900–2003 (Record Group 306) includes documentation of Voice of America radio as well as other jazz activities. There are film and audio recordings as well as photographs and textual materials in the collection. Willis Conover, a deejay on Voice of America for many decades, presented jazz to an avid audience outside the United States. Conover also was active in local DC jazz activities dating back to the 1940s as a radio broadcaster and concert organizer, and he was musical coordinator and master of ceremonies at the 1969 White House celebration of Duke Ellington's seventieth birthday. NARA holds a variety of materials about this event in the USIA collection. Several photographs and the evening's program have been digitized and are available online. Presidential libraries are also part of NARA and jazz events at the White House are found collected under the particular president. For example, materials from the gala 1978 jazz concert on the South Lawn of the White House are housed in the Jimmy Carter Library and Museum in Atlanta, Georgia.

Repository

National Archives and Records Administration
700 Pennsylvania Avenue NW, Washington, DC 20408
www.archives.gov/dc-metro/
(866) 272-6272
National Archives at College Park
8601 Adelphi Road, College Park, MD 20740
(301) 837-2000

Each of the numerous National Archives locations holds different groups of records. Two of the most important Washington-area locations are listed above. A variety of sophisticated searches of the collections can be performed via the Online Public Access system, and every item is specifically identified to allow for more efficient retrieval and access. Note that on-site access to materials requires a researcher identification card.

Peabody Institute Friedheim Music Library

A short trip to Baltimore is required to investigate the life and legacy of guitarist Charlie Byrd, who for most of his life was based in Washington and Annapolis. In addition to performing and recording, Byrd was also involved in several jazz nightclubs including the Showboat and Charlie's Georgetown in Washington and the Showboat II in Silver Spring. Shortly before his death in 1999, he donated his own collection, which includes music scores, tour itineraries, concert programs, photographs, and correspondence to the Peabody Institute (The Charlie Byrd Collection).

Repository

Peabody Institute of the Johns Hopkins University
Arthur Friedheim Music Library
21 E. Mount Vernon Place
Baltimore, MD 21202-2397
http://musiclibrary.peabody.jhu.edu/
(667) 202-6655

Research appointments are strongly encouraged. Finding aids for archival collections exist but are not currently available online.

Historical Society of Washington, DC

The society has vertical files and archival collections with ephemera, photographs, and postcards. Materials date back to the 1920s and extend to nearly the present day. Of particular interest are the National Music Center and Foundation Ephemera, the People's Congregational United Church of Christ Ephemera, and the Remembering U Street Collection. The society also holds some copies of *Tailgate Ramblings*.

Repository

Historical Society of Washington, DC
801 K Street, NW, Washington, DC 20001
www.dchistory.org/
(202) 249-3955

The society welcomes researchers by appointment. A patron registration form must be completed, and photo identification is required. A new catalog is online, but the old catalog, which provides slightly different results, including more on jazz, is also still available.

Howard University, Moorland-Spingarn Research Center

With a mission to preserve information on Africa and people of African descent, the Moorland-Spingarn Research Center has significant holdings on pre-jazz music and culture and the African American experience in Washington. The sheet music collection includes thousands of items, not only ragtime, spirituals, and jazz but also classical music by black composers. The Howard Jazz Studies program, founded in 1968 by Dr. Donald Byrd (though earlier student ensembles date back to the 1940s), has long played an important role in the District's musical life, and materials on it, including numerous sound recordings, are held in the Howardiana collection.

Repository

Howard University
Moorland-Spingarn Research Center
500 Howard Place, NW, Founders Library, Washington, DC 20059
www.howard.edu/msrc/
(202) 806-7239

Research is by appointment only, and seating is limited. Many collections are stored off-site and advance notice is required to retrieve them for use. All researchers must complete a research register form and provide photo identification.

Notes

1.   In general, archives are not designed for casual browsing but for focused research. Most require an appointment, and some need up to two weeks' notice. Contact each institution or check its website for specific instructions. At many archives, rare and delicate analog materials (even if they are not unique) may first need to be digitized before they can be used, so plan to

allow enough time to submit your request before you visit. This applies to sound recordings as well as photographs in some cases.

2.   The Martin Luther King Jr. Memorial Library is undergoing modernization until 2020. See the library's website for more information on interim services available. https://www.dclibrary.org/node/56887.

Contributors

Bridget Arnwine is a freelance writer and photographer currently residing in Reisterstown, Maryland. She has written bios for the Tri-C Jazz Festival and Jazz at Lincoln Center, and she served as the National Jazz Artists Examiner and DC Jazz Music Examiner for examiner.com for more than three years. Her other published work has appeared in allaboutjazz.com, jazzpolice.com, jazzjournalists.org, *The Encyclopedia of Hip Hop Literature*, and her newly formed Beets & Bebop Media at beetsandbebopmedia.com. She is a native of Cleveland, Ohio.

Bill Brower is a founding partner of JBV Production, LLC, an event-production company based in Washington, DC. He has been active in jazz as a journalist and commentator; festival producer and stage manager; oral historian and photographer.

Anna Harwell Celenza is the Thomas Caestecker Professor of Music at Georgetown University, where she teaches courses in jazz history and the music industry. She has published on a wide array of topics, and her most recent book, *Jazz Italian Style: From Its Origins in New Orleans to Fascist Italy and Sinatra*, appeared with Cambridge University Press in 2017. In addition to her scholarly work, she has published an award-winning series of children's books, which includes the title *Duke Ellington's Nutcracker Suite* (2011).

Michael Fitzgerald is electronic services librarian at the University of the District of Columbia. He hosts the Jazz Forum lecture series at UDC and is active as a jazz researcher. He is coauthor of the award-winning book *Rat Race Blues: The Musical Life of Gigi Gryce*, jazz research director of the www.jazzdiscography.com website, and founding editor of the online journal *Current Research in Jazz* (www.crj-online.org).

Rusty Hassan has been the producer and host for weekly jazz radio programs for over fifty years. He currently hosts *Thursday Night Jazz* on WPFW 89.3 FM. He was a union representative with the American Federation of Government Employees for thirty-four years. He has taught jazz history courses at Georgetown University, American University, University of Maryland University College, and the Smithsonian Institution. He currently teaches at the University of the District of Columbia. The DC Commission on the Arts and Humanities recognized him with a special award for his contribution to the community with his years of broadcasting in Washington, DC.

John Edward Hasse is an author, pianist, museum curator, and lecturer. He is Curator Emeritus of American Music at the Smithsonian Institution's National Museum of American History, where he founded the Smithsonian Jazz Masterworks Orchestra and Jazz Appreciation Month, now celebrated in all fifty states and in forty countries. He is the author of *Beyond Category: The Life and Genius of Duke Ellington*, the editor of *Jazz: The First Century*, coauthor of *Discover Jazz*, and the coproducer/coauthor of *Jazz: The Smithsonian Anthology*. He has earned a doctorate, two honorary doctorates, the Nica's Dream Achievement Award, two ASCAP-Deems Taylor Awards, and two Grammy Award nominations. A contributor to the *Wall Street Journal* and eight encyclopedias, Hasse has lectured on jazz, the arts, and leadership in twenty-five countries.

Maurice Jackson teaches history and African American studies at Georgetown University. He is author of *Let This Voice Be Heard: Anthony Benezet, Father of Atlantic Abolitionism* and coeditor with Jackie Bacon of *African Americans and the Haitian Revolution: Selected Essays and Historical Documents* and with Susan Kozel of *Quakers and their Allies in the Abolitionist Cause, 1754–1808*. He wrote the liner notes to the Charlie Haden and Hank Jones CDs, *Steal Away: Spirituals, Folk Songs and Hymns* and *Come Sunday*. In 2009 Jackson was inducted into the Washington DC Hall of Fame. He is at work on *Halfway to Freedom: The Struggles and Strivings of African Americans in Washington, DC*.

Willard Jenkins is artistic director of the annual DC Jazz Festival. He has been a jazz programmer at WPFW since 1989. He is coauthor of the award-winning *African Rhythms: The Autobiography of Randy Weston*, and recipient of the 2013 Lifetime Achievement in Jazz Journalism award from the Jazz Journalists Association. He can be contacted at www.openskyjazz.com.

Judith A. Korey is a professor of music at the University of the District of Columbia and curator of the Felix E. Grant Jazz Archives (www.jazzarchives.org) and JAZZAlive series (www.jazzaliveudc.org). She joined the faculty of the university's predecessor institution, the Federal City College, in 1972 and has been an observer and participant in the evolution of jazz studies at the university.

E. Ethelbert Miller is a writer and literary activist. He is the author of several collections of poems and two memoirs. *The Collected Poems of E. Ethelbert Miller*, edited by Kirsten Porter, was published by Willow Press in 2016. Miller's forthcoming book, *If God Invented Baseball*, will be published in February 2018 by Pragmatix Press. In April 2015 Miller was inducted into the Washington, DC, Hall of Fame.

Blair A. Ruble is a Distinguished Fellow at the Woodrow Wilson Center. He is former vice president for programs and director of the Wilson Center's Program on Global Sustainability and Resilience and author of six monographs, including *Washington's U*

Street: A Biography (2010). A graduate of the University of North Carolina at Chapel Hill, he completed his doctoral studies in political science from the University of Toronto.

Lauren Sinclair is on the faculty at American University in the School of Professional and Extended Studies. She completed her PhD in international education at New York University. She has played violin as a community member with the Howard University Symphony Orchestra since 2014.

Photo Credits and Permissions

I.1: Photograph by Addison Scurlock, courtesy of the Archives Center, National Museum of American History, Smithsonian Institution.

1.1: Courtesy of the Library of Congress, Prints & Photographs Division, Lomax Collection, LC-DIG-ppmsc-00660.

1.2: Courtesy of the Moorland-Spingarn Research Center, Manuscript Division, Howard University, Washington, DC.

1.3: Photograph by Addison Scurlock, courtesy of the Archives Center, National Museum of American History, Smithsonian Institution.

1.4: Photograph by Delia Potofsky Gottlieb, courtesy of the William P. Gottlieb / Ira and Leonore S. Gershwin Fund Collection, Music Division, Library of Congress.

1.5: William P. Gottlieb / Ira and Leonore S. Gershwin Fund Collection, Music Division, Library of Congress.

2.1: Photograph by Addison Scurlock, courtesy of the Archives Center, National Museum of American History, Smithsonian Institution.

2.2: William P. Gottlieb / Ira and Leonore S. Gershwin Fund Collection, Music Division, Library of Congress.

2.3: Courtesy of the Moorland-Spingarn Research Center, Manuscript Division, Howard University, Washington, DC.

3.1: Courtesy of Ruth Ellington Collection, Archives Center, National Museum of American History, Smithsonian Institution.

3.2: Photograph by Addison Scurlock, courtesy of the Archives Center, National Museum of American History, Smithsonian Institution.

3.3: Courtesy of the White House.

3.4: William P. Gottlieb/Ira and Leonore S. Gershwin Fund Collection, Music Division, Library of Congress.

4.1: Photograph © Michael Wilderman/jazzvisionsphotos.com.

4.2: Photograph © William A. Brower.

4.3: Photograph © William A. Brower.

4.4: Photograph © Michael Wilderman/jazzvisionsphotos.com.

5.1: Photograph © Michael Wilderman/jazzvisionsphotos.com.

5.2: Courtesy of the William P. Gottlieb/Ira and Leonore S. Gershwin Fund Collection, Music Division, Library of Congress.

5.3: Photograph by Mike Gillispie.

5.4: Photograph © Michael Wilderman/jazzvisionsphotos.com.

6.1: Courtesy of the Duke Ellington Collection, Archives Center, National Museum of American History, Smithsonian Institution.

6.2: Courtesy of the Marshall W. Stearns Collection, Box 12 Folder 17, Institute of Jazz Studies, Rutgers University–Newark.

7.1: Courtesy of the Felix E. Grant Jazz Archives, University of the District of Columbia.

7.2: Courtesy of the Moorland-Spingarn Research Center, Manuscript Division, Howard University.

8.1: Courtesy of Fred Irby III.

8.2: Courtesy of Fred Irby III.

8.3: Courtesy of Fred Irby III.

9.1: Photograph by Leon Gurley, courtesy of the Felix E. Grant Jazz Archives, University of the District of Columbia.

9.2: Courtesy of the Felix E. Grant Jazz Archives, University of the District of Columbia.

9.3: Photograph by Andrew Elwell, courtesy of the Felix E. Grant Jazz Archives, University of the District of Columbia.

9.4: Photograph by Ana Spoljaric, courtesy of Felix E. Grant Jazz Archives, University of the District of Columbia.

10.1: Photograph by Vincent A. Finnigan, courtesy of Felix E. Grant Jazz Archives, University of the District of Columbia.

10.2: Courtesy of the Library of Congress, Prints & Photographs Division, Carl Van Vechten Collection, LC-USZ62-117880.

Index